THE MODEL RAILROADER'S GUIDE TO
FREIGHT YARDS

ANDY SPERANDEO

KALMBACH
BOOKS

Printed in the United States of America

06 07 08 09 10 11 12 13   10 9 8 7 6 5 4 3

Visit our Web site at
http://kalmbachbooks.com
Secure online ordering available

Publisher's Cataloging-In-Publication Data
(Prepared by The Donohue Group, Inc.)

Sperandeo, Andy.
    The model railroader's guide to freight yards / Andy Sperandeo.

    p.: ill. ; cm.
    ISBN: 0-89024-576-2

1. Railroads—Models. 2. Railroads—Yards—Models. 3. Railroads—Freight—Models. I. Title.

TF197 .S64 2004
625. 1/9

ISBN-10: 0-89024-576-2
ISBN-13: 978-0-89024-576-7

Art Director: Kristi Ludwig
Book design: Sabine Beaupré

CONTENTS

Welcome to one of my favorite parts of model railroading: the freight yard. When it comes to operation, to making a model railroad perform like a true replica of the real thing, the freight yard is most often where I want to be. I've been extremely fortunate to have made a lot of friends who have allowed me to operate their model railroads in many different parts of this country. If you ask my friends about operating with me, most would probably say something like, "Oh, Andy likes to run the yard."

One reason for that is the pleasure of organizing cars into trains and sending them on to their destinations. That's the real business of a freight yard. It's not, or it shouldn't be, a place for cars to collect or to be stored. It's a machine for getting cars going to similar destinations into blocks and arranging the blocks in order for delivery down the line, whether that means across town or across the continent. That's an enjoyable and rewarding kind of activity, even though we're just pretending that the cars really carry freight or go anywhere besides the far end of the basement. It makes running the yard fun.

Another source of satisfaction is that the yard often sets the pace for operations on the entire layout. If the yard can't get trains out or if it backs up and can't take trains in, the main line—always too short on the largest of our layouts—can pretty quickly turn into a static display. Your friends will be coming to the operating session to enjoy getting the through freights over the road and switching the locals. For those events to happen the yard has to remain fluid and keep trains moving. Getting that done is fun too.

When you're operating with a group, it's good to interact with as many of your friends as you can. Yard operation at its best is truly a cooperative effort, as yard operators coordinate their actions with each other, with train crews, and with the dispatcher who controls movements on the main line. You get to work with almost everybody on the system, except maybe the yard crew at the other end of the road. In this kind of situation it's the people who make running the trains fun, and in the yard you get to deal with most of them.

Appreciating yard operation as I do, I've learned from experience in every yard I've ever run. My aim in this book is to share that experience with you. I'm going to concentrate on the small to moderate-sized yards that most layout builders can aspire to. These as a rule are flat-switched yards, where the work is done by switch engines going back and forth on leads and ladders.

On real railroads the big yards are almost all gravity operations, where cars are pushed over an elevated hump, uncoupled, and allowed to roll downhill into one of many classification tracks in a giant bowl. It's the most efficient way of sorting cars, but not necessarily as much fun for the engineer of the hump engine, who has only to push cars up to the hump at a steady speed to accomplish the mission. And anyway, these yards tend to gargantuan proportions well beyond the average model railroader's layout space.

A flat yard, on the other hand, can do a lot of useful work with only a few tracks, and it offers the play value of having to start, stop, and reverse the engine over and over again. Though yards do tend to take up more real estate than any other part of the railroad, flat yards lend themselves to selective compression, squeezing into less length and width while still following the functional pattern of the prototype. In fact, if you really need a layout for the absolute minimum of space, my preference would be for a freight yard with some adjacent staging or fiddle tracks, as the way to pack the most operating enjoyment into the smallest area.

As you read through the following chapters, I'll explain what yards do and how to think your way through designing them track by track. I'll show you some of my favorite model railroad yards and detail why they were successful. And I'll show you how model yards really can replicate the features of specific prototypes. While my main purpose is to cover onstage, working model railroad yards, I'll share some thoughts on staging yards too, since they play a vital role in allowing our limited physical plants to function as parts of a far-flung railroad system. Finally, I'll offer an introduction to freight yard operation, explaining how to enjoy the results of all the design, construction, and modeling you put into the yards on your layouts.

I started out by saying that I've learned a lot from operating with my friends, and I'd like to end this introduction by thanking all of them. Specifically, these are the people whose yard designs and other good ideas I've incorporated in this book: David Barrow, Bill Darnaby, Frank Ellison (who I never met, but whose writings set the tone for my life in this hobby), Keith Jordan, Tony Koester, Bill and Wayne Reid, and Whit Towers. I'd also like to thank John Allen, who let me discover the fun of too many cars and not enough tracks, and John Armstrong, for opening me up to the enjoyment of model railroads imagined on paper. I hope this book can convey some small part of what these and so many others have given to me.

Ten tips for freight yard design and operation

1. Cars don't belong in freight yards. Cars can't be loaded or unloaded in a yard (intermodal yards being the main exceptions), and cars standing in a yard aren't generating transportation. The purpose of a freight yard is to organize cars into trains, interchange transfers, or switch cuts so they can be taken somewhere else for loading or unloading.

2. When space is tight, use something other than a straight ladder. Compound ladders, pinwheel ladders, and ladders on the angle of the next smaller frog will allow longer body tracks in a given length.

3. Include a drill track as long as the longest body track. Allowing a switcher to drag out an entire track for sorting generally expedites classification switching.

4. Allow trains to arrive and depart without interfering with yard switchers. More can be accomplished when switch engines don't have to stop work to let road trains in or out. Also, operators won't have their plans interrupted.

5. Use staging tracks to provide off-layout destinations for trains and cars. Let staging be the "somewhere else" where cars in a yard are supposed to go, over and above the industries on your layout. Staging can represent any place not displayed on your layout: a distant terminal, a connection with another railroad, or an industrial district (or large industry) just out of sight.

6. Operate with paperwork that deals with cars in the order they stand on the track. Whether you choose hand-written switch lists, car cards with waybills, or computer-generated lists, you'll save time and confusion if you can handle cars in sequence as they come in trains, blocks, and switching cuts.

7. Sort arriving cars by where they go next. Cars classified as they arrive into outbound blocks and trains require less handling in the yard between arrival and departure.

8. Model a yard located at or near a junction. Consolidating traffic from and separating traffic for different lines adds interest to the switching, even if most trains just pass through the yard. And the junction can be merely "notional" or "conceptual," off the modeled layout in staging.

9. Assign multiple operators to help the yard keep up. A common complaint is that trains cross our too-short main lines so quickly that the yard inevitably falls behind. But does it make sense to expect one yardmaster to keep ahead of six or eight road engineers? Additional yard operators can run a second yard engine, hostle engines at the roundhouse, switch local industries and interchanges, or any combination of these tasks.

10. Double-endedness is a good thing. The more through tracks a yard has, the more flexible it will be for handling trains in both directions. And since the real railroads overwhelmingly prefer through yards, a double-ended model yard will look more realistic.

BASIC YARD FUNCTIONS

W e're going to look at freight yards as sorting centers: facilities with the main function of grouping individual cars into blocks or trains going to the same destination and dispatching them as trains, transfer runs to connecting railroads, or switching jobs serving local industries. Our basic assumption is that most cars in a yard at any time are supposed to be somewhere else. They're just passing through, and the work of the yard is to move them along to wherever it is that they're really going. We don't want to think of yards as places to store cars, except for certain special cases I'll explain later in the book.

Let's take a closer look at yard functions and their model railroading potential.

Woodsriver Yard on Paul Dolkos's HO scale Boston & Maine layout is a sorting center that builds both originating trains and blocks of cars for pickup by through trains. *Paul J. Dolkos*

Left: Even a mid-sized prototype yard, such as the Southern Pacific's Bayshore Yard on the San Francisco Peninsula, can be a sprawling affair. A model railroad might not approach a prototype in size, but it can duplicate its function of sorting cars by flat switching.
David P. Morgan Library collection

Below: Here is a freight yard in action as a sorting center, with flat switching on parallel leads in the Southern Pacific's West Oakland Yard. Notice the cars at the right being cleaned.
David P. Morgan Library collection

Building trains for departure

This is the payoff in yard operations, and the way yard crews earn their keep. Cars going to a single destination, or to a series of destinations along one route, are put together in one train. A caboose is tacked onto the rear end—if we're modeling any time before the mid 1980s, that is, otherwise an end-of-train device is hung on the rear coupler—and the assigned locomotive is brought over from the engine terminal and coupled on. After performing the required terminal air test (our trains don't have working air brakes, but taking time for such tests can add an extra touch of realism) the train is ready to pull out onto the main line. For the yard crew, that's a trainload of cars out of the yard and moving toward their destinations.

And note that other kinds of departures can have the same happy effect. A transfer run taking cars to be interchanged to another railroad or a switching job pulling out to deliver cars to "in-town" industries are also departing "trains" from the yard crew's point of view. Any kind of departure gets cars moving toward the places where they're wanted or needed.

Of course, before any of this can happen, the yard has to get

the right cars put together into whatever trains the railroad wants to run. That's the next function we'll look at.

Above: The payoff in yard operation is getting trains out of town. Here a switchman gives a "roll-by" inspection to a northbound Louisiana & Arkansas freight departing from the L&A's New Orleans yard behind Mikado no. 564. *Leon Trice*

Classifying cars

"Classification" in a railroad yard means sorting cars into different tracks by destinations. "Blocking" means putting the sorted groups of cars, known as "blocks," into the required order for a given train. If departures are the payoff, classification and blocking are the basic everyday work that makes the payoff possible.

How detailed the classification of cars and blocking of a train have to be can vary a lot depending on location, era, and a yard's role in the overall railroad system. Even the largest railroad yards won't have enough tracks to sort cars for every possible station and industry location, and it wouldn't be efficient to try to do so anyway. Railroads typically lump a number of destinations together into one classification, and sort cars into blocks that can be further refined at some distant yard down the line. This is especially useful to model railroaders, as it helps us make the most of our limited number of tracks.

The most basic classification

scheme for a yard handling traffic in both directions is to put westbound cars on one track and eastbound cars on another. The next step might be to separate westbound and eastbound local cars (cars that will be going between here and the next terminal) from through cars (cars going at least as far as the next terminal in either direction). Now we're up to four classifications.

Suppose that east of our yard is a junction where our railroad splits into two routes. One might go to a seaport on the East Coast, and the other might go to an inland city where it connects with other railroads. To sort traffic for these routes we'd add at least two more classifications, so we'd have two eastward through classifications and two eastward local classifications. That gives us four eastward classifications and two westward classifications.

That inland city might be an industrial center itself, and the destination for enough cars to warrant its own classification. The railroad might then divide the

Above: Departures to local industries and interchange connections are also the goals of freight yards. The Southern Pacific diesel in the center is about to leave Dolores Yard near Long Beach, Calif., with traffic for the City of Industry yard a short distance inland. *Bruce Kelly*

classification for that destination in two, one for Inland Center "propers" (cars being delivered in the city) and one for Inland Center connections (cars to be interchanged to the other railroads there).

You can see how classifications can grow, but also how the diverse destinations can be grouped for simplicity. This can give us the flexibility to tailor classification operations to suit the capacities of our model yards.

When space is tight in real yards, tracks may have to be reused for other classifications after the cars first sorted there have departed, or cars for some classifications may keep arriving after their class tracks are full. Yard crews will often designate a "for-now" track or "slough" track as a place to put cars that can't be classified until other cars move out. Later, as classification tracks are cleared, the cars on the "for-now" track can be sorted into them. This is a great example of a prototype procedure that can be used in crowded model yards.

Blocking trains

Blocking or organizing departing trains can be as simple as moving all the cars in one classification to a departure track, or it may require more switching. If we've put all the cars for our west local on one track, we may want to switch them into station order to help the local's crew as they work their way from town to town. Or not—it's not unusual for a local to depart from its initial terminal with cars in any order and spend some time at its first stop getting organized. It usually depends on how busy the originating yard is and whether it has higher-priority traffic to handle.

For through trains, blocking can be a way to help with work farther down the line. Referring to the earlier example, a through freight for Inland Center might have four blocks. From the head end back, block one might be Inland Center propers, and blocks 2, 3, and 4 could be interchange cars for three different connecting railroads. That would let the yard crew in Inland Center quickly pick off the interchange cars from the rear of the arriving train, switch them into appropriate transfers, then go back to deal with the cars to be delivered to in-town industries. Or a through freight might need to have a block of cars on the head end for convenient setout at an intermediate yard or interchange along its run.

Commodity types can influence blocking as well. Roads that handled a lot of livestock usually blocked loaded stockcars at the front of any train, regardless of station order. That subjected the

critters to a lot less slack action, and made it simple to set out the stockcars when necessary for rest and water. Railroads carrying perishables in the old iced refrigerator cars would typically block all of those cars on the head end of a train for handier spotting for re-icing along the way. If the "reefers" didn't make up a full-tonnage train by themselves, other freight moving the same direction could be added in other blocks to the rear.

Depending on the number of classification tracks available, blocking might simply be a matter of pulling the cars from certain tracks in the necessary order to assemble the departing train. With fewer tracks, further switching might be needed to get the cars classified for an outbound train into block order.

Receiving terminating trains

The object of a yard may be to get cars moving to somewhere else, but it has to have cars to work with. Besides, our yard IS "somewhere else" to other railroaders up and down the line, and they will be sending cars our way. A yard has to receive cars in order to classify them and send them out again. When yard space is at a premium, this may take some dealing between the yardmaster and the dispatcher, as in "take my outbound train onto your main line and then we'll have a track clear for your arriving train." Ideally the yardmaster will be informed of trains bound for the yard and be able to plan ahead for their arrival.

When a train arrives, the process of the departing train is reversed. The engine is uncoupled and moved to the engine terminal, and when cabooses were in use they would usually be taken to designated caboose tracks to be out of the way and safe from the shocks of switching. Meanwhile, car inspectors walk the train to bleed the air from the brake

systems and note any defects needing repair—again, this is something we can simulate with a little extra time. The yard crew will receive a switch list from the yardmaster or yard clerk, and the foreman or yard conductor will plan his moves to classify the arriving cars.

Classifying cars as they arrive is the key to keeping a yard fluid and well organized. The ideal is to sort cars for outbound trains as they come in, so they only have to be switched once, or twice at most if the departing train has to be blocked from one class track. This makes breaking up arriving trains and building departing trains into one seamless process.

To support this process on a model railroad, it's important to have a car routing system that gives arriving cars destinations beyond the yard. The yard itself should never be a destination. The only exceptions would be empties routed to the yard to be reassigned for loading, as we'll see below. Even so, if empties can be assigned to loading points while they stand on the arrival track, they can be classified for outbound movement right away.

Through trains

Some yards will handle trains passing through rather than originating or terminating. These trains might set off blocks of cars to be hauled out of the yard on other trains, and also may pick up cars from the yard to be taken to the through train's destination. The yard will work to classify the cars to be picked up and spot them on a convenient track before the through train arrives. Getting them onto the through train counts as another kind of departure. If the through train also sets out cars, that's another kind of arrival, and the yard will work to classify the arriving cars for outbound movement.

On the real thing, whether the road engine or a yard engine does

this setting out and picking up usually depends on work rule agreements and where the crew is in their day's work. If the yard is a crew change point, or if the train crew will have other work to do along their run, the yard crew will usually do the work. If the yard is an intermediate point between the road crew's terminals, and the yard setout and pickup is the only work they have along the way, the crew may do the work with the road engine. Many other factors may apply, but for model railroads it usually helps to have some logical understanding of who is expected to do the work and why.

Through trains may require other kinds of handling at a yard, including changing locomotives or cabooses, or both. In steam days it was common to change locomotives at every division point because of the amount of maintenance required, especially on older locomotives. With more modern steam, engines might run over more than one division but still have to go to the roundhouse

to take on fuel and water, and to have the ashes dumped and the fires cleaned on coal burners. Even with diesels there were cases where four-axle power that handled a train over a flat territory was exchanged for six-axle units at the approach to a mountain district, or where power was relayed for servicing.

In the days of cabooses being assigned to particular crews or conductors, which lasted into the 1960s on some roads, the caboose had to be changed whenever a new crew took over. This is a great excuse for some extra switching on a model railroad, and for owning twice as many cabooses as the number of trains you run!

Other kinds of through train handling might include re-icing refrigerator cars, setting out stockcars to rest livestock, and cutting out "bad-order" (defective) cars for repair. If the departing train will be facing a steep grade, the yard might be the best place to add pusher locomotives, either mid-train or ahead of the caboose.

Above: Yards also handle trains that pass through on their way to another destination, like this St. Louis-bound Chicago & North Western train changing crews in Nelson Yard. Such trains are often blocked so intermediate setouts and pickups can by handled by a yard switcher working from the rear of the train. *T.H. Cole, Jr.*

Through-train handling in a yard is popular on model railroads. It takes a little less yard capacity than terminating and originating trains, so it can be a better fit with smaller model yards. Our yards may also be more convincing as intermediate yards than major terminals. It can also be useful to schedule some freight trains that bypass a model yard entirely, such as unit coal or grain trains and intermodal hotshots. This can help make the main line busier without overloading an already busy yard.

Other yard functions
A lot of other interesting things go on in and around freight yards,

Above left: The caboose tracks in the Santa Fe's Barstow, Calif., yard were conveniently located between the eastward and westward classification tracks. Note the string of small buildings along the ladder in the Santa Fe's Barstow, Calif., yard. At least four of them are converted freight car bodies. *Santa Fe Ry.*

Above right: City freight stations could be large and imposing structures. This example is in New Orleans, and the medallion and painted sign leave no doubt as to its ownership. *Leon Trice*

Right: Pocatello, Idaho, wasn't a large city, but it was an important transfer point for less-than-carload (LCL) freight. The Union Pacific freight station was served by seven tracks with four loading/transfer docks. *M.D. Helmer*

and we can model as much or as little of it as we choose. Consider these possibilities:

• **Locomotive service and repair:** Where trains come and go, engines will need care and handling, including turning in the proper direction for steam and single-cab diesels. Even an intermediate yard that doesn't originate or terminate many trains will usually have a track for storing and servicing switchers and way-freight power. This is a fascinating subject, but we don't have to spend a lot of time on it here since it's covered in detail in *The Model Railroader's Guide to Locomotive Servicing Terminals* (Kalmbach Books) by Marty McGuirk.

• **Caboose service and storage:** Cabooses were shelters for the conductor and flagman/brakeman at the rear end of the train, rolling offices for the conductor's online paperwork, and occasionally living quarters at the train crew's away-from-home terminal. When cabooses were assigned to crews, the cars couldn't be used while the crews were off duty, so dedicated caboose storage tracks were needed to keep them out of the way. Even when cabooses were pooled to be used by the next crew out on any train, they still required enough special service to make caboose tracks convenient. Consumables such as water, stove fuel (coal or oil), and lantern and marker-light oil had to be replenished, and air brake gauges and valves had to be inspected and kept in good order. Depending on the nearness of storerooms and

car shops, there might be small buildings near the caboose track for storage and workshops—an opportunity for adding a couple of structures to a yard scene.

• **Car loading and unloading:** Freight houses and team tracks were often adjacent to freight yards. Both were for the use of customers who didn't have their own rail sidings. The freight house was a warehouse for handling mostly less-than-carload (LCL) freight, and might require that cars be pulled and spotted at scheduled intervals to connect with trains and delivery trucks. The team track was simply a track with a roadway alongside it, where cars could be loaded and unloaded directly from or into wagons and trucks. (The name "team track" comes from the association with the teams of horses that pulled the wagons,

and with the teamsters who drove the horses and later the trucks.) Many different kinds of cars can be loaded and unloaded at a team track, even tank cars, hoppers, and covered hoppers. Either a team track or a freight house might have an end-of-track ramp for handling vehicles and machinery on flatcars or automobiles in automobile boxcars. Modern multilevel auto-rack cars are usually loaded and unloaded with movable ramps in special fenced lots with space for vehicle parking.

• **Intermodal terminals:** Loading and unloading trailer-on-flatcar (TOFC) and container-on-flatcar (COFC) equipment is a special case. Originally, the handling of this equipment involved end ramps and cranes that were often adjacent to freight yards. As intermodal traffic grew, the terminals it served became yards unto themselves. These generally had paired tracks and paved roadways for yard tractors and rubber-tiered cranes. See *The Model Railroader's Guide to Intermodal Equipment & Operations* (Kalmbach Books) by Jeff Wilson for more information.

The ideal model railroad yard

Here's an example of an "ideal" yard you can use as-is on your own model railroad. You can adapt it from the track plan or follow its schematic to fit a yard into a different shaped space.

It includes double-ended arrival/departure tracks so trains can come and go from either direction. This is a good idea even if the yard will be at the end of the line on your layout.

Remember, a yard isn't a destination. If your road ends here it needs connections to other systems, or to industrial complexes represented by staging.

The classification tracks are single-ended

to save space. A second ladder at the far end of the yard will add that much more length, although if you have the space for it it's a great investment in flexibility. More tracks for sorting and short-term storage would also be welcome.

The switching lead or drill track allows the yard engine to keep working while other traffic, such as passenger trains that won't enter the freight yard, passes by on the main line. The drill track has to be on the ladder end of any single-ended tracks.

Extending the drill track through the back-drop in this case lets it

be as long as the longest yard track. That lets the switcher clear any track in one move, then sort those cars into any other tracks in the yard.

Crossovers allow trains to come and go from the arrival/depar-ture tracks also without interrupting switching on the lead and ladder. The optional crossover would let the switcher on the lead work a through train stopped on the main line.

There's a roundhouse, a caboose track, a RIP track, a freight house, and a few small industries. There's even a passenger station so this doesn't have to be a freight-only railroad.

Interchange at this yard would be represented with transfer runs to and from a stub-ended staging track.

This yard is shown as a complete layout in itself, with staging tracks behind the backdrop to provide trains for the yard to work. That's not a bad concept for a compact but action-packed layout, but either or both ends of this yard could be connected to the main line of a larger layout. Since it can perform all the basic yard functions, it could function just as well as part of a more complete system.

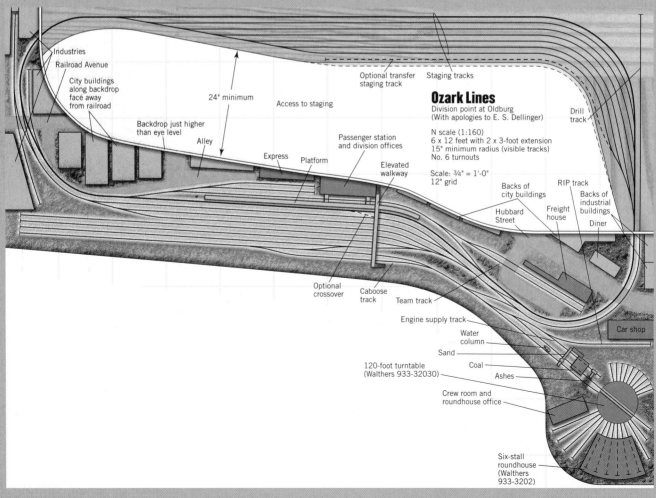

• **Adjacent industries and interchanges:** Whether yards are in urban or rural areas, they're often adjacent to industrial property that attracts businesses needing rail access. These may be served by a yard switcher during breaks in classification, or if there is sufficient work an industrial switching job may be established. The yard switcher would classify cars for the industry switcher to deliver, but as a yard job the industry crew might help in assembling its own cars. Always keep in mind the railroad itself when you're looking for industries around a yard. The engine terminal will need deliveries of fuel (coal, fuel oil, or diesel fuel) and sand, and ash from coal burners has to be hauled away. Shops and storehouses will receive shipments of materials, and items like wheelsets and traction motors may be shipped to another shop for heavy work. If another railroad crosses or passes adjacent to your yard, there can be an interchange track right at that spot. Interchanges are rightly called "universal industries" for a layout because any kind of car might move through such a connection.

• **Car repair and cleaning:** Almost any yard will have a simple repair-in-place (RIP) track, and at larger yards there may be more extensive car shops. Since any actual repairs will be done on our workbenches this may not seem much of an operational opportunity, but we can use card decks or some other random selection to simulate the need to repair cars arriving in our yard or found defective in a terminal air test (see Chapter 6.) That can make for interesting if unexpected switching to get bad-order cars to the RIP track, and later to pull them out and reclassify them. Empty cars may need to be cleaned or otherwise prepared for loading, and a clean-out track can add another switching spot to maneuver cars to and from.

• **Weighing cars:** Most real yards include a track scale for weighing cars, as this is often the basis for billing shippers. Almost any kind of car can be weighed if necessary, but yards that handle a lot of bulk traffic, like coal, grain, minerals, or cement, will need to weigh many cars. Even with dummy track scales, this can be an extra switching move that can add interest to the process of getting cars on their way. Older scales required each car to be

Above: The road locomotive of this northbound Richmond, Fredericksburg & Potomac train has pulled right in alongside the icing dock so carloads of Florida perishables can be re-iced. This icing station was next to Potomac Yard in Alexandria, Va. *David P. Morgan Library collection*

Right: By the mid-1950s railroads began to mechanize refrigerator-car icing, even as they were also becoming interested in mechanical refrigerator cars. *Santa Fe Ry.*

individually spotted on the scale's "live" rails. The newer weigh-in-motion scales can weigh the cars while they are slowly but continuously pushed or pulled through the scale track.

• **Resting livestock:** Back when railroads hauled livestock, the law limited the animals' confinement in railroad cars to 28 hours at a time, though that could be extended by shipper's waiver to 36 hours. Railroads had to keep track of when livestock was loaded and provide stockyards at intermediate points where the animals could be unloaded, rested and watered, and reloaded. A stockyard for this purpose can serve as another "industry" adjacent to a yard on your layout.

• **Icing and precooling refrigerator cars:** Before the mechanical refrigerator car came into service, railroads operated ice-making plants and car icing docks to supply and service reefers hauling perishables. The cycle of servicing refrigerator cars could vary greatly with the shippers' specific requirements. A typical sequence included pre-icing the empty car before spotting it for loading, precooling the loaded car by blowing refrigerated

Above: In some locations railroads provide lodging and reading rooms for crews laying over away from their home terminals. This picturesque example is the Union Pacific clubhouse at Yermo, Calif., a true oasis in the desert. *Union Pacific*

air through flexible ducts and into the car hatches, and re-icing to top off the ice bunkers before sending the car on its way. Once the perishables were on the road, the reefers would need re-icing typically once every 24 hours, perhaps at long icing docks arranged to service a whole train at once. Or, if the perishables were moving into an area with colder weather, the railroad had to put charcoal heaters into the ice bunkers to keep the loads from freezing. This was also done at an ice dock.

• **Car storage:** Storage can be an important function of real yards, whether needed for holding empty cars during the off time for seasonal movements, holding loaded cars awaiting sale or delivery schedules for the commodities they contain, or gathering empty cars for loading at nearby shipping points. Given the limited real estate of most model railroads, however, storage is a function

we'd prefer not to model. It offers relatively little action and operating interest in return for the space stored cars will occupy. In general it's best represented by off-layout staging tracks, or even off-track storage systems. For example, you can keep a few dozen more boxcars or covered hoppers than you'd normally run on shelves or in drawers, and bring them onto the railroad through staging tracks and/or interchange connections when you want to stage a grain rush. This avoids clogging the onstage yard tracks with cars that really aren't going anywhere else. In addition, and as we'll soon see, there are many more enjoyable things we can do with our yard capacity.

The one storage function that usually is worth modeling is the last one I named: gathering empties for loading. As long as you can generate requests for empty cars on a fairly short cycle,

collecting empties, assigning them for loading, and then sorting them into the outbound trains going to the loading points will add to the fun. The obvious examples of this are empty coal hoppers collecting in a coalfield yard that dispatches mine runs, or empty refrigerator cars gathered at a terminal in a fruit-growing area.

That of course takes us back to the principle that a yard's function is to send cars somewhere else. Once the empties are assigned to be loaded at mines or packing sheds or grain elevators, they have someplace to go and it's the yard's job to sort them into appropriate trains and move them out.

Build a scale track
Add a prototypical operation to your layout

By Bill Darnaby
Photos by the author

Scale tracks are infrequently seen on model railroads, but when I added several to my HO scale Maumee Route, I increased its realism and operating potential.

Railroad scales are used to weigh cars—such as those with bulk lading like coal, stone, or grains—for billing purposes. Without the scale it would be difficult to determine exactly how much of these materials are being shipped or received. (For more on railroad scales, see "Tipping the railroad scales" on page 21.)

Though my scales don't actually measure anything, my scale tracks really operate and have added the fun of switching cuts of cars for weighing in a prototypical manner.

Considering space requirements

To add the scale track, I needed a space large enough to include the points for two no. 6 turnouts, the concrete scale foundation, and room to mount a Kadee uncoupling magnet on both ends of the scale.

The approach at each end of the scale track uses a no. 6 turnout, but only requires the portion from the points to where the rails have diverged a scale 21"

The yard crew pushes a Southern Pacific boxcar onto the live rails in front of the scale house for a weigh-in. Bill Darnaby built this prototypical scale track to add realism to operations on his HO layout.

apart (approximately ¼"). They do not need frogs as the rails merely step to the side and never cross.

For the scale itself, I built my version on a 54-foot concrete pad to accommodate 50-foot freight cars. The space requirements for a scale this size, allowing for enough room for the uncoupling magnets to work properly, comes to 21" measured between the turnout points.

The dimensions and layout for the scale track are shown in fig. 1.

Laying out the scale
With the necessary dimensions in hand, I selected the area to place my scale and marked off the track center lines, turnout positions, and scale location as fig. 2 shows.

For my application, I used N scale cork roadbed that I mortised into my extruded foam subroadbed. Though your application will probably be different than mine, make sure the area for the scale track is dead-level, or the cars will roll away when you attempt to spot them.

Because the two tracks are so close to each other, I offset the uncoupling magnets ⅜" from the center line of

the through track. That way, cuts of cars passing over the through track will not unexpectedly uncouple, but cars switched over to the live scale rails will uncouple at the ends of the scale.

Building the styrene base
I made the foundation out of .080" styrene and added .010" styrene rail base plates. The final thickness matches the height of Micro Engineering full-profile wood ties.

I cut the base a scale 54 feet long and 13'-6" wide. The width includes an extra foot of clearance on the scale house side of the

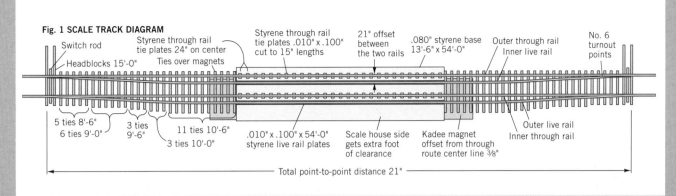

Fig. 1 SCALE TRACK DIAGRAM

Switch rod

Headblocks 15'-0"

Styrene through rail
tie plates 24" on center
Ties over magnets

Styrene through rail
tie plates .010" x .100"
cut to 15" lengths

21" offset
between
the two rails

.080" styrene base
13'-6" x 54'-0"

Outer through rail
Inner live rail

No. 6
turnout
points

5 ties 8'-6"
6 ties 9'-0"

3 ties
9'-6"

11 ties 10'-6"
3 ties 10'-0"

.010" x .100" x 54'-0"
styrene live rail plates

Scale house side
gets extra foot
of clearance

Kadee magnet
offset from through
route center line ³⁄₈"

Outer live rail
Inner through rail

Total point-to-point distance 21"

Fig. 2 LAYING OUT THE LOCATION. Before beginning construction, Bill made sure he had enough room for his scale track by drawing the dimensions directly on the layout.

Fig. 3 INSTALLING THE ROADBED AND FOUNDATION. In this view we see the cork roadbed, Kadee uncoupling magnets, and styrene scale foundation ready for the next step. Do not glue the scale foundation in place until after the rails have been laid.

foundation. Using a sharp pencil, I marked the center line of each through track and live track rail on the styrene foundation.

The through rails sit on base plates of .010" x .100" styrene cut 15" long. I cemented the through track base plates to the foundation using liquid styrene cement and spaced them on 24" centers. I used a straightedge to ensure all the pieces were properly aligned.

The live rails sit on .010" x .100" strips of styrene cut to the length of the foundation. I laid the styrene strips on

their center lines and cemented them in place. To finish, I painted the foundation a gray concrete color and the rail base plates a grimy black color.

The completed styrene base, Kadee magnets, and cork roadbed are shown installed in fig. 3.

Adding the track

Though I handlaid all of my scale track, you could use ready-made no. 6 turnouts cut at the 21" diverging point. The track portions in between the turnouts will still need to be handlaid due to the close proximity of the

through and live rails.

For my project, I used Micro Engineering full-profile wood switch ties that I cut to the required lengths as shown in fig. 1. I glued the ties in place with white glue. Once the glue was set I lightly sanded the tops of the ties to knock down any high spots.

Using Micro Engineering weathered code 70 rail, I began by laying the outside through track rail. (For a complete lesson in hand-laying turnouts, see *Trackwork and Lineside Detail for Your Model Railroad* published by

Kalmbach Books.) First I marked off the locations of the points and filed the point's seats in the side of the rail. Next I hand-spiked the rail in place with Micro Engineering spikes and used a straightedge to keep it aligned properly.

Kadee says that its magnets will accept spikes, but they don't accept them easily. I was able to force the spikes about halfway into the magnets with a pair of small pliers. Then I pulled the spikes out, cut them to half their length, and reinserted them, adding a bit of

Fig. 4 ADDING TIES AND STOCK RAILS. Bill used full-profile switch ties and code 70 rail from Micro Engineering for his project. At this point the ties have been glued in place and the outer through and live rails have been added, forming the stock rails for the two turnouts.

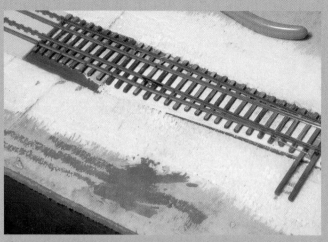

Fig. 5 FINISHING THE TURNOUTS. With the addition of the inner point rails and switch rods, this turnout is finished and ready for turnout controls. Though Bill uses a manual turnout linkage, you could use any type of ground throw or switch motor.

cyanoacrylate adhesive (CA) as insurance.

With the first rail spiked in place, I adjusted the position of the foundation, centering the rail over its base plates. The foundation will be secured later, so do not use spikes to attach the rail to it.

I laid the outside live rail next as shown in fig. 4. Again, I marked off and filed the point seats in the side of the rail and laid it so that it was centered on its base on the foundation.

Though I used a straightedge to maintain alignment, it's important not to kink the rail where it diverges from the turnout to run parallel with the straight route. The rail should form a shallow S curve. On a turnout, these two outer rails are called the stock rails.

With the stock rails in place, I moved to the inside rails, which are called the point rails. I started with the straight inside through rail, cut it to length to fit between the point seats in the outside live rail, filed a switch point at each end, and spiked it in gauge with the outside through rail. I then repeated the process for the inside live rail.

The inside rails shouldn't be spiked any nearer than 4" from the point ends to allow good point movement.

I completed the turnouts by soldering switch rods made from PC board to the points. At this step, you may add almost any type of turnout control and linkage you wish. Figure 5 shows the completed turnout with a manual control system in place, but a switch motor would also work well.

Finishing the scale

After centering the rails on their base plates, I secured them in place with CA. As an additional detail, I added a pre-painted strip of .010" x .100" styrene against both sides of the live rails underneath the rail-heads. These simulate the baffles that prevent debris from falling into the gaps and fouling the scale mechanism.

You'll want a scale house (for the operator and equipment) as well. I constructed mine using Evergreen novelty siding and Grandt Line windows and doors based on standard B&O plans. However, you could use any small shed with a window facing the scale tracks, such as Depots by John kit no. 114, a Fairbanks-Morse scale house.

To finish, I weathered the scale foundation and track and added ballast and scenery.

Using your new scale track

To get a proper reading, cars need to be uncoupled and set on the live rails individually. To start, a switcher shoves a cut of cars onto the scale track and allows the Kadee magnet to uncouple the first car. The switcher crew then backs the cut of cars away so that the couplers move into the delay position before returning to shove the first car onto the scale for weighing.

After the car is weighed, the switcher crew pushes the string of cars forward to move the first car beyond the scale. The magnet on the other side uncouples the car and the crew backs the rest of the string up to repeat the process, spotting each car on the scale in succession. But remember, never run the engine onto the scale!

Bill Darnaby is a regular contributor to *Model Railroader* magazine and a prolific author on model railroading subjects. His HO scale Maumee Route is the beneficiary of his many innovative modeling ideas.

Tipping the railroad scales

Many railroad scales today are weigh-in-motion scales that weigh each car as the whole train rolls over them. Perhaps of more interest to modelers, however, are the older weigh-in-place scales that require cars to be spotted on the scale one at a time.

A weigh-in-place scale is built under a set of overlapping tracks. The normal or "straight" route's rails are solidly fastened to the scale's foundation.

The pair of scale or "live" rails are offset from the normal route 16"-21" using switch points without a frog. By means of balance beams, the live rails are attached to the scale itself, installed in a small house adjacent to the tracks. Because locomotives are too heavy, they are prohibited from running over the live scale rails.

A scale typically required calibration twice a year, so railroads owned scale test cars—basically weights on wheels—to check them.—*B.D.*

This prototype Soo Line scale house was built into the back wall of the Waukesha, Wis., roundhouse. The scale's "live" tracks are the set closest to the scale house. *Rick Johnson*

Left: A freight yard in a large city can be a bustling center of operations. This is the Southern Ry. yard at Bluff City (Memphis, Tenn.), on Allen Keller's HO scale Bluff City Southern. *Lou Sassi*

Below: The East La Salle industrial district on the North American Protoype Modelers HO club layout in Milwaukee is adjacent to a small yard at Kimball Avenue. The "ELA" switcher can spend most of an operating session delivering and picking up cars here, easily the equivalent of a way-freight run over the main line. *Jim Forbes*

Above: A small western branch line's terminal may run right along the town's main street, as at Pandora, Colo., on Ken Ehlers Sn3 Pandora & San Miguel. ("Sn3" indicates S scale, 1:64 proportion, with three-foot narrow gauge.) *Ken Ehlers*

Right: The payoff in yard operation is getting cars out of the yard and moving on to their destinations. Here a Baltimore & Ohio freight heads west out of Grafton, W. Va., on Ed Lorence's HO layout. We can also see that Ed has taken advantage of the opportunities yards present for adding structures and small details. *Lou Sassi*

To see how to provide basic yard functions on a model railroad, we'll go through the process of designing a yard track by track. This will be a somewhat abstract approach without reference to a particular layout space, but I'll point out space concerns and general layout design issues as we go.

The runaround track at left allows engines to escape after pulling into the stub-ended Woodsriver Yard. Most of the sorting is done on the five body tracks.
Paul J. Dolkos

TWO

Right: This aerial photo at Avondale, La., reveals two of the classic yard shapes. The Texas Pacific-Missouri Pacific yard at the left and the Southern Pacific yard in the center are both "pyramid" types, with ladders sloping toward each other and progressively shorter tracks. The SP yard at the right is a "diamond" or parallelogram, with parallel ladders and all body tracks of equal length. *Missouri Pacific*

Runaround

Start with a runaround track—a double-ended track that allows the locomotive from an incoming train to escape to the other end. It will serve equally well if the yard receives trains from both directions. This is about as basic as a yard can get and might well be the basis for a small branchline terminal with adjacent industrial spurs. For all its simplicity, this type of track allows cars to be rearranged in any desired order by switching them between the two tracks. The runaround track also allows cars to be placed on either end of a locomotive as needed.

If used in a stub-end situation with a limited tail track beyond the runaround turnout, the minimum length should be that of the largest locomotive or locomotive consist to be handled in the yard. Any length in addition to that will

come in handy as long as it doesn't take away from the length of the runaround track itself. The runaround track should be as long as the usual train to be operated in and out of the yard. Longer trains can be handled, especially if there's plenty of headroom on either end, but for convenience and efficiency most trains should fit the runaround.

One more track

The next logical step in expanding the basic yard is to add another track. If there's room to make the track double-ended that's the best choice, and real railroads always

prefer to construct double-ended tracks whenever they can. On model railroads we may not have that option, and we can usually make stub-ended yard tracks a little longer than if they had switch ladders at both ends. So while a completely double-ended yard is the most flexible and realistic, the usual model railroad compromise is to have a few double-ended yard tracks for flexibility and more single-ended tracks for the greatest possible capacity.

That mix is not a bad compromise as long as we're aware of the limitations of the approach and plan to work around them. The

Sorting and storage track

West

Main track

Runaround track

Optional storage or RIP track

East

most important consideration is which end of the yard should have the ladder. (I know we're only looking at one additional turnout so far, but this will be the foundation for further development.) If the yard is at the end of the line for our railroad, the ladder should point out toward the main line. This allows a train built on the stub-ended track to pull directly out of the yard and allows us to use the main line for whatever headroom we need to switch long cuts of cars.

Other factors apply if the yard will be in the middle, with the main line extended away in either direction. Where the yard operator will have room to sit or stand might be the most important, keeping in mind that this person will want to be next to or at least near the ladder while working. If there's plenty of aisle space next to the yard site, take the planned traffic into account. If there will be more classifications for one direction than the other, the ladder should point in that direction.

Even though we're still talking about a minimal yard with only three tracks, such a layout can do a surprising amount of work. That's essentially all there was to handle the mainline, local, and

branchline traffic arriving and departing at Port on John Allen's famous HO scale Gorre & Daphetid RR. When I operated there in 1970 and 1971, a yardmaster had to be adaptable and ready to improvise to keep the cars moving in and out. Most of us would like more to work with, but that experience showed me that you can do a lot of railroading with a little track.

Classification tracks

Of course it's more convenient and efficient to sort cars if you have more tracks to sort them into. How many tracks you can fit in a given space in your favorite scale is pretty much determined by turnout geometry and minimum track centers (I'll explore more of that on page 30). For now let's look at how you might want to use additional yard tracks.

Above: The photographer wanted the view of the Amtrak train from the cab of this Southern Pacific locomotive, but we can also observe the placement of switch stands to allow switchmen to work from the right-hand side of this yard ladder.
J. Parker Lamb

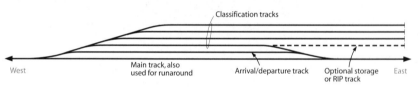

Classification tracks

West

Main track, also used for runaround

Arrival/departure track

Optional storage or RIP track

East

A really basic classification scheme (as described in the first chapter) would use four tracks, one each for through freights and way freights in each direction. You might easily think of more classifications or other ways to define them on four tracks, but let's take that as our example and go on from there.

Also, let's make the first classification track double-ended for a little more flexibility. With our ladder on the east end of the yard, we'll use the double-ended track for our westbound through freight classification. That way we can build a train on that track and have it depart to the west while leaving the runaround track free for other uses. And just to make clear what kind of use we have in mind, let's change the name and

start calling the runaround the arrival/departure (A/D) track.

Drill track

The drill track or switching lead tails off from the yard ladder to allow a switch engine to work while staying clear of the main line. Ideally the lead should be long enough to let the switcher pull all the cars from the longest yard track clear of the first turnout in the ladder. This allows any car to be switched to any track. Should the yard crew need to make an even longer pull, they can use the main track, but the idea is to let the switcher spend most of its time on the drill track.

Many real-life yards don't have such tracks, especially smaller ones on light-traffic lines. They aren't needed if mainline traffic

won't conflict with the yard job very often, and if the business isn't there, the yard engine may not work around the clock anyway. There can be situations like that on model railroads too, but with fast clocks and short distances between terminals, a drill track off the main line is often worthwhile.

Model railroad drill tracks are usually stub ended, with a bumper or electrically dead track section to stop the switcher when it reaches the end. On the real thing, the drill track often connects back to the main line. Remember, the big roads prefer double-ended tracks. With a turnout at its far end, the drill track can serve as an alternate yard entrance and even a place to let an inbound train clear the main line so an outbound train can clear a yard track.

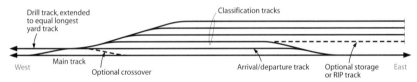

Above: Look at that yard ladder on a curve in the Union Pacific's small yard in Lincoln, Neb. In this post-steam-era photo, the old turntable and its leads are being used to store freight cars. *Jim C. Seacrest*

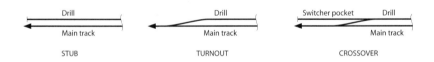

Having a turnout at the end of the drill track may depend on whether the yard engineer will be able to see it on your layout. If not, the stub-end bumper is probably the way to go, but if it's visible I'd probably go for the extra flexibility. For the cost of a second turnout you can put a crossover near the end of the drill track and have the best of both options. Leave enough drill track past the crossover to serve as an engine pocket for the switcher—it needs to be behind any train arriving though the crossover, or it may be trapped and unable to work.

As in the "ideal" yard example from chapter one, the optional crossover between the A/D track and the main line allows the switcher to work a train on the main line from the drill track. The added flexibility will help keep the yard fluid, especially if you can make the A/D track long enough to hold a complete train of normal length clear of the crossover.

Arrival/departure tracks

It's great if you have room for more classification tracks. But before using up all the available real estate, I would want to add at least one more A/D track. Every additional A/D track equals one more train the yard can handle before it gets too full to do its work, and that will help keep things moving on the main line as well. It's particularly useful to have two or even three A/D tracks when most or all of the class tracks are single-ended.

For the cost of some additional yard length, you can provide access to the main line from the A/D tracks without interfering with classification switching from the drill track. The diagrams show a couple of ways to arrange this. When the switch engine crew has a lot of classification work to do, they'll appreciate not being tied up waiting for trains to pull into the yard or out onto the main line. In the interest of flexibility, I also

Right: The curves beyond the turnout frogs show that the Chicago & North Western yard in Nelson, Ill., is laid out with ladders on steeper angles than the turnout frogs. The two-story structure on the left is the yard office. *Wallace W. Abbey*

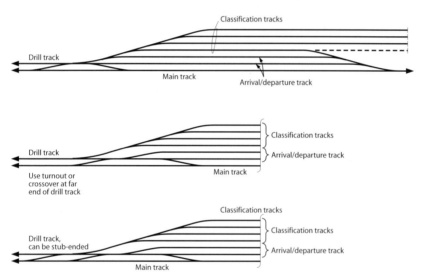

like to make sure there's a direct route from any of the yard's class indication tracks to the main line.

When considering any published yard design, look for direct routes to and from the main line that don't require back-and-forth "sawing" movements. These are real time-wasters that can kill the efficiency of your model yard.

Double-ended yards and thoroughfares

If you can afford the length for a double-ended yard, it will be well worth it. Development of the second or "other" end of the yard can be the same as we've just seen.

Besides gaining realism and flexibility, you can have switch engines working both ends of the yard at the same time for a big improvement in yard efficiency.

One important addition for a double-ended yard is a "thoroughfare" track, also called a "running" track or just a "runner." This track connects to the ladders at both ends and is normally kept empty. It also lets engines get from one end of any yard track to the other (the runaround function). It's also useful to let the switch engines swap cars from one end of the yard to the other for convenient classification and blocking.

Adding the extras

Once you have tracks laid out to serve the basic yard functions, you can add the ancillary tracks and facilities. If the engine terminal can be connected to the thoroughfare track of a double-ended yard, locomotives will be able to move easily between any yard track and their servicing tracks. With a single-ladder yard, access from the engine terminal to the ladder is usually the most convenient.

The caboose track can parallel the drill track or one of the yard tracks. Making it double ended will facilitate keeping cabooses in a first-in, first-out rotation.

If you have an RIP track, you'll want to be able to get cars in and out of it as directly as possible. The scale tracks will need to be convenient, too. This will become useful as you have more cars that need to be weighed. A yard handling a lot of bulk traffic will need its scale in a very handy location.

The same kinds of considerations apply to ice docks. If only a few cars will need re-icing, the dock can be located in an out-of-the-way corner. But if you'll be spotting lots of cars for their initial icing and precooling, you'll want direct access from the yard ladder. And if you want to re-ice cars on through trains, you'll

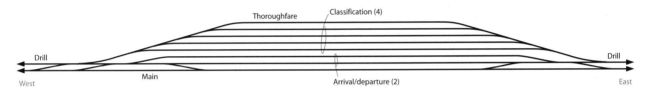

Thoroughfare
Classification (4)
Drill
Drill
West
Main
East
Arrival/departure (2)

probably want the ice dock on a double-ended track so the entire train can pull in and pull out.

Intermodal traffic involves similar concerns. A single track or small ancillary yard may suffice if only a few trailers or containers are to be handled. But if you want to give the impression of a modern intermodal hub, plan for a separate double-ended yard to handle solid trains of flats, spine cars, or well cars. Fortunately for model applications, there are many instances of such yards being adjacent and parallel to what is now sometimes called the "carload traffic" yard.

If you want to have local industries adjacent to a yard, try to arrange the tracks serving them to be switched with the minimum of interference with the classification and train makeup switching. I'd include freight-house and team-yard tracks in that requirement, especially if there will be an extensive LCL operation that involves re-spotting the freight house more than once in an operating session. Being able to serve the industries without conflicting with lead switching will make it easier to establish a separate industrial switching job.

Design process

When you have a good grasp of these various functions, you can look at freight yard design more or less all at once and balance the activities that most satisfy your operational and modeling interests against those you consider to

Photo above: At 40th Street in Chicago the Chicago & North Western yard has both a diamond-shaped yard and a pyramid yard around a curve. *Chicago & North Western*

be not as important. When that seems to get too complicated, however, you can always rely on the track-by-track approach to lay out a practical yard that works.

Yard geometry

The requirements of yard design involve turnout angles, track spacing, car and train lengths, and the length of ladder tracks. There was a tendency—especially in older track plans—to use the sharpest possible turnouts, such as no. 4. (Turnouts are classified by number; the lower the number, the sharper the angle.) This would give the shortest ladder and the longest yard tracks for a given space, but at the expense of operating reliability because of sharp radii and S curves.

Experienced model railroad operators now prefer longer turnouts, with no. 6 frogs being common and anything sharper than no. 5 being avoided. This involves a sacrifice of some yard capacity, but allows for smoother and more reliable operation.

Track spacing is another variable. In straight yards with reliable automatic coupling, and uncoupling handled either automatically or with some form of pick, track spacing can approach the minimum for whatever scale you use. This allows you to squeeze extra tracks in a given width.

Curved yards will need more clearance between tracks, unless the curvature is extremely broad. Real railroads usually prefer to avoid curved yards, but they can't in every situation. Curving a model yard makes it seem larger and opens up scenic opportunities, and the operation can still be reliable if the ends of tracks where cars are coupled and uncoupled remain straight or very gently curved.

Reading car reporting marks on tracks in the middle of a yard should not be a consideration in track spacing, as I'll explain later when we look at yard operation.

Locating uncoupling magnets in a yard

I prefer to use electromagnets on double-ended yard tracks and sidings as well as on mainline tracks so I can control them. Electromagnet uncouplers (which activate when you press a button to energize the magnet) are also a good idea in locations where you'll be working over two magnets at once. Otherwise, I use permanent magnets on single-ended yard and spur tracks.

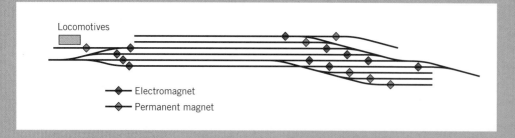

Locomotives

◆ Electromagnet
◆ Permanent magnet

Ladder tracks

Railroads prefer straight ladder tracks primarily for safety in operation. There's no need to cross the ladder track to line switches, and locomotive and ground crews can see each other clearly. For a given frog number, however, these will be the longest ladders and allow the shortest tracks in the body of the yard.

A common answer to this in the prototype—but one too rarely used on model railroads—is to set the ladder at a steeper angle than the frogs and continue the curvature of the turnouts past the frogs. A ladder with no. 6 turnouts, frog angle 9.5 degrees, can be built on the 11.5 degree angle of a no. 5 turnout, with a short but large-radius curve leading into each body track. This is a good way to gain a few extra car lengths in the body tracks while enjoying the advantages of large turnouts and a simple ladder.

More complicated forms can also be used to shorten the length of yard ladders. The compound ladder isn't as common in real yards, except for hump yards where the switch points are power operated. With the usual hand-operated turnouts, a compound ladder can require the ground crew to cross active leads, increasing the danger of their work. Where compound ladders are used in flat-switched yards,

the switch rods are often extended to allow all the switch stands to be outside the main ladder track, thus reducing the need to cross the ladder while switching.

The pinwheel ladder is even less common on real railroads, but is nevertheless a useful design tool for modelers. It offers a way to wrap a ladder around the inside of a curve, and in some situations that may be the only option for extending body tracks. As long as the turnouts and curve radii are large enough, pinwheel ladders can operate reliably, and they have the virtue of eliminating the S curves that are so troublesome for the longest cars.

With double-ended yards, a common arrangement is to have ladders slope toward each other and toward some theoretical crossing point. This produces "pyramid" shaped yards, with tracks of decreasing length as you move farther up the ladder. This may not be a problem with only a few tracks or when some classifications will normally see fewer cars than others. The least-used classifications can be assigned to the shortest body tracks and the shortest track of all can be used for the thoroughfare.

For body tracks that are equally long, the "diamond-shaped" yard

is best. The ladder tracks are parallel, with turnouts branching the same way at both ends of each track. This forms a parallelogram with equal length body tracks.

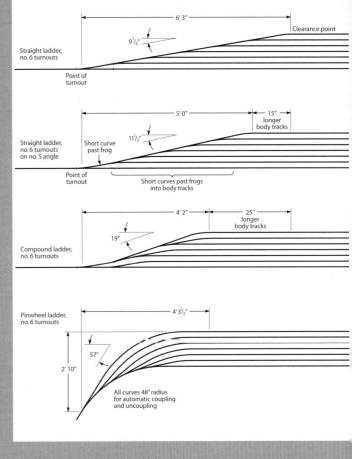

Photo: Above: Shiny new E1 diesels lead a Baltimore & Ohio passenger train past a real-life example of a pinwheel freight yard ladder.
C. Raymond Brandt

Yard throats for operation
An experienced model railroader offers several "domino" designs

By David Barrow

I've recently been planning layouts using what I call "dominos"—standardized, segmental building units. This approach was described in the June, August, and October 1995 issues of *Model Railroader*, and I used it for the South Plains District HO scale project layout I described in the September through December 1996 issues.

I rebuilt my own railroad, the HO scale Cat Mountain & Santa Fe, from 1992-1993 using this method. In my case, the building units are typically 12" or 18" wide and 48" long. These dominos make it easy for me to design a linear layout quickly in a given space and tell me right away what fits and what doesn't.

One of the most interesting features of the domino planning method is that it has allowed me to build up a collection of track planning elements that fit on various numbers of connected dominos. Once I began to see what I could typically fit into two, three, or even four units, I could readily estimate how many dominos would be needed for a specific yard or town.

A potential bottleneck

Here I'd like to concentrate on an aspect of yard design that wasn't discussed in the 1996 issue of *Model Railroad Planning*: yard throats. It's quite possible to do an excellent job designing a classification yard for a model railroad, only to have it become a

bottleneck because of poor yard throat design.

I'll use the domino approach as the basis for this discussion. In addition to reviewing the yard throats on my own model railroad, I've included one based on a Santa Fe prototype. I've also included some good examples of the art from other designers of model railroads.

Among the designs I drew from for this collection are the Mesa and Summit yard throats from my CM&SF as well as the west throat on the

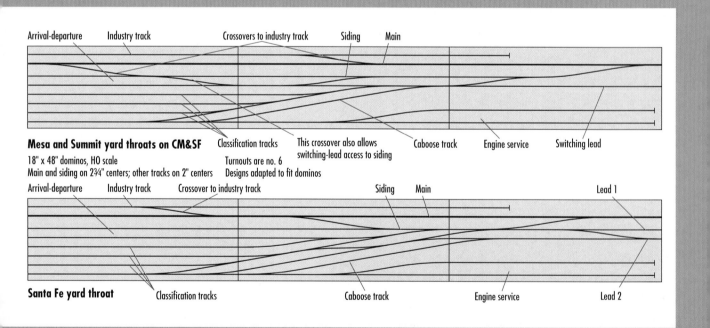

Mesa and Summit yard throats on CM&SF
18" x 48" dominos, HO scale
Main and siding on 2¾" centers; other tracks on 2" centers

Arrival-departure | Industry track | Crossovers to industry track | Siding | Main | Classification tracks | This crossover also allows switching-lead access to siding | Caboose track | Engine service | Switching lead

Turnouts are no. 6
Designs adapted to fit dominos

Santa Fe yard throat
Arrival-departure | Industry track | Crossover to industry track | Siding | Main | Lead 1 | Classification tracks | Caboose track | Engine service | Lead 2

Milwaukee, Racine & Troy (the HO scale club layout designed and operated by employees of Kalmbach Publishing Co.). I also diagrammed a yard throat based on a plan by Tony Steele for a special yard design issue of the *Layout Design Journal* of the Layout Design Special Interest Group. (That issue is available for $10.50 from Bruce Strickland, 10766 Tullamore Ct., Manassas, VA 22111.) Please note that I've modified the original designs slightly to fit on 18" x 48" dominos.

Design requirements
The 18" depth I selected for these examples limits the number of tracks, of course, but all these designs feature an industry track next to the back wall, a main line, a passing track, arrival and departure tracks (the passing siding can also be used this way), classification tracks, a switching lead, a caboose track, an engine terminal, and a thoroughfare or runaround track. Not bad for a foot-and-a-half, eh?

My operational requirements for yard throats are to allow trains to use arrival and departure tracks without interfering with the switching lead, and to provide access to the arrival, departure, and classification tracks from either the main line or the passing track.

Also, crossovers are required to allow a yard engine to go from the yard across the passing track and main to get to the industry track without using the yard entrance switch or switches, which may be signaled. In Santa Fe yards, such as those at Amarillo, Texas, within yard limits on the main tracks and under 10 or 15 mph speed restrictions, these crossover moves may be made at any time without dispatcher authority as long as opposing trains are able to stop well within sight distance.

I also avoid locating turnouts on a section joint, and I recommend a minimum no. 6 turnout frog even for yard and industry tracks. The yard throats in these diagrams follow both restrictions.

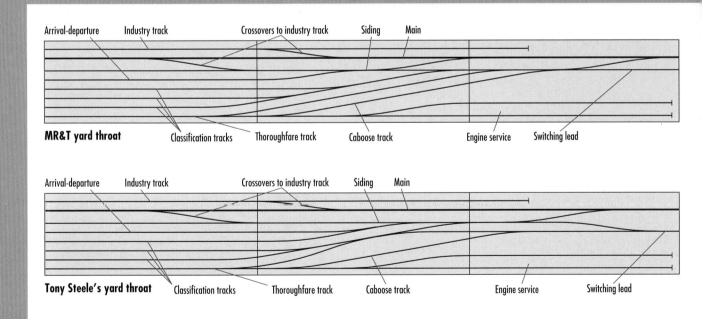

MR&T yard throat

Tony Steele's yard throat

Building a yard ladder

The basic element of any freight yard is the ladder track, where a series of turnouts gives access to parallel tracks used for sorting cars and building trains. The same techniques used for any tracklaying apply just as well to yards, as you'll see in this example.

I built this ladder with ready-made turnouts and flextrack, specifically Atlas HO scale code 83 track, but the methods and materials apply to any scale. The track is laid directly on a plywood surface without any elevated roadbed—Homasote paperboard, sheet cork, or plastic foam insulation board could also be used.

I drew guidelines on the surface for the parallel tracks and the angle of the ladder, and I drilled holes for switch motor actuator rods under the turnout switch rods ("throw bars"). Even if you plan to operate your switches with manual ground throws, you might want to drill the holes in case you ever decide to power the turnouts in the future. Then I glued the track in place with latex adhesive caulk.

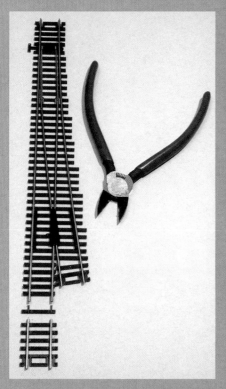

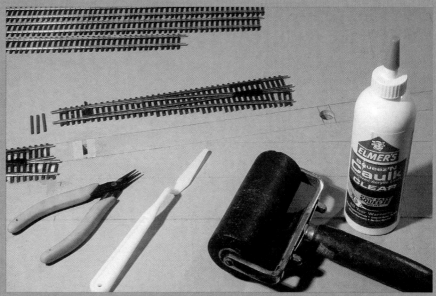

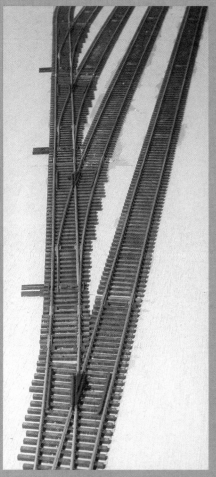

Top left: I wanted the body tracks on scale 14' centers, so I had to trim the Atlas no. 6 turnouts to fit closely enough for that spacing. The short length of track has been trimmed off with rail nippers—flush-cutting pliers—and one tie removed from the remaining turnout lead to make room for the rail joiners.

Bottom left: With adhesive caulk you can build a ladder very quickly. The track sticks to the caulk right away, and no pins or nails are needed to keep it in line, but you have about 15 minutes to make adjustments. This ladder of no. 6 turnouts is laid on a no. 5 angle to save a little space. The ladder diverges from the base line at 12 degrees instead of 9.5 degrees, and the short curve at the beginning of each diverging track brings it back parallel to the base line. I've used half-lengths of Micro Engineering wooden ties to extend the molded ties on each side of the switch rods. These represent the longer ties, called "headblocks," that support the switch stands. Some turnouts come with headblocks molded in place, but you may need to trim and relocate them depending on the layout of your yard. In a simple ladder like this, all the headblocks are normally on the same side of the track to give crews easy access to the switch stands without crossing tracks.

Above: Here I'm ready to add another trimmed turnout to the ladder. I've used short strips of masking tape to cover most of the hole for the turnout motor, so there'll be just a narrow open slot under the switch rod. The next step is to apply narrow beads of adhesive caulk, except beneath the switch rod and switch points, and spread it thin with a spatula. Then I'll slip the rails into the rail joiners, align the ties on my pencil guideline, and press the track down onto the caulk. Finger pressure is all it takes for the adhesive to grab, but I like to run a rubber roller over the rails to be sure the turnout and track are in even contact with the flat surface. The extra stained wooden ties are from Micro Engineering. I use them to fill in under the rail joiners where the ends of turnouts or other tracks have been trimmed.

Top right: After all the yard tracks are laid, wired, and tested, the next step is to paint the track. I airbrushed the rails and ties with a mixture of Polly Scale Railroad Tie Brown and Tarnished Black. This water-based acrylic paint won't fill the air with dangerous solvents, so it's a good choice for spray painting on a layout. I cleaned the railheads shortly after I'd sprayed them, while the paint was still soft and easy to remove. Since the points of the Atlas turnouts don't depend on contact with the stock rail for power, it isn't necessary to mask these mating faces. For other types of turnouts you can insert small blocks of wood or plastic foam between the open point and its adjacent stock rail to keep paint off the mating surfaces for electrical contact.

Bottom right: When the paint is dry the yard tracks can be ballasted. I used crushed stone ballast secured by the bonded-ballast method. That is, I spooned dry ballast onto the track and turnouts. After spreading and shaping the ballast with disposable foam brushes, I glued it down. Ballast is easy to add but harder to subtract, so start with a small amount and spread it out before adding more. Be especially sparing with ballast under turnout points and around switch rods, so the turnouts will still operate freely after the ballast is secure. Using a magnifier and a small brush, I made sure that not even a single grain of ballast could interfere with turnout operation. Then I used a spray bottle to soak the ballast with a 70-percent solution of isopropyl rubbing alcohol and dribbled on white glue thinned 4-to-1 with water. Alcohol is better than water at soaking into the ballast without disturbing its careful placement, and the thinned glue will flow in wherever the alcohol goes. If glue does pool or bead, spritz on more alcohol and the diluted glue will soak right in. Give the ballast 24 hours to dry thoroughly, and it will be firmly secured but still look loose. After ballasting the yard I added some basic scenery around it and built a gravel road across the yard lead to add a point of interest. The planked crossing is built with layers of Evergreen Scale Models scribed styrene. This is meant to be a private, railroad-owned access road, so the grade crossing doesn't need to be protected.

Above: Even if they are
powered by motors under the
roadbed, yard turnouts need
switch stands to look realistic in
your yard. I used Detail West
no. 916 kits to add these
details. Many railroads used
numbers on switch targets to
identify yard tracks, so I added
decal numbers to the
targets to help my yard crews
find the right track. There are
many other ways to do this,
including separate markers
attached to the headblocks next
to the switch stands, or even
numbered signs attached to an
overpass or footbridge above
the tracks.

The empty hopper train entering Shire Oaks Yard is the center of attention here, but take a look at that curving, compound yard ladder at the upper left where the switcher is working. Rob Enrico built this space-saving layout for his O scale Penn Central Monongahela Division layout.
Paul J. Dolkos

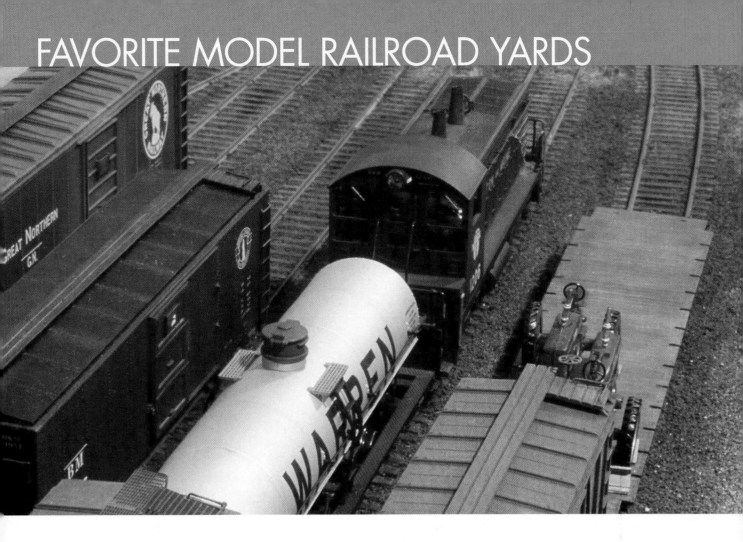

Woodsriver Yard can efficiently support operations on the rest of the model railroad and provide hours of enjoyment for its yardmaster. *Paul J. Dolkos*

My favorite way to learn about model railroad yard design is to operate yards on a variety of model railroads. If you have the opportunity, I encourage you to try it. You'll quickly develop a feel for what you like. You'll learn that there can be a wide variety of ways to accomplish the same basic objectives. In addition, if you like yard operation even half as much as I do, you'll have some really good times.

But this is a book, not an operating tour, so the next best thing is to share with you a few of my favorite model railroad yards. I'll explain what I like about each design. This way, you'll be able to see how each could fit in with your own goals and requirements. A good shortcut to a workable yard for any model railroad is to copy or adapt someone else's successful design. I've done it myself, as I'll show you on page 45.

THREE

Colbert Yard on the Delta Lines

Frank Ellison was one of model railroading's pioneers, and his O scale Delta Lines was a groundbreaking layout. It had three major yards—Chapelle, Colbert, and Fillmore—named for streets in the New Orleans subdivision where he lived. (His home was on Colbert St. between Chapelle and Fillmore.) Chapelle and Fillmore were the southern and northern terminals, and Colbert was a division point yard in the middle of the main line.

Even though I grew up in New Orleans, I'm just a little too young to have had a chance to operate Colbert or even visit the Delta Lines. However, Frank wrote about his division point so vividly that I could clearly grasp its potential. I adapted the design for use on a friend's layout and found that it lived up to my expectations.

The main purpose of Colbert Yard was to handle through traffic, though it originated and terminated way freights as well. It was an actual crew-change point, as different engineers ran trains on the Delta Lines' Northern and Southern Divisions, and most of the trains changed engines as well. At one point in time, the Northern Division was electrified, and trains through Colbert exchanged steam for electric power, or vice versa. (In fact, all of Frank's steam, diesel, and electric locomotives carried shoes to pick up current from an outside third rail.)

In its original form Colbert was extremely compact, so it makes a great example of how to provide

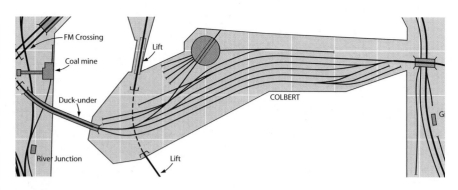

essential functions within a limited space. It was double-ended, so it was not only flexible but had a very railroady look. The S curve through the yard added a little more visual interest. In its earliest published form it had no drill tracks, but Frank had added them by the time the entire layout plan was featured in *Model Railroader* magazine in 1956.

One feature of Colbert Yard that I haven't mentioned in earlier chapters is the pair of engine pockets found at each end. These short spurs allow an arriving engine to uncouple from a train and quickly get into the clear, while the outbound engine waits in position to back directly onto the continuing consist. Their inclusion shows that this was an important function at Colbert, and it must have helped to let trains spend as little time as possible stopped on one of the yard's few tracks.

The freight operation was limited by the track space and the emphasis on through trains, but Colbert did handle what would now be called "block swapping" between through freights and peddlers (way freights). It worked like this: A through freight would

arrive from the north with a block of cars for local destinations on the Southern Division. Railroaders call these "shorts," since they are going to places short of the train's final destination (in this case Chapelle). At the same time, the Northern Division peddler freight would have tied up at Colbert with cars picked up along its run and destined for Chapelle and points south—let's call them "throughs."

As the road engines were being exchanged, the Colbert switcher pulled the shorts off the through freight and added throughs from the north peddler. With its new engine tied on, the southbound train was soon ready to depart with a solid consist of cars for Chapelle and connections at that terminal. The switcher could then build the southbound Southern Division peddler from the shorts it took from the through freight in addition to any Southern Division shorts picked up by the peddler from the north.

Colbert would probably dispatch the south peddler with a Southern Division engine and caboose that had arrived earlier on a peddler that came north from Chapelle. Meanwhile, the peddler

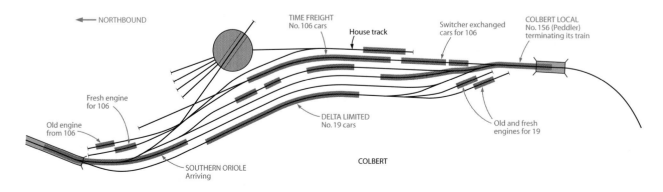

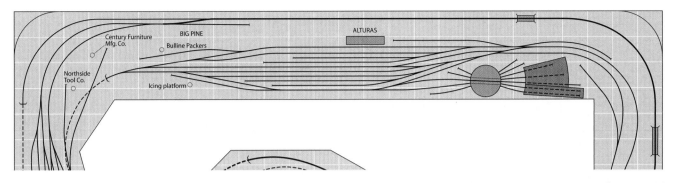

Century Furniture
Mfg. Co.

BIG PINE

Bulline Packers

ALTURAS

Northside
Tool Co.

Icing platform

engine and caboose from Fillmore would be laying over until a northbound through freight arrived with a block of shorts destined for Northern Division points.

Besides a turntable and small number of engine stalls, Colbert had few other facilities and no local industries. It was division point railroading pared down to its lean essentials.

Alturas Yard on the Alturas & Lone Pine

Whit Towers was another pioneer model railroad operator, and his HO scale Alturas & Lone Pine RR appeared in *Model Railroader* magazine many times from the 1960s through the 1980s. I was lucky enough to know Whit and got to operate the ALP with him on a visit to Southern California in the 1990s. I always liked his Alturas Yard for its railroady, through-yard layout and its nice mixture of railroad and industrial structures. When I got to know more about railroading and model railroad operation, I appreciated the yard all the more for its location and function on the ALP.

At first glance, Alturas might seem a lot like Colbert, but instead of being in the middle it was at the north end of the fictitious line's route. The line continuing north into loop staging tracks wasn't the ALP but a connection from the Western Pacific. Traffic moved north from the ALP's lines onto the WP to connect with points north and west. This is a great example of how even a terminal yard moves railcars through to "somewhere else."

Because most cars coming north into Alturas would be interchanged with the WP, this town's very modest industrial base did not have to provide destinations for all of the ALP's northbound traffic. Likewise, cars that came from the WP were the mainstays of most of the ALP's southward trains. Alturas was at the end of the line as far as the ALP was concerned, but in terms of the railroad's connections beyond Whit's train room, it was just as much in the middle as Colbert.

Whit enhanced the role of Alturas Yard by operating what today's modelers call a live interchange connection. Southbound trains arrived from the hidden loop storage tracks at the railroad's extreme north end behind WP diesels and trailing WP cabooses. These came off the train at Alturas, having added to the realism of Whit's free-lanced model railroad by portraying a recognizable link with reality.

An ALP switcher pulled any shorts from the consist and added through cars for Lone Pine. There might also be blocks for setoff along the way at Auburn, where a switcher was stationed to service a concentration of industries, and at Sonora, the junction with the Trojan Logging Co. RR which operated the branch line to Railroad Flat.

An ALP caboose would be tacked onto the rear of the southbound through freight, and an ALP steam locomotive would roll off the roundhouse ready track to transport the train to Lone Pine. Alturas also built southbound way

Alturas Yard was a terminal with a working connection to off-layout destinations.
Whitney K. Towers

freights to serve stations between the terminals, but it didn't have to make up northward locals for the WP. Northward trains might bring in a few cars for local spots at Alturas, but most traffic in that direction would be going straight to the connecting railroad.

Speaking of those local spots, Alturas did have a couple of industry and servicing spurs that added to the switch crew's work. At the south end there was an icing platform and cattle loading

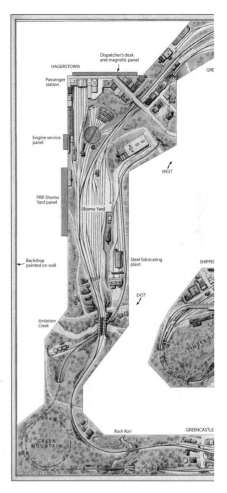

Western's Shenandoah Division at Shomo Yard in Hagerstown.

Shomo Yard does not represent the prototype track arrangement. It is actually based on plan 82 from *101 Track Plans for Model Railroaders* (Kalmbach Books) by Linn Westcott. It's well adapted to its role in Cumberland Valley operations, however.

Freights from Enola Yard in Harrisburg, Pa., (staging) run over the CV line through Shippensburg and Greencastle, Pa., to arrive in one of Shomo Yard's long through tracks. The Pennsylvania power, usually Electro-Motive or Alco cab diesels, is hostled to the adjacent diesel servicing tracks and the PRR cabin car (caboose) is then switched to the cabin track.

The Shomo switcher next cuts off a block of shorts for locals and branchline trains originating in Hagerstown, in addition to any Hagerstown propers for the local industries. That generally leaves a block of cars going through to the N&W at Roanoke, Va., and the Shomo switcher will add a similar block built from cars that have arrived on PRR local and branch-line trains. The transformation from a PRR to an N&W train is complete when the switcher tacks on an N&W caboose from the cabin track.

Since the N&W Shenandoah Division is still all steam, its power is serviced and turned at the roundhouse across the main line from Shomo Yard. Most southbound freights get a Y6 class Mallet-compound 2-8-8-2, making a strong contrast with the rapidly dieselizing Pennsy. The Mallet then leads its train out of the yard past Hager Tower and through Clearbrook to Roanoke (staging). Northbound through trains originating from Roanoke reverse these procedures at Shomo Yard.

In addition to these through freights, Shomo Yard also makes up PRR locals and branchline trains. The mainline local freight runs north to Harrisburg (via

staging), serving Greencastle and Shippensburg. Its opposite side is a southbound local to Hagerstown that originates in staging. Pennsy branchline trains operate south from Shomo to the Virginia towns of Winchester and Martinsburg and return.

A freight station and icing dock at Shomo Yard may be served by the switcher there, but another switcher assigned to the passenger station is available to help out when not required for passenger switching. The station switcher also serves the industries along the station lead and the coal, sand, and ash track at the round-house, making up its delivery cut from cars brought into Shomo on the various trains. Shomo also makes up transfers for the WM interchange at Hager Tower and classifies the inbound interchange cars received from the WM.

The varied through, terminal, interchange, and local switching operations at Shomo make it interesting and challenging to operate, but its efficient layout of through tracks allows it to handle a lot of traffic smoothly. Generally the two long tracks nearest the main aisle are used as arrival and departure tracks, while the four shorter tracks in the middle off the yard are used for classification. Cars for two or more classifications may have to be blocked together on these tracks, but the ability to reach them from either end, especially when both switchers can work together, gives this yard great flexibility.

Port Marquette Yard on the Milwaukee, Racine & Troy

The largest of the model yards in this tour is Port Marquette Yard on the Kalmbach Model Railroad Club HO layout, the Milwaukee, Racine & Troy. Like San Diego, Port Marquette is a true terminal. Nevertheless, this yard features a double-ended arrangement for a prototypical appearance—espe-cially worthwhile on a free-lanced

pens; the Wallace Mat Co. factory was at the north end of the yard lead. The icing platform served the purpose of re-icing refrigera-tor cars in transit, while the latter two generated a few carloadings for the ALP.

Shomo Yard on the Cumberland Valley System

Brothers Bill and Wayne Reid built an N scale model railroad that combines the best of scenic appearance and operating action. Their Cumberland Valley System models two parallel rail lines through its namesake valley and Hagerstown, Md. One line is the Western Maryland. Even though the WM had a fairly large yard in Hagerstown, the brothers decided not to model it. They did decide, however, to represent the mighty Pennsylvania RR which utilized the original Cumberland Valley line to connect with the Norfolk &

Above: Shomo Yard makes the connection between the Pennsylvania RR, its owner, and the Norfolk & Western.
Andy Sperandeo

layout—and for expeditious handling of traffic in both directions.

Port Marquette is envisioned to lie to the southwest of downtown Milwaukee, at the east end of a main line that runs to Rockford, Ill., and Fort Madison, Iowa, site of its main connection with the Burlington Northern Santa Fe. Most road freights arrive from and depart to the west, but there's also a brisk traffic in transfers and local switchers in and out of the west end of the yard. The transfers represent connections with CP Rail and Union Pacific while the local switchers serve customers in the city proper and on the heavily industrialized Kelly's Island.

Port Marquette Yard features a three-track arrival-and-departure yard with independent access to the double-track main line in both directions. Trains arriving or leaving from either end can enter or leave the yard without interfering with lead switching on the adjacent classification ladder.

The next six tracks toward the aisle form the classification yard. That gives the yard about as much width as we thought we could

handle in HO scale, but since Port Marquette will sort cars into at least ten classifications, it will still be crowded enough to present a challenge. (A yard is more fun when the work isn't too easy!)

The last track next to the aisle is the thoroughfare track, meant to normally be unoccupied so locomotives can move efficiently to and from the engine terminal connected to the thoroughfare at its east end. The thoroughfare will also be handy for letting the switchers at opposite ends of the yard pass cars back and forth for the most direct sorting into the inevitably doubled-up classification tracks.

A pair of short double-ended tracks parallel to the east ladder is left over from times past—the caboose tracks. Perhaps one will still be used to store a few cabooses for locals and trains that have to make long backup moves. The other will make a convenient runaround track, or it may see use as an engine pocket when the engine leads are occupied.

The west end has a long drill track, long enough to let the

switcher pull the longest track in the yard and deal the cars out to any other track. This will be the main classification lead. It's not connected to the main line at its far end. It might be more realistic to connect the end of the drill track to the main with a turnout, but on the model railroad the yard engineer will usually be back at the ladder and might not see when the engine had backed out too far. The stub-end lead will avoid that kind of trouble.

The shorter lead on the east end is double-ended. The east-end switcher usually handles the shorter cuts of cars, assisting the west-end job that does most of the sorting. The double-ended lead allows for the occasional long pull when the dispatcher allows use of the connecting main line. It's also an alternate way in or out of the yard from the mainline connection near the passenger station.

43

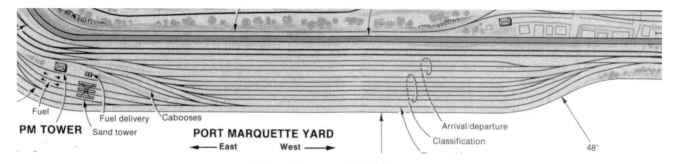

Fuel

PM TOWER Fuel delivery 'Cabooses
Sand tower **PORT MARQUETTE YARD**
◄——— East   West ———►

Arrival/departure
Classification

48"

The only industrial spots serviced by the Port Marquette crews will be on the locomotive supply track—cars hauling fuel, sand, and more rarely, lubricants and other supplies. The other nearby industries will be served by a "City Switcher" on its way to and from "Allis" (the east-end staging yard, taking its name from the industrial community of West Allis) and by the "Kelly's Island Job" working that industrial branch from Port Marquette.

Cars arriving from the west will mostly be destined for Milwaukee industries either modeled on the layout or represented by staging, or for transfer to connecting railroads also represented by staging. The connecting roads include CP Rail (formerly Soo Line) and Union Pacific (formerly Chicago & North Western), both of which are simulated by the Allis staging yard, and Canadian National (which was formerly Wisconsin Central), represented by its own staging track connecting to the MR&T main line at GO Tower west of Mukwonago. The CN transfer will operate on trackage rights over the MR&T from GO Tower into Port Marquette Yard.

At Port Marquette most westbound cars will be built into trains for Rockford, Ill., which we imagine to be home to the MR&T's main classification yard. It also originates a BNSF run-through with cars destined for Kansas City and points west. The Mukwonago Turn, an MR&T way freight, runs between Port Marquette and its namesake station. The Williams Bay Switcher, the other MR&T way freight, is headquartered at

that station, where it exchanges cars with through freights bound for Rockford or Port Marquette.

With traffic moving in and out in this variety of trains, Port Marquette will be a busy sorting center. As with our other examples, this freight yard will handle cars moving in both directions even though it represents the eastern terminus of the MR&T's mainline route.

By now it should be obvious that I've chosen these examples of model railroad yards to show how they handle cars moving through to destinations beyond. Those des-

Above: *Model Railroader* editors Cody Grivno (front) and David Popp operate the Port Marquette Yard. *Bill Zuback*

tinations can be other subdivisions of the same railroad, connections with other railroads, or local industrial customers, and any combination of these three. But all these yards perform the mission of sending the cars they receive to somewhere else, and none of them is operated as a destination in itself.

Ellison Yard on the Cat Mountain & Santa Fe

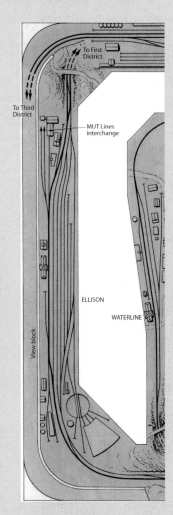

When I designed Ellison Yard on the early versions of David Barrow's Cat Mountain & Santa Fe, I based it on Frank Ellison's Colbert Yard. Both David and I admired the Delta Lines and thought following Frank's example would be both fun and effective. Compare the track plan here with that of Colbert Yard on page 40 and you can see the similarities and differences.

At Ellison, the engine terminal was a little more developed and there was a setout track

at the passenger station. There was a caboose track, and a long yard lead or drill track which paralleled the main line and disappeared off-scene to the west. It also had a couple of industry and interchange tracks. On the other hand, we omitted the engine pockets since we didn't need to make quick changes between steam or diesel and electric locomotives.

Even though Ellison was at one end of the CM&SF main line, instead of in the middle like Colbert, it still functioned like a division point. In Santa Fe terms it marked the divide between one crew district to the east (represented by staging) and another to the west, the modeled segment of the CM&SF. The freight yard received setouts

from through trains and built blocks for them to pick up. It also built the daily local freight that ran west from Ellison to Belo Horizonte, the other end of the onstage district. The eastbound local freight and occasional extra trains terminated at Ellison.

The through tracks allowed traffic to move freely in both directions, and the stub tracks faced west, the direction of most originating trains. Engines had free access from the roundhouse leads to both ends of the yard via the thoroughfare track. The drill track allowed switchers to pull the longest track and deal cars out into any other freight yard track. For the kind of relatively laid-back West Texas traffic we were modeling, the yard was

effective and efficient, and it had an authentic look that we enjoyed.

For me, Ellison Yard remains an excellent example of what can be accomplished by adapting a successful model yard design for another model railroad.

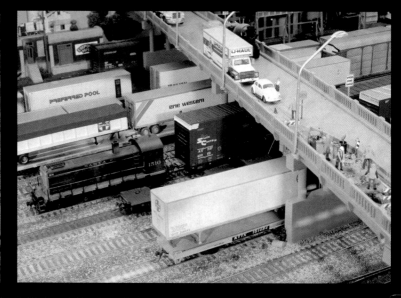

Overpasses across yards are a feature of many cities, and they offer a way to break up large expanses of track in model scenes. There's added interest, too, in seeing cars and trains pass under them. The steam-era yard is at Fellsburg, Mass., on George Sellios's HO scale Franklin & South Manchester RR (top left), while the Santa Fe S-4 diesel switcher is working in Emporia Yard on Stephen and Cynthia Priest's HO scale Emporia Subdivision layout (top right). *Dave Frary and Tom Danneman*

Right: The two-story yard office at White River Junction, Vt., is the focal point of activity on Don Janes' HO scale Green Mountain Division of the Boston & Maine. This building also serves as a train-order office, as we can see by the dual semaphores rising above the roof on the track side of the building. *Don Janes*

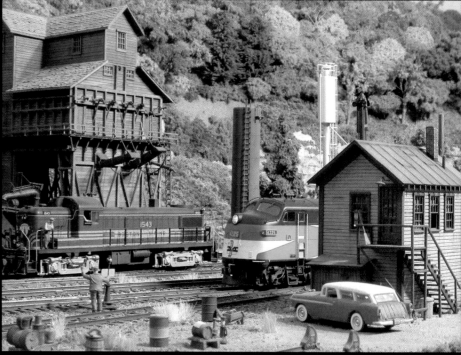

Left: Claymont Yard on John Wilkes' Louisville & Nashville layout is part illusion. The yard tracks curving out of sight under the overpass in the left distance were actually the exposed end of the railroad's through staging yard. It gave the appearance of a busy yard while serving as a ready source of through traffic for the main line, like the Seaboard Coast Line run-through train pulling past the servicing tracks. *Paul J. Dolkos*

If you're modeling your favorite prototype railroad or free-lancing with a strong prototype influence, one of the most rewarding design approaches can be re-creating track layouts used by the real railroads. The track arrangement can help build the authenticity of your model scene, and the operation will be authentic because it must follow the pattern of the track. For small-town stations and junctions this can be relatively easy, but you may feel overwhelmed by the challenge of modeling a prototype yard.

Yet it can be done, and can lend your model railroad the same realism in appearance and functionality as following the track layout of a rural station.

Jack Burgess models the Yosemite Valley RR, a California short line, and was able to build his HO scale El Portal yard as an almost exact duplicate of its prototype near the gateway to Yosemite National Park. *Jack Burgess*

FOUR

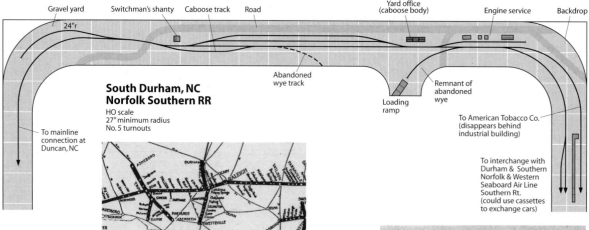

Gravel yard · Switchman's shanty · Caboose track · Road · Yard office (caboose body) · Engine service · Backdrop

24"r

Abandoned wye track

South Durham, NC
Norfolk Southern RR

HO scale
27" minimum radius
No. 5 turnouts

To mainline connection at Duncan, NC

Loading ramp

Remnant of abandoned wye

To American Tobacco Co. (disappears behind industrial building)

To interchange with Durham & Southern Norfolk & Western Seaboard Air Line Southern Rt. (could use cassettes to exchange cars)

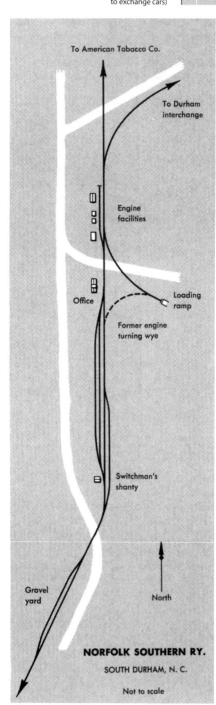

To American Tobacco Co.

To Durham interchange

Engine facilities

Office

Loading ramp

Former engine turning wye

Switchman's shanty

Gravel yard

North

NORFOLK SOUTHERN RY.

SOUTH DURHAM, N. C.

Not to scale

Strategies that work for model yard design are to pick smaller prototype yards when you can, to concentrate on dominant characteristics of the track arrangement and its surroundings, and to represent the functionality of the prototype even when you can't model every track.

In Chapter 3 we saw some examples of model railroad yards that weren't directly copied from particular prototypes. Here we'll see examples of yards modeled on actual railroad installations.

South Durham on the Norfolk Southern

This isn't today's giant system built from mergers of already-large railroad companies, but the earlier regional railroad of the same name that once connected Norfolk, Va., with Charlotte, N.C. A 40-mile branch left its east-west main line at Duncan, N.C., and ran north to Durham, where it served the American Tobacco Co. plant and had interchange connections with four railroads. These included the Norfolk & Western, Seaboard Air Line, and Southern Ry., as well as the short-line Durham & Southern. The terminal of this branch at a small yard at South Durham offers a prototype that can be modeled almost exactly. My design for an HO scale yard is based on the profile of South Durham by Francis H. Parker that was published in

Model Railroader in June 1974.

The yard is simplicity itself: two double-ended tracks on the west side of the through track and a short double-ended track opposite the south end of the yard. I've labeled this short track for caboose storage, but that's really just my guess as Parker didn't identify its purpose. It might also have served as a scale track at some time. No separate lead or drill track was needed on a one-train-a-day branch line.

A single spur was dedicated to servicing the two Baldwin road switchers that worked the branch, and a tank car was normally kept on the end of the spur to supply diesel fuel. In steam days there was a turning wye on the opposite (east) side of the through track, and part of its north leg was retained to serve an end-loading platform. The turning wye could be modeled in full if you wanted to backdate the line; a spur parallel to the tail track would allow you to retain the "industry" spot.

The gravel yard to the south was a good customer that received gravel in hopper cars. The gravel track was really double-ended too, but I made it a spur to better suit its location on a curve.

The major industry for the South Durham branch, however, was the American Tobacco Co. plant located five miles north of the yard. I've indicated it as a spur extending out of sight behind an industrial building flat—in effect a staging track representing the off-layout industrial plant. We could imagine that the plant would receive tobacco and paper products in boxcars, and coal for its power plant in hopper cars. It could also ship its products in boxcars. To add switching interest, we could specify a required order for cars serving these different purposes and block them in order at South Durham before shoving them onto the hidden spur. Outbound cars pulled from the spur could be blocked for east- or westbound connections at Duncan.

The interchange tracks in front of the tobacco company flat could extend for whatever length you have available, or they could end in cassettes. These can be simple: wooden strips with track and perhaps low sides to make it easy to lift the cars delivered to other railroads off the layout. Additional cassettes could hold other cars to be received in interchange. This stratagem allows for a greater variety and number of cars than the layout itself might be able to accommodate. Most of us end up with more cars than we really need, and this approach can keep them circulating between the layout and storage shelves.

South Durham's modest yard won't be able to generate multiple trains to support group operating sessions, but for a railroad meant for solo operation it has all the essentials. It also provides the satisfaction of knowing that the model layout's operations almost have to duplicate those of the prototype, since the track layout is practically identical. The other yards in this chapter offer the same rewards in busier settings.

To review the three strategies I started with, South Durham is a small terminal that can fit on a model railroad. It was out in the pine woods on the south side of the city, so its surroundings would be easy to represent, and its track arrangement directly reflects that

San Diego Yard on the Santa Fe

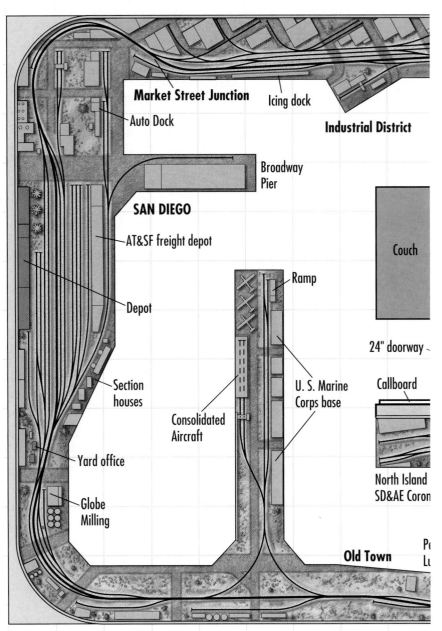

of the real yard. The use of staging and fiddle-yard techniques to represent the major industry and interchanges up the line allows us to replicate the real yard's functions without having to model a sprawling factory or the other railroads.

San Diego on the Surf Line
Keith Jordan's HO railroad represents the San Diego terminal of the Atchison, Topeka & Santa Fe's "Surf Line," formally known as the Fourth District of the Los Angeles Division, as it was in 1940. The track layout is closely based on the prototype, and at that time the Santa Fe's freight operation was centered in a relatively small yard between downtown San Diego and the waterfront. It was adjacent to the ornate passenger station built for the Panama-Pacific Exposition of 1915, a practically ideal setting and size for a model railroad yard.

In 1940 the Fourth District line would typically see only two daily freight trains in each direction.

Eastbound (moving away from Los Angeles) train 136 operated from the City of Angels over the Third District main line to the junction with the Fourth District at Fullerton, and from there down the Surf Line to San Diego. Its westbound opposite, train 135, was known as the "Night Coast" for its late-evening departure.

For traffic from points east and north, symbol freight SDX (San Diego Extra) originated in San Bernardino. It then ran west on the Third District to the junction with the Olive District at Atwood and took that line to reach Orange on the Fourth District. From there it ran "timetable east"—geographically southeast—to San Diego. Its opposite side was the SBX (San Bernardino Extra), which originated in San Diego and used the reverse routing to travel to San Bernardino.

Although all four of these San Diego freights were nominally through trains, the Night Coast and San Bernardino Extra both handled local work between San Diego and Oceanside, 41 miles up the coast. There was one short-distance way freight originating in San Diego and working out and back to Del Mar, and consequently was known as the Del Mar Turn.

That might seem to leave San Diego's yard relatively quiet, and in terms of mainline freight traffic it certainly was. The outbound road freights were made up in the evening and left at night, and the inbound road freights arrived in the early morning. But during the daylight hours the San Diego yard was the hub for several local switching jobs. Switchers serving the Old Town area to the north worked the large Consolidated Aircraft Factory and the U.S.

Marine Corps base along with a number of smaller industries. Other switchers working the industrial district to the south also handled cars to and from the interchange with the San Diego & Arizona Eastern Ry., a subsidiary of the Southern Pacific. The National City switcher moved cars to and from the extreme south end of the Fourth District, which on Keith's railroad is represented by staging. A major source of traffic at National City was the Santa Fe's own tie-and-timber-treating plant, which supplied the needs of the railroad's Coast Lines grand

Above: At the A Yard in San Bernardino, Calif., on the Santa Fe, the powerhouse smokestack and the Mt. Vernon Avenue overpass were recognizable from many angles. And notice the many brake shoes that have been replaced on freight cars that had just descended Cajon Pass.
R.S. Plummer

San Bernardino B Yard

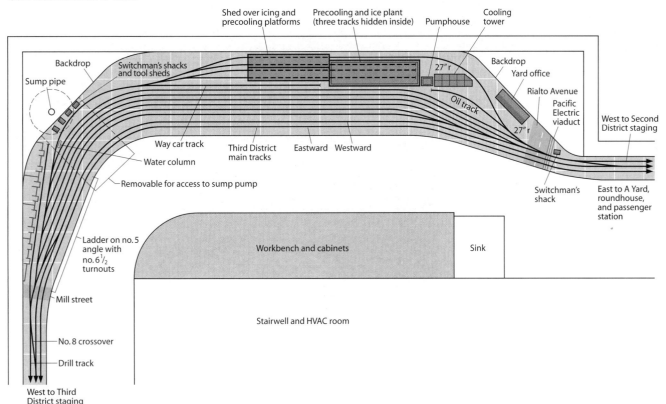

division, including all AT&SF lines west of Albuquerque, N.M.

Adjacent to the San Diego yard are a few industries, the Santa Fe freight house, and the Broadway Pier. These are switched by the yard switcher, which also handles the passenger station switching and couples to the rear end of departing San Diegan streamliners to pull them backwards to turn on the Old Town wye.

The yard's prototypical track arrangement includes two double-ended tracks alongside the main line to use for arrivals and departures, and four stub tracks available for classifying cars. A fifth stub track next to the freight depot is ordinarily used for passenger car storage.

The double-ended track connecting the passenger station lead with the top end of the station ladder is used to store cabooses. This is one of those cases that breaks a "rule" about convenient location of such tracks, especially since it's

across the main line from the yard. However, prototype photos show that this is where the Santa Fe stored the few cabooses needed for the daily freights, so Keith follows that practice.

The engine terminal for San Diego was to the south in National City, so it's represented by storing engines in the staging yard. The light-engine movements between the National City staging yard and downtown San Diego add some prototypical interference with the

tasks of the industrial switchers.

The SD&AE line has trackage rights on the Santa Fe from Market Street Junction to the station, allowing its passenger trains to share the Santa Fe depot.

Since San Diego really is a terminal, all cars arriving on 136 and the SDX are moving either to customers served by the AT&SF between Old Town and National City, or to customers served by the SD&AE. Even in this extreme end-of-the-line situation, the yard itself isn't the destination, and the yard crew sorts the arriving cars into cuts for the various switching jobs to deliver.

Cars brought back to the yard by the returning switchers must be sorted for departure on either the Night Coast or the SBX, but Santa Fe procedures add extra complexity to the blocking of these trains. The first block behind the engine on each will be "protective service" cars, meaning any loaded stock and refrigerator cars. Other loads for the Night Coast are blocked for the Santa Fe's two Los Angeles freight yards, Hobart and First Street, while SBX loads are all blocked together for San Bernardino and beyond. Finally, both trains are filled to the

tonnage rating of their assigned power with empty cars, with the majority of those moving on the SBX to return to connecting lines to the east and north.

Keith's San Diego yard illustrates all three of the strategies we can use to base model yards on particular prototypes. It's a small yard to start with, and while the scale length of Keith's yard is foreshortened in comparison with the real thing, he was able to model it track for track. Its distinctive setting, between the ornate Santa Fe passenger station and the San Diego waterfront, lends credibility to the model. Even the grade crossings of Broadway and Ash Street—south and north of the

yard, respectively—add to the verisimilitude. And even though Keith couldn't model the roundhouse at National City, the light engine movements to and from the staging yard reproduce the functionality of the actual San Diego terminal.

San Bernardino B Yard

On my own Santa Fe layout I modeled San Bernardino, the headquarters of the Los Angeles Division and the base for helper operations over Cajon Pass. The most important feature of the "San Berdoo" yard arrangement was that there were two separate yards. The A Yard was laid out along the east-west beginning of

Above: How about snow-covered Mt. Shasta to set the scene of a model railroad yard? And notice the river on the right. This is Dunsmuir, Calif., on the Southern Pacific. *Mac LeFebre*

the First District main line between the San Bernardino passenger station to the south and the locomotive and car repair shops to the north. The A Yard handled westward freight traffic, including through trains to Los Angeles via the Third District line through Riverside and Fullerton, San Diego trains by way of Fullerton to the Fourth District "Surf Line," and local freights and fruit pick-ups for the Second (Los Angeles via Pasadena) and Third Districts.

A second yard known as the B Yard stretched north and south (timetable east and west) along the Third District line between San Bernardino and Colton. This was also known as the Precooler Yard because it was adjacent to a large refrigeration plant that made ice for refrigerator cars and "precooled" produce loaded in reefers. In the precooling process, cold air was blown through ducts fitted over the open ice hatches at each end of the refrigerator car to lower the temperature of the perishable lading before it was dispatched to its destination.

The B Yard received perishable carloads from packing houses along the Second, Third, and Fourth District main lines and Los Angeles Division branch lines, switched the refrigerator cars to be precooled and iced according to individual shippers' instructions, and then assembled them into trains. Most of the loaded reefers were bound for Kansas City, Chicago, and connections to Midwestern and Eastern railroads. They were blocked into trains designated GFX (for Green Fruit Express). A smaller number were consigned to points west of Kansas City but east of Belen, N.M.—ranging from Colorado to Texas—and blocked in CTX (California-Texas Express) trains. A few reefers traveled north by way of Barstow and Bakersfield in cars designated NCX (Northern California Express) trains. Add in through freights running east from Los Angeles, also handled in the B Yard, and you've got more than enough prototypical action for a model yard.

Keep in mind that the base for Cajon Pass helpers was San Bernardino. Pusher crews picked up their engines at the round-house on the north side of the A yard, and then backed light (without cars) to the south end of the B Yard to couple on behind eastbound trains. A switcher added the way car (caboose) behind the pushers to complete the train. Union Pacific trains operating over the Santa Fe's First District by trackage rights also stopped in the B Yard to add pushers stationed at the UP's own San Bernardino enginehouse.

In terms of setting, the dominant features of the B Yard were the precooler plant on its west side and the double-track Third District main line on the east. During the 1940s the main line was relocated further east and the yard expanded to more than 25 tracks, but a 1938 plan of the B Yard shows only six double-ended body tracks and four icing and precooling tracks at the south end off the precooler plant. This gave me a starting point of "modelgenic" size for a prototype-based freight yard, even though my layout is set in 1947. I think of this as another aspect of the "selective compression" we use all the time in designing model railroads.

My HO scale plan reproduces those dominant features of the B Yard in a 3'-6" x 19'-0" basement alcove. The precooler plant is against the backdrop with the precooling and icing tracks under the adjacent shed. I plan to extend these tracks inside the model building for extra car capacity, using the structure of the shed to conceal this compromise with reality. The double-track Third District main line along the front edge defines the size of the yard.

The six through body tracks, though curved at each end, follow the diamond grid pattern of the actual yard. All tracks are the same length, and the ladder at the south end is located around the curve at Rana to help make them long enough for what I call my "design freight train." I've built the passing sidings along my eastward main line to hold a train consisting of a three-unit 100-class diesel (Santa Fe terminology

for the Electro-Motive FT), 22 nominally 40-foot freight cars, a 3800-class 2-10-2 steam pusher, and a standard steel way car. Even though the main line is double track, my freight trains need to fit in the passing tracks to clear the numerous passenger trains in the Santa Fe schedule. A train of this size can be assembled in the B Yard without fouling other tracks. Any train that fits the yard tracks will also fit the passing sidings.

At the north (timetable east) end, the main lines and yard lead run along a narrow shelf to reach the A Yard, the San Bernardino passenger yard, and the First District main line over Cajon Pass. At the south (timetable west) end, the main lines traverse another narrow shelf to reach the Third District staging loop hidden under the main level of the layout. The B Yard drill track extends along these main lines toward the loop to make it long enough to let the switcher pull any one track in the freight yard.

The stock track, with stockyards represented on the backdrop, was used to rest and water stock approaching the 28-hour

limit that the animals could be confined aboard the cars. The livestock in such cases was most likely to be westbound, so the stockcars would be brought over by a switcher from the A Yard.

There may not have been a way car (caboose) track at the B Yard in 1938, as bulletins from about

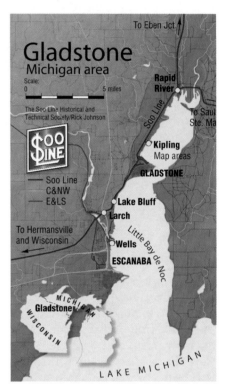

Gladstone, Mich., on the Soo Line

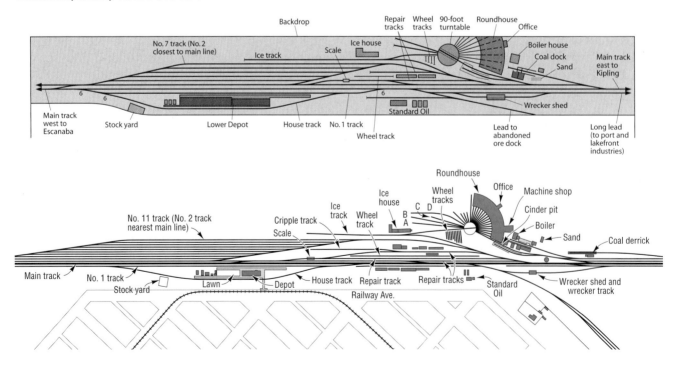

that time refer to engines off arriving trains bringing their way cars with them to the A Yard on their way to the roundhouse. That changed when the yard was expanded, so I'm including one of the two stub tracks that were just west of the precooler shed to serve as a way car track.

Way cars were assigned to specific crews on the Santa Fe's Coast Lines until 1955, with separate pools for the "Valley," meaning the Second and Third Districts, and the "Hill," meaning the First District. That means cabooses that arrive in the B Yard on eastward trains from the Second and Third Districts have to be moved to the A Yard to be used on westward trains. Likewise, way cars arriving in the A Yard on westward trains off the First District will have to be shifted to the B Yard to be used on eastbound freights. Transfers like this were common practice where railroads operated separate eastward and westward yards in the time before labor agreements allowed pooling of cabooses. When appropriate, as it is for my San Bernardino yards, it makes an interesting addition to the challenges of yard operation.

Gladstone, Mich., on the Soo Line

Let's look at another prototype example. Gladstone, Mich., on the Minneapolis, St. Paul and Sault Ste. Marie (the Soo Line) is a classic steam-era division point. Located roughly midway between the Twin Cities and the Soo, Gladstone was developed as a Great Lakes port on the Lake Michigan shore of the state of Michigan's Upper Peninsula.

The Gladstone yard layout looks as if it were meant for a model railroad, and it could be modeled almost track for track in one of the smaller scales. I've drawn an N scale Layout Design Element for a 2 x 15-foot area. (A Layout Design Element or LDE is a prototype-based layout segment that can be incorporated into a larger plan or used as the basis of a small layout in itself.) This LDE includes the diamond-shaped yard, the car repair tracks, the roundhouse, and the simple passenger station with its siding (the "No. 1 track") and house track.

In the actual yard arrangement there is no clearly defined switching lead or drill track, as is often the case in smaller prototype yards. With small steam switchers

the tendency was to work with short cuts of cars, and the north lead extending past the roundhouse would have been adequate most of the time. When it was necessary to make longer pulls, the traffic probably allowed ample time for switchers to use the main line within yard limits. If you wanted longer leads for a model yard, the north yard lead could be connected to one of the two engine leads. At the south end of the yard a drill track could be extended along the main line from the south end of track 2.

The Long Lead track paralleling the main line was the industrial lead to the port of Gladstone. It served grain elevators, warehouses, an extensive coal dock, and a large sawmill, the Northwestern Cooperage & Lumber Co. The Soo Line typically carried grain, flour, and other agricultural products from the Twin Cities to the Great Lakes. At Gladstone it also received coal from lake steamers for distribution along its lines, predominantly to the west. The lake port industries served by the Long Lead could be the basis of another LDE or two. If that appeals to you, see the Fall 2003 issue of *The Soo* magazine of the Soo Line Historical & Technical society. Alternately, the Long Lead could simply run into a staging yard where switchers operating out of the Gladstone freight yard could exchange cuts of cars.

At one time there was also an iron ore dock at Gladstone. Its lead branched off the wrecker track opposite the roundhouse and climbed to cross above the other port tracks. The dock itself had a single track and extended perpendicular to the shoreline for 768 feet. Constructed in 1887, it was damaged by an ore boat in 1900

Frankfort, Ind., on the Nickel Plate Road

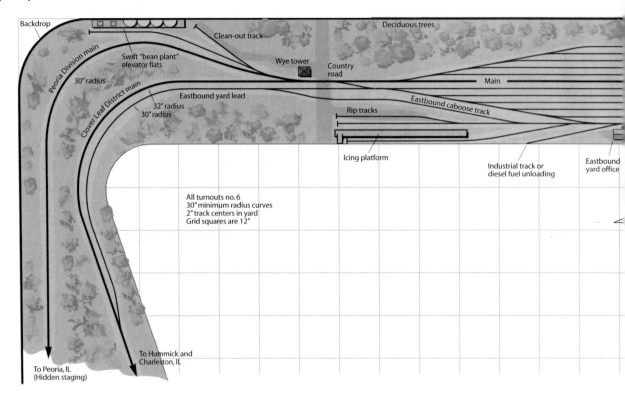

and removed in 1905. Afterwards the Soo's iron ore traffic was rerouted. However, many modelers would grant themselves the historical license to maintain an ore dock connection from a model of Gladstone in a later era.

As Gladstone shows, modeling an actual freight yard can be a practical possibility. The key factors can be the choice of a prototype and the choice of scale.

Frankfort, Ind., on the Nickel Plate Road

One more example of a prototype-based yard design comes from *Model Railroad Planning* editor and *Model Railroader* columnist Tony Koester. In the 1998 edition of *MRP*, Tony presented an LDE for the Nickel Plate Road's yard in Frankfort, Ind. It accompanied a detailed look at the prototype's operations in "Around the clock at Frankfort Yard" by retired NKP railroader Don Daily.

Frankfort was a hub where the Nickel Plate's western lines from St. Louis and Peoria connected to routes stretching eastward to

Toledo and Cleveland in Ohio and Buffalo in New York. It handled fast freights in both directions, but the heaviest traffic was eastbound from the NKP's western connections. To balance crews and power, the NKP ran local freights westbound only on its St. Louis and Peoria lines, originating from Frankfort.

Frankfort switched blocks on through trains, combined some trains heading east, and switched "shorts" on through trains into station order for setout down the line. It also changed locomotives and cabooses on through trains.

The yard was on the western edge of the city. It featured separate yards for eastward and westward traffic on opposite sides of the single-track main line. In addition, a roundhouse and machine shop maintained the stable of Berkshires, Mikados, and 0-8-0 switchers that were the core of the NKP's steam-era roster. There were also a car shop, RIP tracks for running repairs, a small ice dock, and a scale track. A cannery and soybean elevator were indus-

tries adjacent to the yard. The passenger station, freight house, and team track were all to the east, closer to the center of the city.

Tony's LDE for Frankfort represents the eastbound and westbound yards with five through tracks each on either side of the single-track main. It includes a caboose track for each yard, two RIP tracks, and the icing platform. The engine terminal is up front—it was on the south side of the east-west yard layout, and this puts it in position to be both a visual and operational highlight.

Tony omitted the shops and their tracks to keep the LDE to a practical width for HO scale, and the passenger and freight stations in downtown Frankfort are off the layout in staging to the east. At the west end the Peoria line takes off at WY Tower for its own separate route to staging, and the Swift soybean plant is modeled with a simplified track arrangement and low-relief structures against the backdrop of the layout.

At 5 x 31 feet the Frankfort LDE is a large yard for a model

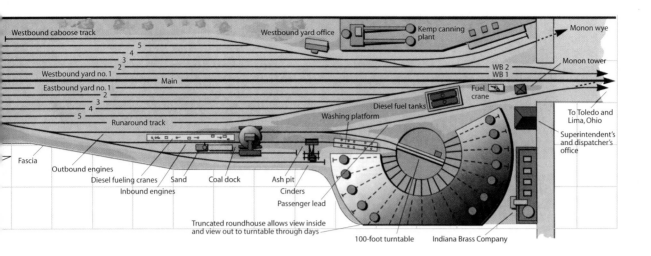

Westbound caboose track
5
4
3
2
Westbound yard no. 1
Eastbound yard no. 1   Main
2
3
4
5
Runaround track

Fascia
Outbound engines
Diesel fueling cranes   Sand   Coal dock
Inbound engines

Westbound yard office
Kemp canning plant
Monon wye
Monon tower
WB 2
WB 1
Diesel fuel tanks
Washing platform
Fuel crane
To Toledo and Lima, Ohio
Superintendent's and dispatcher's office

Ash pit
Cinders
Passenger lead

Truncated roundhouse allows view inside
and view out to turntable through days
100-foot turntable   Indiana Brass Company

Left: Looking west at Frankfort, Ind., in 1944, we see the westbound yard with its east-end ladder angling off to the right, and in the distance the eastbound yard's east ladder running the other way. Beyond the east yard ladder are the icing platform and the ice plant. *Jay Williams*

railroad, big enough to give a sense of the prototype's "out in the country" expansiveness. As Tony's plans for a Nickel Plate Road St. Louis line layout developed, he was able to expand on this LDE and get even closer to the actual track arrangement. His plan also includes a downtown Frankfort scene. You can see his expanded version of Frankfort in the September 2000 issue of *Model Railroader*. These examples can serve as inspiration for your own model yard based on a prototype.

Remember the three key strategies:
• Pick a prototype of modelgenic size.

• Look for characteristic features of the yard layout and its surroundings to establish the model's prototypical identity.
• Design the model yard to support the prototype operations you want to re-create on your layout.

Weathering your yards

Most prototype yards are eyesores, so why shouldn't yours be too?

By Paul J. Dolkos
Photos by the author

We model railroaders love our yards. On many layouts they are the centerpiece. The Woods River yard on my Boston & Maine layout is about 10 feet long with seven parallel tracks. It holds about 80 cars on the classification tracks. There are two tracks for arrivals and departures.

As I worked on it I really looked forward to its completion. I put a light cosmetic curve in it such as those found in yards that bend along a riverbank. I varied the tie coloring, painted the rails, and neatly spread the cinder ballast. Voilà! The masterpiece was complete.

But what a letdown. It worked fine, but it really didn't look as great as I had imagined it would. It was kind of dull. But then maybe seven parallel tracks don't have that much visual potential.

Then I looked at a prototype yard in my city. The very things that make these facilities the neighborhood eyesore and the bane of city beautifiers were what was missing in mine. Ballast materials varied, and it was dirty. There was spillage from a variety of loads. There

was trash, and grass and weeds were growing here and there. The place was a mess.

So I messed up my new yard. I proceeded with the same trepidation that you have when you take your weathering brush to your newly painted locomotive.

Some sources of yard weathering or texturing that I observed included the following:

• Spillage of cargo such as coal, cement, ore, and grain

• Oil drippings from rolling-stock bearings and turnout lubrication (and maybe even tank cars, but let's hope not)

• Trash, including paper, chunks of wood, and metal banding

• Vegetation—including a variety of colors and heights, dead and alive

• Ballast in many variations due to reballasting, tie replacement, or raising of a rail

• Soil, as opposed to or in lieu of ballast, from erosion, road grades, and construction

I avoided littering the yard with rail sections or loose ties. While they certainly may be present

during a maintenance project, the areas where switchmen walk are generally kept clear of such objects. A crewman could easily trip over them, especially at night. So keep safety in mind when you litter your yard.

The materials I used for my yard weathering were much the same as those you would use on any scenery project. For spillage I used crushed materials such as rock ballast, sand, or sifted dirt, as long as the color contrasted with the cinder ballast. You should vary the spillage patterns too. Materials leaking from hoppers tend to drop between the rails, while those that come from boxcars drop outside the rails. Drippings are probably best done with paint. For trash, use whatever turns up; although, I must confess, I really haven't thrown little scraps of paper around my yard yet. You can use ground foam or tufts of rope or carpeting for the vegetation.

I did not weather all tracks equally. l left the arrival and departure tracks relatively clean on the theory that perhaps they receive a little more maintenance. But the track in the back that would be used for dead car storage is covered

with vegetation and soil washed down an adjacent embankment (nobody takes care of the drainage ditches).

Between these two extremes there is the normal spillage and a few weeds. The variation is just another way of providing a range of contrast to add more interest.

Yard weathering could also be used to mark the location of under-the-track Kadee uncoupling ramps. A patch of grass or a tuft of weeds can be a distinctive, yet unobtrusive, marker when nothing else seems right. The plastic yard limit signs that come with the ramps aren't appropriate in the middle of the yard.

Yard weathering is something you should do in stages. Grow a little grass, spill a little coal, pile up some dirt. Stand back and see what you think. Add litter as the mood suits. After all, that eyesore railroad yard in your town didn't get to be that way all in one day either. The railroad might have taken some nice public relations photos of the yard when they opened it long ago showing how nice it was. Yards just don't stay that way.

Above: Here's Alco S-4 switcher no. 1270 working in the Woods River yard. The boards between the foreground rails cover a Kadee electromagnetic coupling ramp. The hand-bar marks the ramp's center. The phone box follows B&M practice, as do the switch stands with rectangular targets.

Top right: The author used a wide variety of textures and colors for his yard weathering. In the foreground is a pile of dirt representing spillage. Soil was washed onto the track in the left background and ground foam was scattered around to represent grass and weeds.

Bottom right: Soil and gray ballast sprinkled between the tracks contrast with the basic cinder ballast. The telephone box marks the location of concealed uncoupling ramps.

GALLERY

Above: Jack Burgess models California's famed Yosemite Valley Ry., and here at El Portal he's modeled the YV yard track-for-track and turnout-for-turnout. Only the length of the yard is compressed. Of course, you usually have to pick a small prototype to accomplish this feat, but there's a great satisfaction in operating an accurate replica of a real yard. *Jack Burgess*

Right: The Burlington Northern-Rio Grande-Santa Fe Joint Line between Denver and Pueblo is the prototype on the lower level of Doug Tagsold's HO scale Denver, Front Range & Western layout. The mixture of road names is therefore quite authentic, and the photo backdrop of the city of Denver lends even more authenticity. *Doug Tagsold*

Left: Bob Smaus's HO layout captures the essence of the Southern Pacific's River Station and Bull Ring Yards in downtown Los Angeles. The typically "LA" concrete viaduct hides a passage through the backdrop, and Bob has used scenery, structures, and a backdrop in what is nominally the "off stage" area to give greater continuity and depth to the scene. *Bob Smaus*

Staging yards are off-scene storage areas for holding trains that will appear on layouts as if coming from somewhere else or that will depart from layouts heading for distant, unmodeled destinations. These yards have very aptly been likened to the wings of a theater stage, the place actors come from on cue to play their parts on stage, and where they go when the action requires them to leave the scene. Think of trains as the actors in the plays of our operating sessions and the comparison will be clear.

The connection between staging yards and freight yard design is that staging provides a place where cars passing through our freight yards will go. Staging can represent a continuation of the same railroad, a connection with another railroad, a terminal or industrial area, or any combination of these possibilities.

This behind-the-scenes stub-ended staging yard supports operation on the Kalmbach employees' Model Railroad Club layout, the Milwaukee, Racine & Troy. *Bill Zuback*

Staging allows us to operate our model railroads as part of the larger railroad network and help to give realistic purpose to the switching and blocking that we do in our freight yards.

Staging and operating patterns

The most important design consideration for staging yards is how they will be located in relation to the onstage yard or yards and the patterns that will be established for the layout's operations. There are many possibilities, and the following list includes a few of the most common:

• **Yard with staging directly off either end; no main line.** This kind of layout would emphasize yard operation at the expense of mainline running. An example of this would be my Ozark Lines track plan shown in Chapter One, and it can be a good choice for packing a lot of railroading into a limited space. A variant would be a stub terminal yard with staging off one end and no main line. This can be effective for representing the end of a branch line, but since cars have only one way in and out, it's a less typical pattern for busy mainline railroads.

• **Yard in the middle of a main line; staging at each end of the main.** With the yard in the middle, the main line is broken into segments that can represent different divisions or subdivisions. One end might be the "Mountain Subdivision," with rugged climbs requiring heavier locomotives. The other end could be the "River Subdivision" with easy grades using lighter engines. There are other ways to differentiate the two segments, but this "yard-in-the-middle" approach suggests a desire to model some distinction.

• **Yard at one end of main line; staging adjacent to yard and at opposite end of main.** Here the focus is on the district or subdivision between the yard and the distant staging yard, with the next district in the other direction

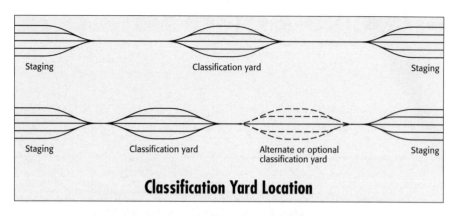

Classification Yard Location

The north staging yard on Tony Koester's Allegheny Midland HO layout was a stub yard, meaning that most of the trains shown would have to be turned before the next operating session. *Tony Koester*

represented by the staging adjacent to the yard. In this and the previous approach, the subdivisions may be assumed to extend some distance beyond the onstage portion of the layout, so entire crew districts don't have to be represented by a short main line.

• **Yard at each end of main line with adjacent staging.** With this pattern the main line can represent an entire subdivision or crew district, with crews "getting on" trains at one modeled yard and "getting off" at the other. This is most effective on layouts with very long main lines. No model railroad I've seen comes close to representing the "100-mile-day" of the steam era in exact scale, but the longer the better if this is the operating scheme you want.

In any of the above patterns, the two ends of a railroad can be tied back together in a single staging yard, which can be efficient in

using space and offer other operating advantages as well.

It's important to note for yard operation that any staging yard can be assumed to represent more than one destination. The most basic application is to imagine a junction just off the modeled railroad. Trains leaving the layout in that direction might be designated as going to either of two widely spaced terminals, such as St. Louis and Chicago. This can give the onstage yard or yards a reason to sort cars into trains for each different destination, or in the other direction, to combine trains from different points of origin.

Onstage junctions with different lines leading offstage, either to different staging yards or to the same one, can reinforce this concept. However, it's a very workable approach that can add considerable operating interest even if the junction is assumed to be offstage.

Types of staging

Staging yards can be built in several different patterns, but most fall into one of three shapes:

• **Stub.** At the end of the main line, the yard entrance fans out into a number of single-ended tracks, each long enough to hold one train. This is the simplest and most space-efficient form of staging, especially if two stub staging yards for opposite ends of the line can be stacked one above the other. Trains are assembled in the staging yard facing out, to depart when called for by the schedule or other operating scheme.

Trains enter the staging yard heading in, and when they arrive they are through for that operating session, at least in the typical passive staging use. Between operating sessions trains have to be backed out, turned, reblocked as desired, and backed in again. Because of the need for this restaging operation, these are sometimes called "muzzle-loading" staging yards.

• **Through.** The opposite ends of the main line run into a single double-ended yard. Trains start and end their runs at the same place, although on the modeled portion of the layout the terminals can appear to be far apart. The great strength of through staging is that loaded and empty open-top traffic (such as coal or ore) can always appear onstage moving in the appropriate directions without having to be restaged. Other trains can be reused too, provided there are no issues with blocking or motive power changes.

To equal the storage capacity of two stub yards, a through yard would need twice as many tracks, which could be a problem if the

yard has to be too wide for convenient reach. If trains are reused in an operating session, however, it will take fewer of them to maintain a given level of traffic. Fewer tracks might therefore be sufficient in a through yard.

Of course, a through yard may be used as if it were two stub yards for manifests and locals, with only open-top trains always circulating in the same directions. On the old Milwaukee, Racine & Troy Kalmbach employees' club layout, we evolved such an operating scheme. The through yard still gave us the advantage of compactness, with all staging in one place, and the double-ended tracks made it easier to turn trains between sessions, especially since most of our freight trains were powered with double-ended diesel consists.

• **Loop.** The main line runs into a reversing loop or "balloon track," as it's commonly called on the real thing. Storage tracks in the form of a through yard may either be wrapped around the loop or located along the lead to it. In other configurations, trains may traverse part of the loop before backing into a stub yard. The "reverted loop" popularized by master layout designer John Armstrong is connected backward to the main track, so trains enter a tail track and back around the loop to the stub yard. This allows a longer onstage main line before trains disappear into staging.

In loop staging trains automatically turn and are stored ready to run back in the opposite direction. This is a particular advantage for passenger traffic, making it easy to reuse these expensive and distinctive trains in an operating session. It can also have advantages for freight operation, especially in modeling "overhead" or "bridge" traffic that will move across the onstage main line with little switching, adding to the traffic density by reusing trains. A similar application would be for trackage rights trains from another

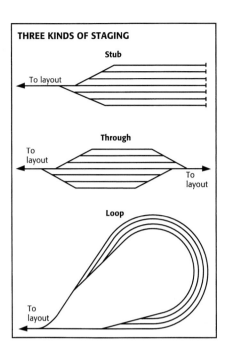

company using our segment of the home railroad.

On my own Santa Fe Los Angeles Division layout, I'll operate fruit pickup trains from the perishable concentration point at San Bernardino running to and from loop staging. These trains operated as turns on the real railroad, running out and back with the same crew, engine, and caboose. They took empty refrigerator cars out to the Southern California packing houses served by the Santa Fe and returned with loaded reefers that would be built into Green Fruit Express trains, designated "GFX," to run to eastern markets. Since no open loads are involved, the same reefers that depart as empties can be treated as loaded cars when they return from a layover in loop staging. It's an ideal freight application for loop staging, and could suit many other prototype operations.

Trains stored in loop staging don't necessarily have to be reused in an operating session, and can be reblocked and restaged in between sessions if you wish. Some operators like the easy turning offered by loop staging, not only for trains but also for steam engines and other single-ended power. This also tends to reduce

Lee Nicholas uses active staging in a through yard on his HO scale Utah Colorado Western. The hidden yard is worked by an operator known as the "Mole" for his concealed location. The Mole breaks up arriving trains and assembles new trains for departure as the operating session proceeds on the rest of the railroad. Lee is shown checking the card files for stored cars that can be used to make up the next westbound freight. Rerailers on each track make it easy to transfer rolling stock from storage shelves to the rails, and the engine storage tracks keep locomotives out of the way until needed. *Lou Sassi*

handling of locomotives and cars, which is easier on the equipment and may also save time.

No one form of staging may be ideal for every purpose, and layouts can combine different kinds of staging for different operations. I know of several coal-hauling layouts that use through staging to handle empty and loaded hopper trains but use a loop or loops to turn passenger trains.

Active staging

I used the term "passive staging" to describe the situation where trains are simply stored in staging yards and aren't changed or handled except between operating sessions. The active staging alternative is to have an off-scene operator restaging trains—breaking them up and making up new ones—while the operating session is going on. British model railroaders have pioneered this technique and call their active staging yards "fiddle yards." In contrast with the onstage part of the layout where realistic operation prevails, the offstage operator is allowed to handle the locomotives and cars, or "fiddle" with them.

Active staging offers two great advantages. Since you don't have to have a track to store every train that will run during an operating session, you can support the

desired level of traffic with a smaller yard. And since active staging goes on continuously, operating sessions can be as long or short as you wish. If the staging operator keeps busy, the railroad never runs out of trains, and there's never a time when you have to run more trains to be ready for the next session.

The downside is that someone has to be the staging operator and fiddle the trains, which isn't a realistic railroad job and is by definition conducted off-scene, away from the realistic setting of the model railroad. The staging operator has to find reward in contributing to the realism of the rest of the layout, and in controlling the pace and character of the operating session. Some layout owners have been lucky in having friends willing to take on this task, and I know of at least one who does it himself. Unselfishly, he hardly ever gets to run a train on his own railroad. Only you can decide if active staging is for you; it's a question that deserves serious thought before you adopt it for your own railroad.

Active staging can be carried out in any form of staging yard, though the through yard with its advantage of compactness is probably the most common. Using a loop or loops in active staging has

advantages for minimizing the handling of passenger equipment and is also convenient for turning locomotives. Some layout owners like to be able to turn engines on the track, using turntables or even wyes if not loops, especially when using steam power.

Sequential staging

A further alternative for staging is sequential storage, with trains lined up one behind the other on a single track. Track planners John Armstrong and Don Mitchell have both suggested sequential staging for situations where length of track offers greater capacity than the typical yard with parallel tracks. One such case would be a helix connecting the ends of the main line on the two levels of a double-deck layout. Adding a second track to the helix generally takes little extra space and may allow several trains to be sequentially staged in each direction.

Obviously, sequential staging is less flexible than a more-typical yard with ladders. Trains must run in the order they stand on the track, although crossovers between parallel tracks can allow trains to run around other trains. And if trains are to leave one end of a sequential staging track and enter the other, all the trains being stored on the track will have to move

Jack Ozanich's HO scale Atlantic Great Eastern also uses a through yard as a fiddle yard for active staging. The shelf units aren't for displaying models, but keep them handy until needed. A turntable at the far right allows hands-off turning of steam locomotives. With active staging such as this, the railroad's operations can proceed continuously as long as the crew's stamina holds out, and Jack has been known to hold some round-the-clock sessions. Even hobbyists who aren't that ambitious can appreciate the opportunity active staging allows to begin and end operations at any time and at any point in the railroad's schedule.
Jack Ozanich

forward one storage section at a time to keep a section open for the arriving trains. This is an unrealistic task for a human operator to manage, but is a good application for computer automation.

Staging design considerations

Some aspects of yard design can be especially important in staging yards. Consider track spacing for example: If a yard is straight, track centers can be the minimum required for clearance, and often that will squeeze an extra track or two into a given width. On the other hand, if a yard is to be used for active staging, it will help to provide extra space between the tracks so cars may be more easily picked up and re-railed.

Ideally, all tracks should be the same length, so any train that fits in the yard can run into any open track. With stub yards, a split-ladder design will keep the number of shorter tracks to a minimum. For through yards, a diamond-shape design works best.

Keeping the yard ladders as short as possible allows the greatest length of storage tracks, and design approaches that may be less desirable for onstage yards can be used to advantage in off-stage storage. We can use the sharpest turnouts consistent with smooth operation, since we don't

have to be concerned with appearance. Other helpful tactics include building the ladder on the angle of the next-smaller-size turnout, using a compound ladder, laying out a pinwheel ladder to take advantage of a curved approach, and starting with a three-way or lap turnout to build split ladders on both sides of a center line.

How long do storage tracks have to be? The minimum is usually the maximum train length. When it's possible to allow extra length, however, it will be useful. It makes it easier to stop trains before hitting a bumper or running past the clearance point at the other end of a through track. Operators may miscount cars, and train length can vary because of extra-long cars and locomotives. A little extra track length is forgiving in these situations.

Access is also an important consideration, especially for a hidden staging yard. If a staging yard will be below another layout level, it can help to arrange ladders so that all turnouts are along the near edge of the benchwork. The clearance below the overhead level should be as great as possible, especially for wider yards. In HO scale, 10 to 12 inches above the railhead is usually workable.

Some layout builders have adopted open staging for the easi-

est access and may even do some minimal scenicking of the staging area. While this can be the simplest approach for operating and maintaining a staging yard, it can also compromise the illusion that trains in staging are on their way from distant origins or to faraway destinations. Hidden staging is better for supporting the fiction of the model railroad as part of a larger transportation network, but it does require more-elaborate controls and indications of the status of offstage trackwork and trains, the equivalent to a large interlocking plant.

Perhaps the ideal solution, when space permits, is to place staging yards in a separate room adjacent to the main layout room. This can combine easy, walk-up access with out-of-sight storage for trains off the layout. For smaller layouts, the behind-the-scenes staging shown on the Ozark Lines layout in Chapter One, with duck-under access, could be a good alternative.

However it's arranged, staging should be designed to support the kind of traffic you want to model through your onstage yard or yards. Staging can make the difference between a model yard that's choked with cars in storage and one that operates as a fluid distribution center.

Visible staging yards
Concerns about hidden staging yards led to an open-air approach

By David Barrow

I've experimented with various forms of staging since 1973, when we built the first version of my HO scale Cat Mountain & Santa Fe. Staging is the idea of providing one or more places where the modeled portion of a railroad connects with the unmodeled segments as well as with the rest of the North American rail network. The 1975 version of the CM&SF, shown in fig. 1, featured hidden staging with a reversing loop at either end of a point-to-point main line.

Problems with early efforts

There were only five spots available to stage trains at each end, so we simulated the through trains by turning the consists on the loops and reusing them. That

is, Santa Fe's 594 train from Houston to Denver would make its run in the morning, turn around in the staging area, and come back in the afternoon with the same power and consist as the 495 train from Denver to Houston.

As you can see from the plan, there was an onstage yard adjacent to each staging yard. The yardmasters had the added duty of running the trains in and out of staging at the proper times. This got a bit tricky, as we sometimes put more than one train on a track.

I put a mirror above the Third District so the operators could see where trains were and that they didn't foul the turnouts at either end of the tracks. The First District staging yard, however, was completely hidden. Need I mention

that incorrectly set turnouts and trains hanging out past the clearance points created more than a reasonable amount of excitement?

A solution in sight

As I revised the CM&SF over several years, I decided I didn't want any staging I couldn't see. Also, I now have enough staging tracks so each train runs only once during a session. The present staging arrangement, shown in fig. 2, features a yard called either "West Mesa" or "East Hill," depending on how it's being used at the moment. I've scenicked this staging yard so that trains waiting out in the open will be seen in a realistic setting.

The concept is that Mesa Yard is located in Lubbock in western Texas, while East Hill

Yard is near the center of the Lone Star State in Brownwood—refer to the map in fig. 3. Just west of the modeled Mesa Yard is the West Mesa visible staging yard, duplicating the actual arrangement of two endto-end yards in Lubbock.

Two operators work here: the West Mesa operator and the Mesa yardmaster. The former uses West Mesa as an arrival and departure yard for trains to and from the west. When eastbounds are due, the West Mesa operator brings them into Mesa from their "arrival track" in West Mesa. He also runs westbounds from Mesa into the West Mesa "departure yard."

The three tracks at the rear of the staging yard are used for departing westbounds, and the five foreground tracks are for arriving eastbounds. If the westbound tracks are filled, westbound trains have to be held in Mesa until a track opens up.

East Hill operations

The story is very different for crews running trains in or out of staging at the east end of the CM&SF. Crews see East Hill as a suburban yard outside Brownwood. When they look to the east (right), they envision trains arriving from and departing to Temple and southern Texas.

There's no yard operator at East Hill. Entry into this yard from the west is through a dispatcher-controlled turnout between Allen and East Hill at the end of Centralized Traffic Control (CTC) territory. The dispatcher routes eastbound trains through the reverse side of the turnout for access to the five frontmost tracks; the train crews then use ground throws to select any open track. There are enough tracks so least one is always open if trains run reasonably close to schedule.

Westbound trains that are leaving the rear three tracks are in "dark" (unsignaled) territory, so their crews must obtain permission from the dispatcher by radio before moving their trains up to the signal. My friend Gordon Locke, a senior conductor on the Santa Fe, tells me that trains are handled precisely this way in Temple, Texas, where signaling begins well south of the yard.

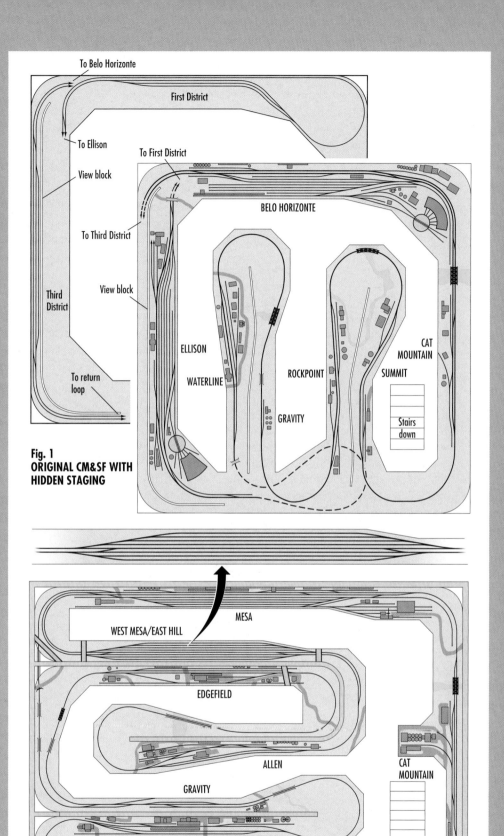

Fig. 1
ORIGINAL CM&SF WITH HIDDEN STAGING

Automatic restaging

One of the best features of this staging design is that the railroad restages itself. That is, at the end of the operating session trains are right back at their starting points, ready to go again. I do have to cycle some waybills (the CM&SF uses the popular four-cycle waybills and car cards printed by Old Line Graphics) for trains that have completed their runs, but this takes very little time.

I sometimes host weekend operating sessions that run almost continuously for many hours. This would be impossible if I used stub-ended staging yards and had to back trains from their inbound tracks and swap ends with the power and cabooses. I could easily run engines around their trains so they could return in the opposite direction, but that's not part of normal operations on the Cat Mountain Line.

I also like the fact that crew changes occur in visible locations at Mesa and East Hill. A crew "gets on" a westbound train at East Hill, runs it to Mesa, and "gets off" there. Eastbound crews reverse this sequence. I find this more realistic from the point of view of what the train crews see and do than having them run trains in or out of hidden staging yards.

Alternatives

If you're still uneasy with the idea of trains not actually disappearing from the portion of the railroad with scenery, let me offer two alternatives to the present CM&SF visible staging.

Figure 4 shows how an addition built onto one end of the room could house two staging yards that, if not hidden under scenery, would at least be out of sight from the rest of the railroad. With this plan a staging operator would run trains in and out of this room to and from crew-change points (marked by shacks) in the main room. Regular road crews still wouldn't run trains in or out of the staging.

Figure 5 shows a way to stack one stub-ended staging yard above the other, as in my present train room. A ramp track could connect the upper and lower levels for continuous running. I'd recommend putting the stacked yards inside a cabinet with sliding doors for access. Tunnels aren't prototypical in this part of the country, but the main line could vanish under a highway overpass. But trains wouldn't obviously leave the railroad room, so I'm not entirely comfortable with this arrangement.

To stay within my comfort zone I like my current visible staging on the CM&SF. There's a prototypical basis for the operation of West Mesa/East Hill, the staging is out in the open where I can get at it and crews can see what they're doing, and the continuous restaging is excellent for frequent operating sessions.

David Barrow told how he'd use "domino planning" to fit a scaled-down version of his CM&SF into a bedroom in the 1996 edition of Model Railroad Planning. *(see pp. 32-33)*

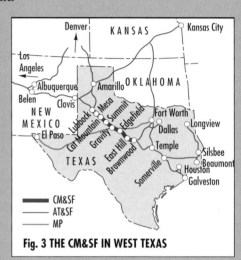

Fig. 3 THE CM&SF IN WEST TEXAS

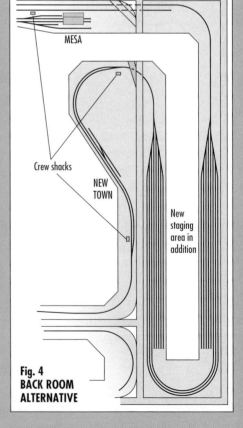

Fig. 4
BACK ROOM
ALTERNATIVE

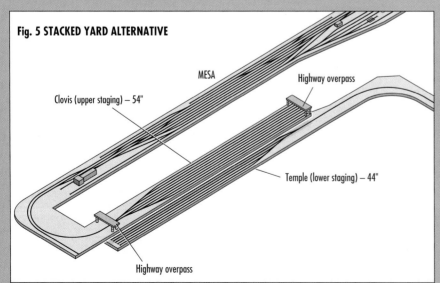

Fig. 5 STACKED YARD ALTERNATIVE

Above: Even if the rest of a layout is built on one level, it can make sense to use double-deck staging yards. The Kalmbach employees' Milwaukee, Racine & Troy HO club layout uses two staging yards stacked 12" apart (10" clearance from the lower-level rails to the upper level's 1x2 supports) represent the east and west ends of a point-to-point main line. Each level has 12 tracks, all a minimum of 20 feet in length. *Model Railroader* photo by Bill Zuback

Left:. A space-saving option for staging tracks is the sector plate. In the British example shown, the entire yard in the foreground pivots at the near end to align any staging track with the tracks running into the onstage scene. Because it uses no turnout ladders, this kind of yard can be much shorter overall for any given train length. Note the convenient knob for manually swiveling the sector plate. *Paul J. Dolkos*

Above: Dave Davenport looks over the stacked staging yards on Allen McClelland's new HO scale Virginian & Ohio RR. Allen has also provided shelves (above) and drawers (below) for convenient storage of extra rolling stock—anyone who's been in this hobby for a few years will see the value of that. *Allen McClelland*

Right: Sometimes something as simple as a curve can help re-create a prototype yard. The Western Pacific yard at Keddie, Calif., curves as it follows the Feather River Canyon above Spanish Creek, a fact Jim Dias used to advantage on his HO WP layout. The real WP yard had only a couple more tracks than Jim's version does. *Tommy Holt*

Above: David Haines modeled actual structures without compression to set the scene for his N scale Raton, N.M., yard. He was especially proud of what he called the Hobbs Hardware group, a nondescript but completely authentic block of buildings whose prototypes stood next to the Santa Fe. The small size of N scale models allows a higher ratio of scenery and structures to track than is typical in larger scales. *Bill Pearce*

Right: A distinctive structure can suggest a yard's locale as well as its specific prototype. John Signor modeled the wide overhangs and screened porches of the Southern Pacific's Indio, Calif., station, a building adapted for railroad operations in the desert. Indio is a terminal on John's HO scale Southern California Ry. *John Signor*

OPERATING MODEL RAILROAD YARDS

Experienced model railroad operators know that yard operation can be the key to a smooth-running railroad or a bottleneck that restricts mainline train movements. We've already seen how track arrangements can support a free-flowing yard operation. Now we'll look at the human side of the equation by considering what people can do to keep a freight yard fluid and how to help them achieve that goal.

The model railroad equivalent of the yard office is often a card file like this one at Woodsriver on Paul Dolkos's railroad. Each car is represented by a card, and information on the waybill tells the yard crew where to send it. *Paul J. Dolkos*

SIX

Top left: Here's a yardmaster at work, in a 1950s-style elevated tower overlooking the Southern Pacific yard in Eugene, Ore. The switchboard in front of him controls telephones, not turnouts. *Southern Pacific*

Top right: A Southern Pacific yard foreman (conductor) waves his switch list to signal the engineer of an Alco diesel switcher. Notice the track number painted on the switch stand target. *Southern Pacific*

Left: The engineer of a Rock Island yard switcher leans out of his cab window looking for hand signals while switching cars in Dallas. *Lee Langnum*

Yard crew duties

A real railroad yard may employ people with a lot of different titles and job descriptions, but for model railroad operation we can focus on three: the yardmaster, the yard clerk, and the engine foreman. The yardmaster is the boss of the yard and supervises all of its operating workers. A yardmaster assesses the work to be done on his shift and plans how to accomplish it, assigns clerks and switch engines to carry out his plan, and keeps the yard in a flexible posture to deal with whatever changes and interruptions the day may bring.

The yard clerk's job is to keep track of the cars in the yard and the paperwork that shows what they're carrying and where they're going. This isn't just an office job, though maintaining waybill files and track lists can be a big part of it. Often a clerk or assistant clerk had to walk a track in the yard, or a number of them, listing every car in order, to be sure the files maintained in the office matched the way the cars stood on the track. The clerk also prepared switch lists for the yard engines according to the yardmaster's directions, listing all the cars to be pulled from a given track and showing which other tracks they were to be switched into in order to build cuts, blocks, and outbound trains.

The engine foreman was in charge of a switch engine and its crew; on some roads he might be called a yard conductor. In addition to the engineer and fireman on the switch engine, he had two switchmen to line switches and uncouple cars and help in passing signals to the engine. The foreman would generally follow the list prepared by the yard clerk but could vary the order of the work for efficiency and safety. For example, when a long cut of cars had to be dealt out to many different tracks, the foreman could elect to sort the cars into blocks using only two or three tracks and then distribute the blocks to the various tracks.

What I've just described was the manning typical in the classic era of railroading. In today's railroading, far fewer people are

Above: Here's an example of a track number painted on a switch stand target, an easy way to help yard and road crews identify tracks in a yard. *Gordon Odegard*

Left: Another way to identify yard tracks is represented by this cast number plate mounted on the headblock next to the switch stand on the New York Central in West Columbus, Ohio. *George Sura*

employed, because of computerization, microwave and radio communications, and reductions in crew size. The trend today is for the engine foreman or yard conductor to work alone, controlling the switch engine remotely with a strapped-on radio unit.

In model operations these yard jobs are often combined in the duties of one person. This is the equivalent of the prototype "footboard yardmaster," an engine foreman who ran a small yard with little or no office support, almost literally from the footboard of the switch engine. In smaller model yards and when traffic is slow, this can work very well, but if the size of the yard or the amount of work to be done starts to overwhelm a single operator, model railroaders can follow the example of the big roads in dividing the jobs. A yardmaster/clerk who updates the car-card file

and writes switch lists for the foreman/engineer can relieve the operator running the switcher from administrative tasks and take time to plan what the engine will be doing at any given time. If the yard layout permits two switchers to work at the same time, the yard will be able to keep up with even the busiest arrival and departure schedules. Model railroad yard crews often have to do the duty of the engine hostler too, but if another operator can be assigned solely to the engine terminal the yard operators can focus on the yard.

Again, only the largest and busiest model railroad yards may need more than a single operator. However, if one yardmaster has difficulty keeping up with four, six, or eight mainline engineers, assigning more people to help with the yard work can definitely be worthwhile.

Yard schedules

To plan their work effectively, the yardmaster and his crew need to know in advance when trains will be arriving and departing. This may involve timetable schedules for second- and third-class freight trains but will also have to allow for extra trains with no timetable authority, as well as switching jobs and transfers that may come and go within yard limits on a relatively informal basis. Even the many railroads that operate all freight trains as extras will have a service schedule to guarantee connections and to provide regular services to shippers.

Since model railroad operators don't have the advantage of doing the same railroad job every day—and thus the chance to get used to its patterns—it's generally best to provide them with a more formal and comprehensive schedule than might be seen in a real yard office.

Above: One communication innovation used in some 1950s yards was the "talk-back" loudspeaker, as here on the Grand Trunk Western in Battle Creek, Mich. These allowed two-way conversation between the yardmaster and road and yard crews, as long as one of the crewmen was on the ground. *Jerry Pinkepank*

Right: In the 1970s railroads used a color-barcode labeling system called Kar-Trak Automatic Car Identification (ACI) on rolling stock. The boxes on poles in this photo are Kar-Trak readers, here near the entrance to the Missouri Pacific's yard in Dolton, Ill. Kar-Trak ACI was supposed to provide electronic data listing every car in a train, taking the place of laboriously handwritten "wheel reports." It was abandoned in the 1980s, however, partly because of difficulties in reading bar codes on dirty, grime-covered freight cars. Today railroads use an electronic transponder system. *David P. Morgan Library collection*

As a minimum the list will probably include the approximate or expected times of all arrivals and departures, including transfers and local switch runs. If all trains are extras the times may be "call times," the time a train is expected to be ready and its crew on duty, which may be well in advance of its actual departure.

The yard schedule may also indicate which trains run through as opposed to originating and terminating, and list the setouts, pickups, and other work to be done on through trains. It can spell out the procedure used on this railroad for calling extra trains and include special instructions for such requirements as weighing coal, icing reefers, resting stock, and any scheduled switching, such as spotting and pulling freight house tracks by a specified time. It can also state train-length restrictions and loco-

motive "tonnage" ratings—usually just the number of cars to be handled by various classes of power.

In addition to the printed or standing schedule, the dispatcher can help the yard operators stay ahead as the operating session progresses. The dispatcher can give advance notification of trains that are approaching, lineups of extra trains or additional sections to be run from other terminals, and information on any special handling needed for particular trains or cars. At its best, model railroad operation should be a cooperative exercise, with everyone working as part of a team to help the railroad function as effectively as possible.

A schedule, or even a planned sequence of trains, will be useful in our often cramped-for-space model yards, where there aren't enough tracks to assign one for every classification. The yard crew can shove cars that aren't scheduled to be leaving for a while into a "for-now" or "slough" track while building trains for more immediate departure on other available tracks. As each early train leaves, the switcher can pull the for-now track and switch the cars for the next train to be built into the newly opened track left by the last departure.

Blocking instructions

Blocking instructions specify which trains take cars for which destinations, and where a train is made up of more than one block, the instructions will give the order of blocks in the train. A fast through freight might consist of only a single block, such as "Kansas City and beyond." Even if all cars in a train are destined for a single terminal, however, they might still be blocked for connections at that point. For example:

• Block 1: St. Louis (or "St. Louis proper," for delivery by the home road in that city)
• Block 2: St. Louis PRR (for interchange to the Pennsylvania RR at that point)
• Block 3: St. Louis NKP (for interchange to the Nickel Plate Road)
• Block 4: St. Louis SOU (for interchange to the Southern Ry.)

Whether St. Louis is actually modeled on our railroad or represented by staging, we can still choose to block trains this way for quicker handling in the distant terminal. This can be a choice of the level of detail you want in your operations and is also something

you can adjust depending on the workload of your modeled yard.

Another approach in blocking trains is to put cars to be set out along a train's run in station order. This is especially common for way freights, such as:

• Block 1: Colton
• Block 2: Riverside
• Block 3: Casa Blanca
• Block 4: Corona
• Block 5: Fullerton

This could be the blocking for the Santa Fe's Third District Local heading for Los Angeles from San Bernardino, but notice that it doesn't include a Los Angeles block. Cars going all the way from San Bernardino to Los Angeles would be handled more efficiently in through freights.

Another approach to blocking common to roads with a lot of perishable and livestock traffic would be to use the first block in any train for "protective service" cars, livestock loads, and produce or meat in iced reefers. For the stock this placement limits the slack action that might harm animals. For the perishables forward placement makes it easier to spot the reefers for re-icing at intermediate points.

However you organize the blocking of your trains, what's most important is how you convey the information to your yard operators. Again, professional railroaders doing the same job every day will learn by repetition which cars go into train 98 and in what order. Our friends coming over to run the railroad once a month will need easy-to-use written guides.

Yard schedules and general instructions can include blocking instructions if they aren't too complicated or extensive. More-elaborate detail can be given in blocking instructions or in a freight train procedures book. For those planning to use card-order systems, I've found it particularly helpful to have cards that fit in the

card file with the blocking instructions for a given train. If these are made a little taller than the car cards, they can also serve as dividers or markers to show where the trains and blocks are being assembled on the track.

Some layout owners like to research and develop elaborate routings for every carload of freight, and their waybills will often give a destination far beyond the modeled railroad with every interchange connection called out. If you enjoy the realism this adds, that's great, but this level of detail may be too much for the frontline yardmaster or engine foreman. That person will be more interested in knowing that a car is eastbound to the next division point than whether its ultimate destination is in Oswego, N.Y., or Waycross, Ga.

Card files

I've mentioned card files. If you use the popular car-card-and-waybill routing system, you'll find that a freight yard needs more-extensive files than a typical station along the line. The basic requirement is a file box or pocket for each track, including tracks like passing tracks and main lines that are normally open but which may temporarily hold a train or cut of cars being worked by the yard crew. That way, wherever cars end up there will be a pocket representing that location to hold the cards representing the cars.

It might seem obvious, but the pockets need to be deep enough to hold as many car cards with waybills as will fit on the track. Ideally they will also have a little extra room to allow for taller blocking cards to serve as file tabs to identify blocks.

You will also need pockets for any auxiliaries such as caboose tracks, cleaning tracks, RIP tracks, or ice tracks. Yard "industry" tracks such as locomotive supply tracks, team tracks, and freight house tracks should be

treated like any other industry tracks on your railroad. If you use a pocket for each industry track, provide pockets for the yard industries as well. If you use a three-pocket box to hold all the cards for a station's industries in a "set out-hold-pick up" sequence, you'll want the same thing for the yard "industries."

In switching model railroad yards I've often felt the need for another kind of box that not many layout owners provide. If you use card packs as switch lists—I'll cover that shortly—then it could help to have a box to hold the cards currently being switched. I'd label that box "Lead" or "Drill," and when I pulled a cut of cars out onto the lead to classify, I'd put their cards into the Lead box. That would be better than holding onto them because it would leave one hand free, and also better than

putting them on an open shelf where they could be accidentally swept onto the floor and out of order. As the cars were classified I could pull their cards and put them into the boxes for the appropriate tracks.

The great advantage that car card systems have over computer-generated switch lists is that it's relatively easy to keep the cards in the same order that the cars stand on the track. To take advantage of that, get into the habit of checking arriving trains and cuts you pull out for switching to make sure that the cards match the order of the cars. Keep the files for each track in order by placing cards in the front of a box as you switch more cards into that track.

When you pull a track to sort it out, the packet of cards from that track's box serves as a ready-made switch list. You can quickly shuf-

fle through it if you wish to plan the work, or simply begin dealing out the cars from the far end of the string. Look at the last card in the pack to determine where it should go—here's where having that "Lead" box would be so handy—then check the next one up to see if it goes to the same place. If the answer to that is "yes" you have the start of a cut and can keep checking the next card up to see if it matches. When you find one that doesn't match, you've found where to make the cut when you shove the cars on the end of your string into the appropriate track. Then pull the cars still attached to the engine back out and repeat the read, shove, and cut process until you've dealt with all the cars.

Notice that with the card files properly organized and matching the way the cars stand on the track, there's never any need to read car numbers on closely spaced tracks in the middle of a yard. The card files always show the location of every car.

If a car or card gets misplaced, it's a simple matter to set things right. Use the engine to slowly pull a track while you check the cards against the cars. First sort the cards to match the cars as they stand, and then re-switch the cars as necessary to get them into the desired track or sequence.

Switch lists

Real-life railroaders are often perplexed when they see modelers switching yards with handfuls of car cards because that's not the way these yard crews work on

prototype yard leads. They're used to having a list of the cars they're supposed to pull from a given track that shows either the car's destination or train assignment, or maybe even the specific track where they're supposed to classify it. Today these lists are printed by the railroad's computer system, but in earlier times they were often hand-written on the railroad's switch-list form (printed on cardstock to stand up to harsh weather and rough handling.)

One of the initial goals in the development of car-card routing systems for layouts was to eliminate this kind of hand-written paperwork. Nevertheless, some model railroad operators have found that using written switch lists along with a card system adds both an interesting level of prototype detail as well as greater convenience and efficiency.

The yardmaster or engine foreman can have just the one piece of paper (or cardstock) in hand while switching cars, and it will be a realistic-looking form with the name of the railroad and perhaps its emblem or herald to add atmosphere. The thinking about where to put each car will already have been done when the list was written out, so the operator can concentrate on making the moves realistically and according to plan. If the work is interrupted by any of the inevitable distractions, it's easy to pick it up again—just check to see which cars on the list are still coupled to the engine.

If you have two or more operators assigned to one yard, the engine foreman can be working

through one list while the yardmaster makes out the next one, so the use of written paperwork actually saves time. Whoever's writing the lists probably won't be running the engine, and this kind or work doesn't appeal to every operator. But a growing number of model railroad operators enjoy the paperwork of dispatching a railroad with written train orders, and switch lists can be seen as the yard equivalent of written orders for the main line. In both cases there's a satisfaction in running a model railroad with authentic railroad paperwork.

Here's how to use switch list forms with car cards: Pull the pack or cards for a cut of cars that needs to be classified from a yard track pocket. List the cars one by one on the lines of the form, in the same order as in the card file, which matches how they stand on

the track. Save time by abbreviating reporting marks wherever possible—it's very realistic to write "AT" for ATSF (Atchison, Topeka & Santa Fe), "Q" for CB&Q (Chicago, Burlington & Quincy), and "P" for PRR (Pennsylvania RR). Similarly, you usually need to list only the last three digits of each car number.

You may skip over the "Load" column unless you want to indicate different handling for empties and loads. If they'll both go into the same blocks it may not matter, but if you can use this extra bit of detail go ahead.

In the "To" or "Destination" column you have several choices. You can list specific yard tracks where the switcher is to put each car, or you may just give stations or even train numbers or symbols. If the cars are being delivered to industry spots instead of classified

in the yard, you may write in abbreviated industry names or spot codes. For lead switching into classification tracks, track numbers will probably be the most useful.

If cars are assigned to specific tracks, you can place each card in the appropriate file pocket after you take the information from the card. If the switch crew will have discretion as to where to place the cars, the engine foreman will have to note the track placements on the list and return it to the yardmaster so the cards can be filed after the work is done.

Either way, the engine foreman (or the yardmaster wearing his foreman's hat) can switch out the cars by working entirely from the list. The written form will clearly show where blocks of cars for like destinations already exist in the cut, so efficiencies in blocking will be obvious and may save a few trips up and down the lead. The foreman can check off or line out cars as the work progresses, so there's always a ready indication of what to do next in case of some interruption, like having to clear the lead for another movement.

Terminal operation details

Additional terminal operations can be modeled to add prototype realism and operating interest. For the most part these will be simulated, but they add time to the process and help keep yard activities from becoming too hectic. One of the most important and basic on the real railroad is the initial terminal air test.

When cars or blocks of cars are being switched in a yard, they are often handled without air brakes for convenience in uncoupling and with the air bled out of their systems. Once cars are assembled in a train, car inspectors (or in their absence yard or train crew members) couple the air hoses, open the angle cocks to allow air to flow through the brake pipe, and check to see that all hand brakes are released. (If a yard is on a grade, some hand brakes may remain set until the train is ready to move.)

The next step is to pump air into the train's brake pipe and charge the system to operating pressure. This may be done by connecting a yard engine to the train, although obviously that will keep the engine from other duties for the time it takes to build pressure in the train. In some large, busy yards, "yard air" is provided to charge outgoing trains by way of brake hoses between the tracks that connect the end car of a train to a stationary compressor. Most typically the train will wait until the road engine arrives from the engine terminal and then charges the train's brake pipe with its compressor(s).

Once the brake pipe is charged, an inspector or the train conductor will make a leakage test to see that the system is holding air, and then the engineer will be signaled to apply the brakes for the first step in a "set-and-release" test. (Even if the brake pipe charging and leakage test are done with a yard engine or yard air, the set-and-release test must still be made with the road engine.) Inspectors or crew members will walk the train to see that the brakes have applied on every car. Then the engineer will be signaled to release the brakes, and a similar inspection will be made to see that all car brakes have released. This last inspection may be performed

as a "roll-by" if the train is ready to leave the yard right away.

There are at least a couple of strategies for simulating all this. One that many modelers have used for years is to back the road engine against the train until the caboose or last car barely moves. Then the engine slowly eases forward until the caboose or last car barely moves again. On the real thing this is called stretching the train, and in both prototype and model it serves the valuable function of ensuring that all couplers are engaged.

You can also simply allow time to pass, perhaps 20 minutes by fast clock, or a period that will vary with the length of the train, such as two minutes per car. This doesn't have to be just dead time for the crews, either. They can put the time to good use by checking the consists of their trains against

the car cards or switch lists; reviewing the schedule, train orders, and work instructions for their trains; and generally planning at least the initial portions of their runs. Thinking ahead like this will usually result in a smoother trip over the main line.

Another wrinkle you can add is the possibility that a "bad-order" car will be discovered in the initial terminal air test and has to be cut out of the train. Typically the yard engine will set the car out and re-couple the train. Then the road engine can tie on again and repeat the air test. The bad-order car will be switched to the RIP track and forwarded to its destination on a later train after allowing time— perhaps an eight-hour shift—for the repairs to be completed.

An easy way to simulate this is to make a pack of cards that a train crew can draw from while

Above: Lacing 'em up! After a train is assembled, all the air brake hoses have to be connected by hand. We can model this by allowing time, instead of just highballing out of a yard as soon as a train is coupled together. *Day Photographers*

making the air test. Most cards will read "No defects" and allow the train to go on its way as built. A few cards will read "Bad order car nth from head end," with "n" being a number from 0 to the number of cars in your longest train. If a crew pulls a card for a high-numbered bad order when they have fewer cars in the train, they can treat that the same as a "no-defect" test.

Car cards and waybills

The car-card-and-waybill system for directing freight car movements consists of three elements: a car card for each car on the railroad, at least one four-step waybill card for each car, and file boxes for organizing the cards at yards, stations, and other industrial areas.

One of the most commonly used car cards is a 2" x 4" card printed with blank lines for the car information. The bottom third of the card folds up and is taped on each side to form a pocket for the waybill card.

Waybills are printed with four numbered steps, one each on the top and bottom of each side. When placed in the pocket of the car card, only the facing top step shows, and that represents the car's next destination. If the car is already at that location, it remains until the waybill is turned to show the next destination or step. When a car has been to all four destinations indicated by the waybill, there are two options: the waybill can be removed and replaced with another waybill for that type of car, or it can simply be turned to show its first step again and repeat the cycle indefinitely.

The first model railroaders to use car-card-and-waybill systems usually had file boxes at each station with three pockets labeled "set out," "hold," and "pick up." By cycling cards through these pockets, they kept cars at their spots for at least one operating session to simulate loading or unloading time. A disadvantage of this procedure was that train crews had to turn the waybill cards and advance the car cards from pocket to pocket.

Now it's more popular to simply provide a box for each industry track or car spot. The layout host turns the waybills as needed or desired between operating sessions, and train crews simply pick up cars with waybills showing another destination and leave those that indicate their present location.

For yards it's always best to have a file pocket for each yard track. The car cards are kept in the same order as the cars stand on the track so they can be used as a switch list for sorting and train makeup. Taller "blocking" cards can be used at the back of the pockets to show classification assignments. These cards can also carry the blocking instructions for their respective trains for easy reference. As an alternative, some operators use magnetic tags to show track assignments.

Printed car cards, waybills, and three-pocket wooden bill boxes

Above: Here are examples of a completed car card (left) and a folded and taped blank card (right). I used the "DESC." line to indicate the Santa Fe car class, but it could also be used for the car color or other descriptive information.

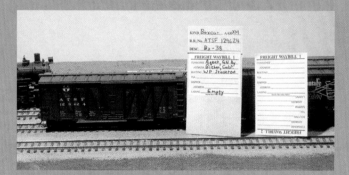

Above: A blank waybill form is shown at the right, with a filled-out waybill shown in the car card for boxcar 129624 at left. In this case the car is consigned empty for loading on the Great Northern Ry. and routed by way of the Santa Fe's connection with the Western Pacific at Stockton, Calif. The waybill can have as much or as little information as you care to provide, but where the car is going and perhaps how it will get there are about the minimum requirements. On my model railroad this would take the car off the layout into staging representing lines to the north and east.

like the ones shown are available from Micro-Mark, 340 Snyder Ave., Berkeley Heights, NJ 07922, www.micro mark.com. The starter set is no. 82916, and additional cards, waybills, and bill boxes are also available. Similar cards and file boxes are offered by Doc's Caboose, Inc., 1400 Union Ave., Kansas City, MO 64101, http://store.yahoo.com/ docscaboose-online/.

The starter kit is the no. 030-82916 Car Routing System.

Software for printing your own car cards and waybills is available from Shenandoah Software at http://members.aol.com/ Shenware/waybills.html. This software lets you enter car and waybill information in onscreen forms before printing, so it can produce especially neat and legible car cards and waybills.

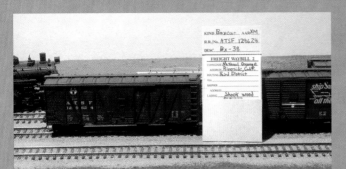

Above: When the car comes back to the Santa Fe it's carrying a load of shook wood (the lumber used to make fruit-packing crates) consigned to a packinghouse in Riverside, Calif. This information allows San Bernardino yard crews to block it into a local freight that will head into staging representing lines to the west and south.

Above: Once more car 129624 is back with a load of shook wood, but this time consigned to a packer on the coast southeast of Los Angeles. This time the yard will classify it into symbol freight SDX bound for San Diego, a destination also represented by staging.

Above: Empty again, the Santa Fe boxcar is heading back north for another load.

Above: Two Micro-Mark bill boxes placed side by side provide enough pockets for this small yard. I labeled them for each numbered track, plus the drill track and the icing track. (I explain the use of the drill-track box on page 76.) The track 2 through 4 pockets each have a yellow blocking card at the back; unused blocking cards are stored in the drill track box. I made the red card in the track 1 pocket for a caboose, and I also made blue "ice" tickets for the reefers in the icing track. After the cars have been spotted for sufficient time, the ice tickets can be pulled and the cars sent on to the destinations on their waybills.

Left: Here's an example of a switch list made out according to the car-card information and waybill instructions. The cars are listed in the order they stand on the track. The switcher will pull the track and sort the cars according to the list. Deciphering the entries is easy: line 1 means the AT&SF ("AT") car with the last three digits "624" is an empty leaving our yard on train NCX (Northern California Express), and the foreman wants it on track 2. Line 4 is a UTLX (Union Tank Line) car with the last three digits "496" also leaving on the NCX, so it's also going to track 2. Line 8 is an SFRD ("RD") refrigerator car, last three digits "676," loaded with citrus fruit. It will go out on the "Green Fruit Express," train GFX, which the crew is building on track 1. The list can be written out quickly, and then all the switching is done without further handling.

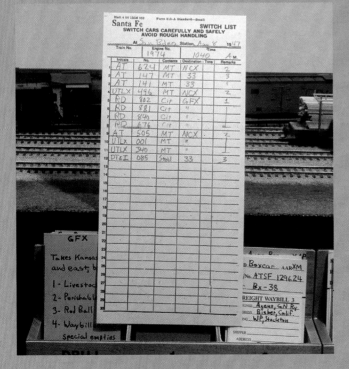

Kitbashing a yard office

There are many kits that can be used to represent yard offices, and some of them may even be called a "yard office" on the box. I wanted a building that would at least come close to one of my favorite prototype yard offices, the Santa Fe's old frame yard office that once stood in downtown San Diego. It has an interesting roofline and a long, narrow shape that fits easily into model yard scenes, and it's clearly labeled "YARD OFFICE" on the front. I've scratchbuilt HO models of this structure in wood and styrene, but this time I thought I'd see what I could do by kitbashing—using kit parts in ways in which their makers didn't intend. It turned out to be simple and pretty effective.

For the main office I used one of the Grandt Line HO scale Reese Street Row Houses, kit no. 5903, and added an extra window along what would be the track side. I omitted the decorative roof trim that comes in the kit, and right away that gave the building the utilitarian, railroady look I wanted. For the windowed front door of the office, I simply cut out the top two panels of one of the Grandt no. 5021 five-panel doors that come with the row house kit.

The crew locker room addition I made from

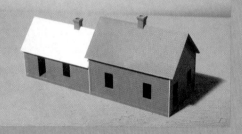

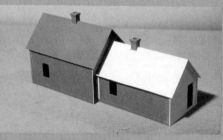

parts of another row house—three come in the kit, so there are still parts left over for other projects. I cut down the two sidewalls for the lower eave line and added a new doorway in the trackside wall. After thinking about how to modify the Grandt peaked walls for this lower, narrower addition, I decided it would be just as easy to cut a new peaked end wall from Evergreen Scale Models no. 4080 V-groove styrene siding. This is .040" thick with the grooves spaced .080" apart, and comes close to the molded siding of the Grandt parts. I used thin styrene strip to add trim to the addition matching the trim of the main office.

The main office has the shingled roof that comes with the kit, but for the addition I built a new roof from plain .040" styrene sheet. After painting under the eaves I covered the top surfaces of this roof with double-faced Scotch tape, and then laid on strips of Builders in Scale no. 261 tarpaper. This textured paper has a black side and a red side, and the red fit right into the Santa Fe color scheme.

The building is still pretty plain and could use some more details, but the railroad herald and sign on the front wall establish its identity. It's ready to be the headquarters of a model railroad yard.

Top: This kitbashed yard office is based on a Santa Fe prototype at San Diego. It might not look like it, but it started out as a Grandt Line Reese Street Row House kit.

Bottom left: The taller main office building is built pretty much straight from the kit. It has an additional window opening cut into the wall on the near side for an extra Grandt no. 5030 double-hung window.

Bottom right: The crew room addition has the same sidewalls as the main building, but I cut them down to give it a lower roofline. I used a second kit floor for the addition but cut it narrower. I cut the new end wall from a sheet of Evergreen groove siding. The plain styrene roof will be covered with simulated tarpaper to give it a different texture than the shingled main roof.

Icing dock and ice house

An icing dock and icehouse make good freight yard auxiliaries if you're modeling the era of ice refrigerator cars. That lasted into the 1960s, so icing the reefers was a service required right through the most popular modeling periods. A yard might need an icing dock if it served nearby meat or produce packinghouses, or a port where produce (such as bananas) was moved from ships to railcars. A division-point yard far away from perishable-producing industries might have an icing dock to re-ice reefers on their way from one end of the railroad to the other, and in that case the dock might be long enough to handle a whole train at once.

Icing reefers can introduce interesting operating requirements in a yard. While being iced the train or cut of cars would be "blue-flagged," meaning that it could not be moved or coupled to until the blue flag or light was removed by the worker who placed it there. This was a safety protection for the men working on top of the cars.

Time is also a factor. It took a crew of six men about two minutes to fully ice a typical 40-foot reefer. At smaller ice docks this might mean a wait of two minutes multiplied by the number of cars to be iced before the cut can be moved. Where re-icing an entire train was required, larger crews were employed to save time. Often these came from section gangs, nominally track workers, who would be pressed into service to keep the perishables on schedule.

Railroads didn't have unlimited manpower, and there were limitations on how fast blocks of ice could be delivered along the dock, so the usual practice was to handle a train in sections of 15 to 20 cars.

For shorter model trains, cars can be iced in groups of 10. So a 25-car train would need about 6 minutes of icing time, plus time to place and remove the blue flags and reposition the crews. The train might spend 10 to 15 minutes standing during the operation. With a fast clock that's not long enough to get boring, but would require planning of yard and train movements around it. That's just the kind of restriction that adds an enjoyable challenge to model operations.

Above: This is the Walthers HO no. 933-3409 icehouse and icing dock. Andy repainted it from the gray and white of the original kit to help disguise its origins as a model of a Pacific Fruit Express prototype. As it comes the dock is long enough to service two-and-a-half 40-foot reefers. For longer docks Walthers offers a no. 933-3050 add-on kit to extend the icing platform.

A model yard in operation

To give you a sense of how yards work I'll describe part of an operating session at the Port Marquette Yard on the Milwaukee, Racine & Troy, the HO layout of the Kalmbach Employees' Model Railroad Club. This isn't the same yard shown in Chapter Three, but the older version that we ran in the old Kalmbach building in downtown Milwaukee. Port Marquette was the MR&T's main freight terminal at Milwaukee, the east end of the railroad, which we imagined ran southwest to Rockford, Ill., and Ft. Madison, Iowa.

The main line extended east past Port Marquette to a through staging yard that served both ends of a point-to-point line. At the east end this yard was called "Allis," and it represented both other parts of the MR&T's Milwaukee terminal and connections from other railroads. Switchers worked at both ends of Port Marquette, with the east end switcher doing most of the classification work because of the longer drill track at that end—it extended into the staging yard.

12:01 p.m. We'll pick up the action just past noon on the fast clock, as the second "trick" (shift) yard crews took over their engines already on the leads. The engineer of the west end switcher also acted as yardmaster, coordinating the two switchers, directing road and transfer crews, and communicating with the dispatcher.

At the start of the trick two westbound trains are ready to leave. On track 1 is an RFX (Rockford Extra), a long manifest freight destined for the MR&T's automated hump yard at Rockford. The first trick yard crew built this train with cars bound for Rockford and points west, but with a block of "shorts" on the head end for the stations of Lake Beulah, Troy Junction, Winter Hill, and Williams Bay on the west end of the onstage part of the layout.

The RFX won't make these local deliveries itself but will set out the block of shorts at Williams Bay for the WBS (Williams Bay Switcher). This local freight job is based at its namesake town but works between there and Lake Beulah along the main line. The second trick yardmaster will identify the setout for the RFX crew when they bring their power over from the roundhouse.

This arrangement allowed us to run some RFX trains that were too long for our staging yard. Only the Rockford block had to fit into staging, as the Williams Bay block would be set off there before the train ended its run. Sometimes the RFX was so long that it would be built on two tracks at Port Marquette, and the road engine would double the train together before departure.

The other train ready to go is the MUT (Mukwonago Turn) on track 2. This local serves industries along the east end of the main line at Hales Corners, Big Bend, and Mukwonago, and then returns to its starting point at Port Marquette. The first trick yard crew blocked the MUT cars in station order, a big help for the local crew who will have to get their work done while dodging through traffic on the busy single-track main line.

While the yardmaster helps the road crews get their engines onto the RFX and MUT and lines them out to depart, the east end switcher gets to work on the next train out. The first-trick crew had begun blocking cars for the SFW (Santa Fe run-through West) on track 3. This train takes traffic other than intermodal for Kansas City and points west on the Santa Fe system and runs through Fort Madison, Iowa, to terminate in the Santa Fe's big classification yard at Argentine, Kans.—a suburb of Kansas City.

Cars for the SFW come from local industries in Milwaukee and along the east end of the MR&T main line, and from interchange connections at Milwaukee. The east-end switcher finds additional SFW cars on tracks 4 and 5 where they were left from earlier arrivals, and adds them to the growing consist on track 3.

12:50 p.m. The outbound RFX and MUT met eastward manifest train PMX (Port Marquette Extra), the Rockford-Port Marquette run that's the opposite "side" of the RFX. The PMX now arrives on track 1, which the departure of the RFX left open. The PMX picked up a block of cars from the WBS at Williams Bay, and it's now too long to fit on track 1. The east-end switcher clears up on the drill track so the PMX can use the main line to double the block from Williams Bay onto track 2. The power off the PMX can then use the main line to get back to the roundhouse at the west end of the yard.

Cars from the PMX may be going to many different destinations, but most will be for Milwaukee interchange connections, local industries served out of Port Marquette, and for industries served by the MUT. The same is true for cars from the Williams Bay block, but they may also include some cars to go west on the next RFX and on the SFW.

The east end switcher goes to work on the PMX proper, while the west end switcher pulls the Williams Bay block off track 2. Any SFW cars will be added to that consist on track 3. The yardmaster designates that track 2 will be used

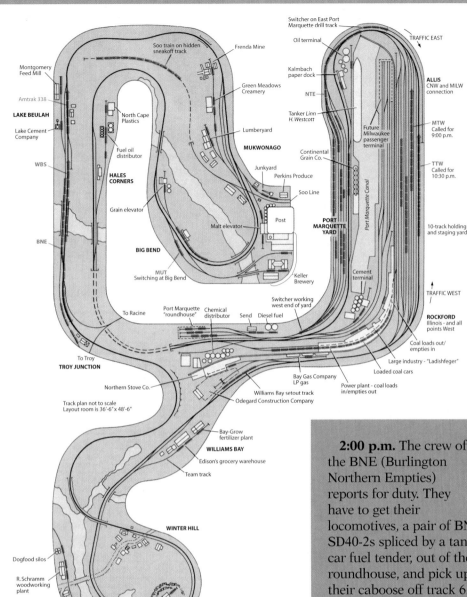

and a few for the next RFX. If necessary the switcher re-blocks those to put the Soos on the west end of track 5 and the Milwaukees and RFXs on the east.

2:45 p.m. The SLW arrives from Allis, pulling in on track 1. It will pick up the Soo cars on track 5 before departing west to reach its own line at Mukwonago. This is why the Soo cars were blocked to the west end of the yard. The SLW doesn't make any setouts. Its opposite number, the SLE (Soo Line East) set out cars at Port Marquette during the morning trick as it ran from Mukwonago to Allis.

3:00 p.m. The crew of the SFW reports for duty and picks up their run-through Santa Fe power, an SD40-2 and an F45, at the Port Marquette roundhouse. The yardmaster coordinates the SFW power's backing move to its train on track 3 with the SLW switching between tracks 1 and 5. The dispatcher lets the SFW out first, and it departs at 3:30; the SLW follows 10 minutes later.

With the departure of the two westbounds, the yard has two clear tracks, 1 and 3. The yardmaster designates track 1 for building the next morning's RFX, and the east-end switcher digs out the RFX cars on tracks 5 and 6 and assembles them on track 1.

4:15 p.m. The lineup in Port Marquette yard is: track 1, RFX; track 2, MUT and WBS; track 3, clear; track 4 NTE; track

for MUT and WBS cars, track 4 for NWT (Chicago & North Western Transfer) cars, track 5 for SLW (Soo Line West) cars, and track 6 for Port Marquette local deliveries. There may also be a few RFX and MTE (Milwaukee Road transfer East) cars—they'll also be stuffed into track 6 and possibly the east end of track 5 until other tracks are clear. Once the east switcher has pulled all the

PMX cars out of track 1, the yardmaster will try to keep that open for an arriving train.

1:40 p.m. A unit train from the Allis staging yard, the CGW (Cargill Grain empties West) runs past Port Marquette on the main line and heads west with empty covered hoppers. The yard engines keep switching on their leads clear of the main line while the unit train rolls by.

2:00 p.m. The crew of the BNE (Burlington Northern Empties) reports for duty. They have to get their locomotives, a pair of BN SD40-2s spliced by a tank car fuel tender, out of the roundhouse, and pick up their caboose off track 6. Then they'll cross over to the main line and put their train together there by pulling a string of empty 100-ton coal gons off the Wisconsin Electric power plant lead. This is a brief interruption for the west end switcher, but soon another westbound unit train is on its way.

Meanwhile the engineer of the east-end switcher is finishing classification of the cars that arrived on the PMX. When that's done it goes in on track 5, which holds both Soo Line and Milwaukee Road interchange cars,

5, MTE; and track 6, Port Marquette locals.

The west-end switcher goes in on track 6 and sorts the local industry cars into order for delivery from east to west. It pulls them west out of the yard and crosses over to the main line. Then it them shoves west with a switchman riding the last car to begin its work at the Kalmbach paper dock and the oil terminal. The switcher will work the Continental Grain Co. elevator, the cement terminal, the Ladishfeger manufacturing plant, and the Ashland Chemical distribution plant before returning to the yard.

While the west switcher works the industries, the east switcher goes in on track 2 and blocks the WBS cars to the west end of the track and the MUT cars to the east. It then begins sorting the MUT cars into station order.

5:30 p.m. The west switcher works its way back into the yard, shoving a cut of cars ahead of it into track 3. It leaves most of them there, then backs out to the roundhouse to spot some loaded sand and fuel cars and pull the empties. As it handles that last industrial work, the east switcher begins classifying the cars left on 3: some for the RFX, a couple each for the North Western and Milwaukee, and some Santa Fes and Soo Lines that won't go out until tomorrow. The latter two groups go into track 6 "for now."

The west switcher comes back from the roundhouse and puts the engine supply empties right into the RFX block on track 1.

6:20 p.m. The NTW (North Western Transfer West) shows up at the east end of the yard and receives instructions to pull in on track 3. Its faded yellow-and-green GP7 drags in a long string of cars, then cuts off and runs around on the main line to come back in at the east end and tie onto the NTE consist on track 4. It's after 7 o'clock by the time the NTE gets air in its train, pulls out far enough to pick up its caboose from track 3, makes another air test, and drags out for Allis.

7:20 p.m. Both yard engines go to work on the cars left by the North Western. The east switcher puts MUT cars into the east end of track 2 and RFX cars into 1. The west switcher shuffles WBS cars into the west end of 2 and also moves some RFX cars onto 1. Anything else, including SFW and Port Marquette local cars, will end up in track 6.

8:15 p.m. Amtrak train 338, the *City of Beloit*, rolls into town past the roundhouse and onto the passenger station lead to arrive at the station on the opposite side of the Port Marquette Canal. The train itself doesn't affect the freight yard work, but its F40PH will cut off and come back out across the west yard lead to reach the MR&T roundhouse, where it will lay over until the next morning.

8:30 p.m. Following the passenger train, the MUT comes home. It pulls in on track 4, and its engine uses track 3 to get to the roundhouse. It brings some cars for the RFX, a couple for the Milwaukee Road, and several for the Santa Fe. There are getting to be too many Santa Fes for track 6, so the yardmaster designates track 4 for building tomorrow's SFW.

While the east-end switcher classifies the cars from the MUT, leaving its Santa Fes on 4, the west switcher goes in on track 6, pulls the track as far as the last Santa Fe car, and then sorts the Santa Fes from 6 into the west end of track 4. It's left with a mixture of Soo Line and Port Marquette cars on the ladder, which it shoves back into 6.

9:15 p.m. The MTW (Milwaukee Road Transfer West) pulls up to the east end of the yard and receives instructions from the yardmaster to yard its train on track 4. When its train is in the clear, the Milwaukee SD9 cuts off and pulls onto the west yard lead. It might use the main to get back to the east end, but the dispatcher has warned the yardmaster that he's clearing the AGT (Argentine Trailers) out of Allis, so the yardmaster holds the Milwaukee power on the lead.

With the other end of the yard on hold, the east-end switcher comes in on track 3 and moves the Milwaukee transfer caboose over to track 6.

Then the switcher goes back in on 3 and pulls the just-arrived cars from the Milwaukee Road back onto the drill track. The Milwaukee transfer engine can now use track 3 to run to the east end of the yard and couple onto the MTE cars on track 5. As it pumps air into the transfer, the AGT, an MR&T-Santa Fe run-though intermodal train, runs past the yard on the first leg of its race west. When the AGT is clear the MTE can pull out to the east from track 5, back into 6 to pick up its caboose, and depart for Allis after its air test.

10:00 p.m. The east end switcher starts dealing out the cars from the MTW. Some go to the RFX on track 1, some to the MUT on 2, and some to the SFW on 4. There are also some WBS cars, which the east switcher shoves back into 3 where the west switcher can retrieve them and add them to the WBS block on the west end of 2. While this classification work is going on, the TTW (Trailer Train West), the MR&T's own piggy-back and container train, heads west on the main line to follow the AGT. The RFX our two yard crews have built will be a long train and will have to double the setout block from track 2 onto track 1 to get its train together. Only after it leaves will the MUT be able to depart from track 2. But that's normal, and what the yardmaster had in mind by building both the WBS and MUT blocks on the same track.

Above: Can't settle on one prototype? Then model a line where a second railroad has trackage rights. The Union Pacific line between Salt Lake City and Los Angeles uses Santa Fe (now BNSF) tracks from Daggett, Calif., just east of Barstow, to Riverside Junction south of San Bernardino. Mike Komosinski models Barstow at the west end of his N scale Santa Fe Needles Division layout, and handling UP traffic adds to the interest of operations in this yard.
Mike Komosinski

Right: Trains that bypass the yard can help keep the main line busy while easing the load on yard operators. On Tony Koester's HO scale Allegheny Midland RR, coal trains bypassed the yard at Sunrise, Va., running to a nearby coal marshalling yard at Mountain Grove, which was represented by staging.
Tony Koester

Left: A RIP ("repair-in-place") track doesn't have to be just a scenic attraction. It can add a challenge to a yard's operation when cars have to be cut out of trains and set aside for repairs. And a car shop can serve as an "industry" requiring shipments of wheelsets, complete trucks, and other materials. This car repair scene is on Dwight Smith's HO scale Northern Vermont Ry. *Paul J. Dolkos*

Further reading and resources

Armstrong, John, "Prototype yards," Model Railroader Special Handbook Series No. 5, June 1955 Model Railroader, pages 47-59.*

Armstrong, John, "Designing model railroad yards," Model Railroader Special Handbook Series No. 7, August 1955 Model Railroader, pages 47-60.*

Armstrong, John, Track Planning for Realistic Operation, Kalmbach Books.

Daily, Don, "Around the clock at Frankfort Yard," Model Railroad Planning 1996, pages 16-23.*

Droege, John A., Freight Terminals & Trains, republished with a new introduction by John Armstrong by the National Model Railroad Association (NMRA).

Koester, Tony, Realistic Model Railroad Design, Kalmbach Books.

Koester, Tony, Realistic Model Railroad Operation, Kalmbach Books.

Kraft, Edwin, "Railroading's hidden half: the yard," Part 1, "What yards do and how they work," June 2002 Trains magazine, pages 46-67, Part 2, "Yards of the future," July 2002 Trains, pages 36-41.

Layout Design Special Interest Group (SIG) of the NMRA, publishes the Layout Design Journal and maintains an online Internet discussion group. Contact Bob Knoll, NMRA-LDSIG Member Services, 7788 East Whileaway Place, Tucson, AZ 85750-7409, or visit the website at http://www.getnet.com/~dickg/nmra/sigs/sig.html

McGuirk, Marty, The Model Railroader's Guide to Locomotive Servicing Terminals, Kalmbach Books.

Operations SIG of the NMRA, publishes the quarterly newsletter, the Dispatcher's Office, and maintains an online Internet discussion group. Contact Bill Jewett, Co-coordinator, Operations SIG, 14 Summit Drive, Dune Acres IN 46304, or visit the website at http://www.opsig.org/

Sperandeo, Andy, Easy Model Railroad Wiring, Kalmbach Books.

Wilson, Jeff, The Model Railroader's Guide to Intermodal Equipment and Operations, Kalmbach Books.

* Photocopies of articles from out-of-print editions of Model Railroader, Model Railroad Planning, and Trains are available from Kalmbach Customer Sales and Service at 800-533-6644, or by e-mail to customerservice@kalmbach.com.

All that is comes from the mind; it is based on the mind, it is fashioned by the mind.
— The Pali'Canon

CREDITS

Design: Steve Winter, with monster updates by Blake Mobley
Editing: Andria Hayday

Black and white illustrations: Terry Dykstra
Chapter illustrations: Dee Barnett
Color photography (used with permission):
    page 1 by Lightscapes, ©The Stock Market
    page 9 by Ken Cooper, ©The Image Bank
    pages 45 and 77 by Steven Hunt, ©The Image Bank

Graphic design: Stephanie Tabat
Typography: Gaye O'Keefe
Production: Dee Barnett, Sarah Feggestad

Playtest coordination and liberal advice: Jon Pickens
Playtesters:
    Rich Brewer with Allen Thomas, Mike Mlczeko.
    Arthur Collins with Phred Cain, Jason Davis, Jeff Pickett.
    Lee G. Irons with Andy Cohen, Matt Harrop, John Whitmer.
    Alan Grimes with Bob Bellamy, Leo Hallack, Shaun Horner, Jeff
        Kennedy, Mike Leibhart, Sam Orlando, Tim Pontallion,
        Alex West.
    Caroline R. McBride with Brenda A. Floyd, Joe Floyd, R. Keith
        McBride, Sarah McBride, Mary E. Noah, Donnie Wolfgeher.
    Mark Middleton with David Boddorf, Tony Caine, Paul Conway,
        Jerry Harper, Ed Isaacs, Liz Neese, Kip Romine.
    Jim Milan and William Tracy with Gay Milan, Jeff Stevens, Justin
        Stevens, Paul Stevens, Teresa Stevens, Jeff Wherry.
    Norm Ritchie with Linda Bingle, Mary Conczyk, Dewey Frech, Mark
        Hougaard, Jim Moeller, Jay Tummelson.

TSR, Inc.
POB 756
Lake Geneva, WI 53147
U.S.A.

TSR Ltd.
120 Church End, Cherry Hinton
Cambridge CB1 3LB
United Kingdom

Copyright ©1991, TSR, Inc. All Rights Reserved.   Fourth Printing: September 1993

ISBN 1-56076-054-0

Advanced Dungeons & Dragons® 2nd Edition

Player's Handbook **Rules Supplement**

The
Complete
Psionics
Handbook

by Steve Winter

Table of Contents

"What do you think I am, a mind reader?"

As a matter of fact, you might be, if you're an AD&D® game character with the right stuff. All you need is brainpower, discipline, and *The Complete Psionics Handbook*.

Psionics—the practice of extraordinary psychic powers—was included in the original AD&D game. Some players favored psionic powers; others found them confusing. Psionics was not included in the AD&D 2nd Edition game.

Now psionics is back by popular demand, and it's better than ever. Powers this great may not be for everyone, so psionics is a completely optional addition to the AD&D 2nd Edition rules. But if you're ready to put mind over matter—to test the limits of inner space—then this book is for you.

The Complete Psionics Handbook is not a reprint of the old psionics rules; it's a complete revision. If you remember the original AD&D rules, you'll find much that seems familiar here. Beware: old words may have new meaning. We've kept a lot of the terminology, but changed the definitions. Read this book carefully before you assume an old rule still applies or jump to conclusions about what certain powers can or cannot do.

What's Changed?

This book contains five major revisions to the original AD&D psionics rules:

1) The psionicist is a character class. Characters cannot pick up a psionic power here and there just because they have a superior brain. Psionicists are extraordinary characters who develop their powers through arduous training. (While members of other classes may occasionally boast a psionic power or two, such characters are mere shadows of true psionicists.) An NPC psionicist has the potential to stand his own against any other class. As a PC in a team of adventurers, the psionicist will complement other classes well. Most of the psionicist's powers are unique. He advances slowly, at a rate somewhere between the fighter and mage. At low levels, however, the psionicist has the potential to be powerful.

2) The list of psionic powers is greatly expanded. Original rules included a menu of 50 powers. This book has over 150.

3) Psionic powers are organized differently. All psionic powers are grouped into six disciplines: clairsentience (expanded senses), psychokinesis (moving matter through space), psychometabolism (altering the body), psychoportation (psionic travel), telepathy (mind-to-mind contact), and metapsionics (an advanced discipline). Within each discipline are major powers, called "sciences," and minor powers, called "devotions." Characters can only learn powers from the disciplines they have access to. At 1st level, a character has access to only one discipline, but with experience he gains access to more.

4) Psionic powers are treated much like proficiencies. Psionic powers do not work automatically. A power is essentially a skill, and using it properly requires a power check.

5) Psionic strength points are not divided into attack, defense, and generic batches. All of a character's psionic strength points come from a single pool.

Numerous other changes, both major and minor, have been made. To avoid confusion, players are urged to read this book carefully.

How Does This Fit My Campaign?

There's no reason why adding psionics to an existing campaign should disrupt anything. As a class, psionicists are no more or less powerful than any other. Guidelines on how to introduce psionics without trauma are given in Chapter 9.

Remember, everything in this book is optional; none of it is part of the core of the AD&D game. If something in here doesn't suit a particular campaign, rule it out.

Is Psionics Magical?

Many people assume that psionics is just another type of magic. The AD&D® game already has two types of magic—one wielded by wizards and the other by clerics. So it is not unreasonable to ask, "Does the game need a third type of magic?"

The answer is no, the game probably does not need a third kind of magic. But the question is misinformed because psionics is not magic. Magic is the ability to shape, control, harness, and utilize natural forces that infuse the game world and surround the characters. It is based on the principle that, through the use of words, gestures, and catalyzing materials of unique power, these external energies can be controlled.

The key element of that statement is *external energy*. Magical effects are produced externally by manipulating outside forces. The power does not come from inside the wizard or priest but from somewhere else.

Psionics is the complete opposite of this. The psionicist shapes, controls, harnesses, and utilizes natural forces that infuse his own being. His effort is focused inward rather than outward. He must be completely in touch with and aware of even the tiniest workings of his body and mind.

This type of knowledge comes from long and intense meditation coupled with physical extremes. The psionicist finds enlightenment in both complete exhaustion and complete relaxation, in both pain and pleasure. The mind and body are only parts of a much greater unity. Indeed, discussing one without the other, as so many people do, seems nonsensical to a psionicist; they cannot be separated. The body produces energy and vitality, the mind gives it shape and reality.

Neither does the psionicist study or pray for his powers. He carries them with him wherever he goes. As long as his mind and body are rested—i.e., as long as he has not depleted his psionic strength—his powers are available to him.

Animate Shadow: A watchman confronts his dark side.

More than a character of any other class, the psionicist is self-contained. Unlike the fighter and thief, he needs no weapons or tools to practice his art. Unlike the priest, he needs no deity. Unlike the wizard, he relies on no outside energies. His power comes from within, and he alone gives it shape.

The psionicist strives to unite every aspect of his self into a single, powerful whole. He looks inward to the essence of his own being, and gains control of his subconscious. Through extraordinary discipline, contemplation, and self-awareness, he unlocks the full potential of his mind.

Requirements

This section describes the requirements all characters must meet to become a psionicist, including restrictions based on ability scores, race, and alignment. The DM may waive these requirements in special circumstances, but players shouldn't count on it.

Ability
Requirements: Constitution 11
                  Intelligence 12
                  Wisdom 15
Prime Requisites: Constitution,
                  Wisdom
Races Allowed: human, halfling, dwarf,
                  gnome, elf, half-elf

Ability Requirements: To be eligible for the psionicist class, characters must have ability scores equal to or greater than those listed above for Constitution, Intelligence, and Wisdom.

Prime Requisites: The pursuit of psionics requires strict mental and physical discipline, so the psionicist has two prime requisites: Wisdom and Constitution.

Wisdom—the measure of enlightenment and willpower—is the psionicist's primary mental characteristic, not Intelligence. Reasoning and memory (two hallmarks of Intelli-

gence) are indeed crucial to this class. However, the essence of psionic ability is the understanding and mastery of the inner self.

Although psionic powers are centered in the mind, acquiring and controlling those powers demands physical fitness. Meditative study places tremendous physical strain on the psionicist, not to mention the sheer drain of projecting psychic energy out of one's body. The psionicist need not be muscular, or even exceptionally strong, but he must maintain his health and fitness at a high level to fully exercise his powers. That's why Constitution is also a prime requisite for psionicists.

Racial Restrictions: Humans, halflings, dwarves, and gnomes often have a high degree of psionic talent. Elves and half-elves also exhibit some natural psionic ability, but they are unable to pursue it to high levels.

Multi-class Characters: As usual, only demihumans can be multi-class characters. Halflings and dwarves can combine psionics with other classes as shown below. Gnomes, elves, and half-elves cannot be multi-class psionicists; characters of these races develop their psionic powers at the expense of all others.

Multi-class Halflings:	Multi-class Dwarves:
fighter/psionicist	fighter/psionicist
thief/psionicist	thief/psionicist

Dual-class Characters: Humans can be dual-class psionicists within the normal rules and restrictions for dual-class characters. (See "Multi-class and Dual-class Characters" in Chapter 3 of the *Player's Handbook*.)

Racial Level Limits: Humans can reach the highest possible experience level as psionicists. Characters of other races have limits, as shown on Table 1. Because of their experience limitations, half-elf and elf psionicists are best suited as NPCs. Players who don't mind this "diminished potential" may still play such characters, however. (The DM may amend these level restrictions for characters with ex-

ceptionally high Wisdom and Constitution scores; see the optional rule under "Exceeding Level Limits" in Chapter 2 of the *Dungeon Master's Guide*.)

Table 1:
PSIONICIST RACIAL LEVEL LIMITS

Halflings	10
Gnomes	9
Dwarves	8
Half-elves	7
Elves	7

Alignment: Psionicists have only one alignment restriction: they cannot be chaotic. Discipline is the foundation of all psionic power. A character whose creed is chaos cannot achieve the level of self-control that psionicists require.

This restriction applies to a character who becomes chaotic for any reason. Such a character will quickly lose his psionic powers. Every day in which his alignment is chaotic, the character must make an ability check against one-half of his Wisdom score, rounded down. Each time he fails one of these Wisdom checks, the character loses access to one of his disciplines, selected randomly by the Dungeon Master. Furthermore, a chaotic character cannot recover psionic strength points. (Disciplines and psionic strength points are explained below.) If the character's alignment returns to normal—or even to another, non-chaotic alignment—he can recover his disciplines, one per day, by successfully making the same halved Wisdom check.

Other Qualifications: If a character meets all the requirements above, and the player wants to play a psionicist, the PC is assumed to exhibit psionic potential. Nothing else is required.

Initial Funds

When psionicist characters begin play, they have 3d4x10 gold pieces. As usual, skill and luck will determine what they make of it.

A Psionics Primer

All psionic powers belong to one of six disciplines: clairsentience, psychokinesis, psychometabolism, psychoportation, telepathy, and metapsionics. Within each discipline are major powers, called *sciences*, and minor powers, called *devotions*.

• *Clairsentient powers* allow characters to gain knowledge that is beyond the normal capacity of human senses. For example, some clairsentients can see and hear events that are miles distant, while others can sense poison.

• *Psychokinetic powers* move objects—from molecules to missiles—across space. A psychokineticist can throw a rock without touching it, or agitate molecules in a piece of paper until it bursts into flame.

• *Psychometabolic powers* affect the body. Biofeedback, healing, and shape-changing are just a few of the powers known.

• *Psychoportive powers* move characters or creatures from one location to another *without* crossing space. The traveler simply ceases to exist in one location, and begins to exist somewhere else. He may even travel to another plane of existence or to another time.

• *Telepathic powers* involve direct contact between two or more minds. Examples include mind reading, personality swapping, and psychic attacks.

• *Metapsionic powers* amplify, augment, or enhance other psionic abilities. This is an advanced, demanding discipline.

Psionic Strength Points: Characters use psionic powers much like proficiencies, with a few significant differences. Every time a psionicist uses a psionic devotion or science, he must pay its "cost." This cost is deducted

from the character's total *psionic strength points*, or PSPs. PSPs are similar to hit points, except that the psionicist spends them willingly, and he can recover them much faster than lost hit points. (Psionic strength points are explained more fully in a section below.)

Power Scores: Like a proficiency, every psionic power that a character knows has a score. In other words, a psionic power score represents the character's aptitude in using that particular power. Power scores are devised exactly like proficiency scores. Every psionic power is associated with one of the character's basic attributes (Strength, Wisdom, etc.). The psionic power score equals the character's score for that attribute, plus or minus a specific amount. For example, a psionic power with a score of "Intelligence −3" has a score three less than the character's Intelligence.

Power Checks: When a character wants to use a psionic power, the player makes a *psionic power check* by rolling 1d20. If the number rolled is equal to or less than the power score, the character succeeds. (In other words, he does what he intended.) The player subtracts the cost of the power from his character's total pool of psionic strength points.

If the roll exceeds the psionic power score, it means the character tried to use his power, but failed. *Failure has a price.* The player must subtract half the cost of the power, rounded up, from the character's psionic strength points. In most cases, the psionicist can try to use the same power again immediately (in the next round). For exceptions, see the individual power descriptions in this book.

Like a proficiency check, a psionic power check yields specific results on a die roll of 20 or 1. A "20" always indicates failure. A "1" always indicates a minimum level of success, regardless of the character's power score. In other words, even if a character's score has been reduced to a negative number by penalties, a roll of "1" still succeeds. That doesn't mean a "1" (or any low number) is the best result. A "1" means the power works—but often

with a quirk or drawback. See the individual power descriptions for specifics.

Players may use the optional "skill score" rule for psionic powers, too. If the die roll for the power check equals the character's power score, special results occur. Chapters 3 through 8 provide the details.

Advancement

Experience Levels and Awards: A psionicist earns experience points and advances in level just as members of other classes do. Table 2 outlines a psionicist's advancement.

The *Dungeon Master's Guide* includes an optional rule for individual experience awards. (See DMG Chapter 8.) Table 3 expands that rule to include psionicists.

Table 2: PSIONICIST EXPERIENCE LEVELS

Psionicist Level	Experience Points	Hit Dice (d6)
1	0	1
2	2,200	2
3	4,400	3
4	8,800	4
5	16,500	5
6	30,000	6
7	55,000	7
8	100,000	8
9	200,000	9
10	400,000	9 + 2
11	600,000	9 + 4
12	800,000	9 + 6
13	1,000,000	9 + 8
14	1,200,000	9 + 10
15	1,500,000	9 + 12
16	1,800,000	9 + 14
17	2,100,000	9 + 16
18	2,400,000	9 + 18
19	2,700,000	9 + 20
20	3,000,000	9 + 22

Table 3: INDIVIDUAL CLASS AWARDS

Psionic power used to overcome foe or problem	10 XP/PSP
Psionic power used to avoid combat	15 XP/PSP
Defeat psionic opponent	100 XP/level or hit dice
Create psionic item	500 XP × level

Gaining Disciplines: Every psionic power belongs to one of the six disciplines listed previously. Before a character can learn a psionic power, he must have access to the appropriate discipline. *Psionic characters begin play with access to only one discipline.* As they progress to new experience levels, they gain access to additional disciplines. Table 4 shows how many disciplines a character has access to at each experience level.

Table 4: PSIONIC POWER PROGRESSION

Exp. Level	Total Discipl.	Total Sciences	Total Devotions	Def. Modes
1	1	1	3	1
2	2	1	5	1
3	2	2	7	2
4	2	2	9	2
5	2	3	10	3
6	3	3	11	3
7	3	4	12	4
8	3	4	13	4
9	3	5	14	5
10	4	5	15	5
11	4	6	16	5
12	4	6	17	5
13	4	7	18	5
14	5	7	19	5
15	5	8	20	5
16	5	8	21	5
17	5	9	22	5
18	6	9	23	5
19	6	10	24	5
20	6	10	25	5

Gaining Sciences and Devotions: Every new, first-level psionicist knows four powers within a single discipline: one science (major power) and three devotions (minor powers). With each new experience level, a psionicist gains new powers. Sometimes he gains both sciences and devotions; at other times, only devotions. (See Table 4.)

A player can select new powers for his character as soon as the psionicist reaches a new experience level. These new powers can be chosen from any discipline the character can access, including a discipline that was just gained.

Note: If the optional training rule is in play, characters must train with a mentor until they reach 7th level. To find the training time in weeks, subtract the mentor's Wisdom score from 21. Beyond 7th level, psionicists can train themselves if they pass the necessary checks to qualify as instructors. The training time for a psionicist instructing himself is doubled.

Players must follow two simple rules when choosing new powers for their characters:
- Within a single discipline, the number of devotions that a character knows must be at least twice the number of sciences.
- The first discipline chosen is the character's *primary discipline*. A character can never learn as many sciences or devotions in another discipline as he currently knows in his primary discipline.

Example: Lena's primary discipline is clairsentience. She knows three sciences and seven devotions in that discipline. This means: a) she must learn an eighth clairsentient devotion before she can learn a fourth clairsentient science, and b) at her current level, she cannot know more than two sciences or six devotions in any other single discipline.

Advancing Mid-adventure: Most Dungeon Masters award experience points at the end of adventures rather than in the middle, so experience levels are rarely gained in mid-adventure. In the unusual event that a new level is gained in the middle of an adventure,

however, the character should have to wait at least until he has a chance to rest and recuperate—long enough to recover all his psionic strength points—before gaining any new psionic powers.

Raising Psionic Power Scores: A character can increase a psionic power score when he reaches a new experience level by "relearning it." (He repeats his studies, and learns something new about a familiar power.) Instead of learning a new devotion, the character can add one point to his power score in a devotion he already knows. Similarly, he can exchange a new science for a one-point increase in a science he already knows.

Psionic Strength Points (PSPs)

Psionic energy comes from within the character. This energy is measured in psionic strength points, or PSPs. When a character uses a psionic power, he expends psionic strength points. The exact cost depends on which power is used, and how long the character uses it.

The total number of psionic strength points that a character has depends on four factors: his Wisdom, Intelligence, and Constitution scores, and his experience level. Wisdom, Intelligence, and Constitution determine the psionicist's *inherent potential.* (Wisdom is the primary factor.) Experience determines how well the character has developed that potential.

Follow these steps to calculate a character's total PSPs:

1) Find the character's Wisdom score on Table 5, then get his base score from that.

2) Add the appropriate ability modifiers for the character's Intelligence and Constitution scores to his base score. This final adjusted number is the character's inherent potential.

Example: Rowina's ability scores are Wis 17, Con 16, Int 12. Her inherent potential is 25 (24 points for her Wisdom score with a +1 modifier for her Constitution score). At 1st level she has 25 PSPs.

Table 5: INHERENT POTENTIAL

Ability Score	Base Score	Ability Modifier
15	20	0
16	22	+1
17	24	+2
18	26	+3

Gaining Psionic Strength Points: Every time a character advances to a new experience level, he expands his total pool of psionic strength points. To determine how many PSPs he gains, find the modifier on Table 5 that corresponds to his Wisdom score. Add this number to 10. The result equals the total PSPs gained.

Example: Rowina has just advanced to a new level. Her Wisdom is 17. According to Table 5, the modifier for this score is +2. Rowina can add 12 PSPs (2 + 10) to her total pool.

Recovering Psionic Strength Points: A character who has expended psionic strength points can recover those points by "taking it easy"—which means engaging in no hard physical activity and refraining from using psionic powers (i.e., from expending any more PSPs). After each *hour* in which a character expends no psionic strength points, check Table 6 to determine how many PSPs the character recovers. A character can never recover more PSPs than he lost.

A character's rate of recovery depends on how much physical exertion he experienced during the hour in question. Psionicists recover the most points when they sleep or meditate for the entire hour of rest. Light activity, such as walking or riding, diminishes the speed of recovery. Rate each hour according to the *most* strenuous physical activity undertaken, even if it lasted only a few minutes.

Option: DMs may allow characters to recover points per *turn* of rest rather than per hour. These rates are also listed on Table 6.

Table 6: PSIONIC STRENGTH RECOVERY

Physical Activity	PSPs Recovered
Hard exertion*	none
Walking, riding	3/hour (1 every 2 turns)
Sitting, resting, reading	6/hour (1/turn)
Rejuvenating**, sleeping	12/hour (2/turn)

* "Hard exertion" includes fighting, running, digging ditches, walking while encumbered, climbing a rope, scaling a mountain, exploring a dungeon, swimming, and any other activity the DM wants to include.
** This refers to use of the psionicist's Rejuvenation proficiency.

Defense Modes

Psionic *defense modes* are special powers which all psionicists acquire naturally in time. All defense modes belong to the telepathic discipline. Psionicists learn these powers automatically as they gain new experience levels—regardless of whether or not they have access to the telepathic discipline. Defense modes do not count toward the psionicist's maximum number of powers as listed in Table 4. Nor are they counted when characters determine the relative number of sciences and devotions they can acquire within a given discipline.

There are five psionic defense modes:
- mind blank
- thought shield
- mental barrier
- tower of iron will
- intellect fortress

Each is described in Chapter 7, "Telepathy." All psionicists automatically know one of these powers at 1st level (player's choice). They learn another defense mode of the player's choice every other level—at 3rd, 5th, 7th, and 9th.

Special Abilities

In addition to ordinary psionic powers, which are the hallmark of the class, psionicists have several special abilities. These include their saving throws, THAC0s, and psionic powers that operate continuously.

Maintaining Powers: Certain psionic powers can operate continuously. (Chapters 3 through 8 specify which ones do.) Such powers can be "switched on" and kept on without interruption, until the user decides to (or is forced to) "switch them off." This is called *maintaining* powers.

Each power that is maintained is handled separately. In many cases, maintenance entails expending PSPs by the hour or turn rather than the melee round (the norm for psionic combat). *If a psionicist is expending PSPs to maintain a power, he cannot recover psionic strength points that hour.* A character cannot spend PSPs to maintain a power when he is sleeping or unconscious; no continuous power that requires strength points can operate during sleep.

A character can maintain any number of powers at one time, but he can "switch on" or initiate only one per round. When maintained powers are deactivated, the character can drop all maintained powers at once, or one per round. He cannot drop two or more in one round and maintain others.

THAC0 and Saving Throws: As shown on Table 7, a psionicist's THAC0 advancement equals that of a rogue. Table 8 lists saving throws. *Psionicists gain a +2 bonus on all saving throws vs. enchantment/charm spells and the like.* This is in addition to their magical defense adjustment for high Wisdom.

Followers

At 9th level (which is sometimes called "name" level), a psionicist becomes a contemplative master. He can build a sanctuary (usually in an isolated place), and use it as his

Table 7: PSIONICIST CALCULATED THAC0s

Level	1	2	3	4	5	6	7	8	9	10	11	12	13	14	15	16	17	18	19	20
THAC0	20	20	19	19	18	18	17	17	16	16	15	15	14	14	13	13	12	12	11	11

Table 8: PSIONICIST SAVING THROWS

Level	Paralyzation, Poison, or Death Magic	Rod, Staff, or Wand	Petrification or Polymorph[1]	Breath Weapon[2]	Spell[3]
1-4	13	15	10	16	15
5-8	12	13	9	15	14
9-12	11	11	8	13	12
13-16	10	9	7	12	11
17-20	9	7	6	11	9
21+	8	5	5	9	7

[1] Excluding *polymorph wand* attacks.
[2] Excluding those which cause petrification or polymorph.
[3] Excluding those for which another saving throw type is specified, such as death, petrification, polymorph, etc.

---

headquarters. Most importantly, he begins to attract followers.

One neophyte psionicist (1st or 2nd level) will arrive each month, coming to study at the feet of the master. These neophytes will arrive regardless of whether or not the master builds a sanctuary. If the master does have a sanctuary, however, he will attract a maximum number of followers equal to his Charisma score. If not, the maximum number is halved (rounded down).

These followers want only to learn. They will serve in any capacity the master chooses. In return, the master must spend at least 10 hours per week instructing his followers, or they will leave.

Restrictions

Like members of other classes, psionicists must abide by restrictions when choosing weapons and armor, and in selecting nonweapon proficiencies.

Weapons: Psionicists tend to disdain weapons of any sort, given the crudeness and imprecision of such tools compared to psychic weaponry. Still, a good sidearm is indispensable for a last-ditch personal defense, and it's essential when a display of psionic power would be inappropriate. Also, in the rough-and-tumble frontier areas where adventurers are common, appearing in public without a weapon often invites ridicule and trouble.

Psionicists can use any of the common weapons listed below. Essentially, these are most small- or medium-sized weapons weighing 6 pounds or less.

short bow	throwing axe
hand crossbow	horseman's mace
light crossbow	horseman's pick
dagger	scimitar
dirk	spear
knife	short sword
club	war hammer
hand axe	

Armor: Psionicists can don armor made of padded leather, studded leather, or hide. They can also carry a small shield.

A psionicist can use his powers while wearing a helmet that is psionically active, or one featuring magical enchantments that affect or simulate psionic powers. But if the psionicist is wearing a normal helmet of any sort, he cannot use his powers. Removing a normal helmet won't affect the character's armor class, but it may have other effects defined by the Dungeon Master. For example, a thief who approaches the psionicist from behind may find the psionicist easy prey. Or, if the DM allows called shots, the character's bare head might present a tempting target.

Optional Rule: A DM may allow psionicists to wear any sort of armor, but impose penalties for heavy armor that's made of metal. (See Table 9.) This rule creates an across-the-board reduction in psionic power scores when a psionicist wears the inappropriate armor.

Table 9: PSIONICIST ARMOR PENALTIES

Armor	Psionic Power Score Reduction
Padded, leather, studded leather, hide	0
Brigandine, ring, scale, splint mail	−1
Chain, banded mail	−2
Plate mail	−3
Field plate	−5
Full plate	−7

Proficiencies

Psionic powers function like proficiencies, but they do not replace them. Psionicists can learn the usual weapon and nonweapon proficiencies regardless of their powers. Proficiencies are acquired at the rate shown on Table 10.

Psionicists can learn a weapon proficiency for any weapon they can use. They can learn any nonweapon proficiency from the "General" group (see proficiency rules in the AD&D® 2nd Edition *Player's Handbook*, page 54, Table 37) or from the Psionicist group, described below.

If the optional proficiency rules in the *Player's Handbook* are in use, psionicists can gain extra nonweapon proficiency slots based on their Intelligence scores. See Table 4, "Intelligence" in the *Player's Handbook* to determine these bonus proficiencies (Chapter 5, page 16). Characters can use these extra slots for languages or nonweapon proficiencies, but never additional psionic powers.

Initial refers to the number of weapon or nonweapon proficiency slots received by psionicists at 1st level.

 # Levels indicates how many levels a psionicist must advance before he receives a new weapon or nonweapon proficiency. Thus, psionicists receive a new weapon proficiency every five levels—i.e., at levels 5, 10, 15, 20, etc. They receive a new nonweapon proficiency every three levels—i.e., at levels 3, 6, 9, 12, etc.

Penalty is the modifier to a psionicist's attack rolls when he fights using a weapon he

Table 10:
PSIONICIST PROFICIENCY SLOTS

Group	Weapon Proficiencies		Penalty	Nonweapon Proficiencies	
	Initial	#Levels		Initial	#Levels
Psionicist	2	5	−4	3	3

Animate Object: Raji turns the tables against his attackers.

isn't proficient with. This penalty is subtracted directly from the character's rolls to hit.

The Psionicist Group: Table 11 lists seven nonweapon proficiencies which psionicists can easily learn. These proficiencies—the "Psionicist group"— are an extension of Table 37 in the AD&D® 2nd Edition *Player's Handbook*.

Table 11: PSIONICIST NONWEAPON PROFICIENCIES

Proficiency	# Slots Required	Relevant Ability
Gem Cutting	2	Dex −2
Harness Subconscious	2	Wis −1
Hypnosis	1	Cha −2
Rejuvenation	1	Wis −1
Meditative Focus	1	Wis +1
Musical Instrument	1	Dex −1
Reading/Writing	1	Int +1
Religion	1	Wis +0

Harness Subconscious: This meditative proficiency lets the psionicist temporarily boost his total PSPs. In effect, the proficiency lets him tap into energy reserves that lie deep in his subconscious—reserves which are usually unavailable to him. It's like enjoying a shot of psychic adrenalin.

Before he can harness subconscious energies, the psionicist's PSP total must be at its maximum. He then must spend two days (48 consecutive hours) gathering this energy, taking only necessary breaks for eating and sleeping. At the end of that time, the character makes a proficiency check. If he passes, he increases his PSP total by 20%, rounded up.

The increase in PSPs lasts 72 hours. At the end of that time, the character loses as many strength points as he initially gained, regardless of his current total. This loss can never reduce his total below 0 points, however.

During the 72 hours of heightened strength, the character cannot recover PSPs if his current total equals or exceeds his usual maximum. Once his current total drops below his usual maximum (i.e., once he has spent all bo-

nus points), he can begin regaining PSPs normally. He cannot recover the lost bonus points, however; he can only recover enough points to return to his usual maximum.

Hypnosis: With this proficiency, a psionicist can hypnotise another character—placing the subject into a relaxed state in which he is very susceptible to suggestions. However, hypnosis is not possible unless the subject is willing and knows he is being hypnotised.

Psionicists with this proficiency can hypnotize humans and demihumans with ease. Nonhumans can be hypnotized, too, but the DM should assign a penalty to the proficiency check. The size of the penalty depends on how inhuman the subject is. A half-orc, for example, could be hypnotized with a −2 modifier, while a lizard man could be hypnotized only with a −8 modifier to the psionicist's proficiency check.

The act of hypnotizing someone takes about five minutes. The subject is then very relaxed and willing to do almost anything that isn't very dangerous or against his alignment. Note, however, that a hypnotized subject can be easily fooled; the subject may be convinced that he's doing one thing, while he's actually doing another. Lawful or good psionicists who trick their subjects in this fashion should beware. Psionicists who use hypnotism to make people do chaotic or evil things may find themselves with alignment problems of their own.

Hypnotism can have the following (or similar) effects:

- A character can be induced to remember things he has forgotten by reliving a frightening or distant event.
- A character can be made calm and unafraid in the face of a specific situation that he has been prepared for.
- A character can be cured of a bad habit or addiction (but not of curses or magical afflictions).
- A character can be prepared to impersonate someone by thoroughly adopting that individual's personality.

Hypnotism cannot be used to increase a character's attributes, give him powers or abilities he does not naturally possess, let him do things that are beyond his capabilities, or give him information that he couldn't possibly know.

Rejuvenation: This proficiency allows a character to recover PSPs while he meditates, as quickly as if he were sleeping. The character achieves a state of deep concentration, in which he focuses and regains his energies. He is still conscious and aware of his surroundings, so he does not suffer any penalties on surprise or initiative rolls, and he is not helpless if attacked. (He still can't *expend* PSPs, however.)

Meditative Focus: Through this proficiency, a psionicist can focus his mental energy on one particular discipline. As a result, his power scores in that discipline temporarily increase, while those in other disciplines decline.

The proficiency requires the character to meditate, *uninterrupted*, for 12 hours. The last four hours of this meditation are spent in a deep, sleeplike trance. The psionicist can recover PSPs normally during the entire period.

When the meditation is complete, the player makes a proficiency check. If the character passes the check, he has successfully focused his mind on one particular discipline (which was chosen when the process began). All of the character's psionic power scores in that discipline are increased by two points for the next 24 hours—or until the character's PSPs have been reduced to zero, whichever comes first. All of his power scores in other disciplines are reduced by one for the same period.

Gem Cutting, Musical Instrument, Reading/ Writing, Religion: See the *Player's Handbook* for a description of these proficiencies.

Wild Talents

A wild talent is someone from any other character class who has natural, latent psionic potential. This potential can be present in any character, regardless of class, alignment, or race. Wild talents can never approach psionicists in skill, but they do boast at least one psionic power—which is known as a "wild power" among psionicists.

Any character can test for wild powers. (The character should be forewarned: such efforts are not without risk, as explained below.) A character can test for wild powers only at specific times: when the character is first created; when the character's Wisdom increases to a higher point than it has ever been; the first time the character goes to a psionicist who can perform psychic surgery on him; when psionics is first introduced to the campaign.

Every character (and NPC and monster, if the DM wishes) has a base chance of 1% to possess wild powers. This is modified as shown below:

Each Wis, Con, or Int score of 18	+3
Each Wis, Con, or Int score of 17	+2
Each Wis, Con, or Int score of 16	+1
Character is 5th-8th level	+1
Character is 9th level or higher	+2
Mage, cleric, or nonhuman*	× 1/2

* Round fractions up. Apply this penalty only once, even if more than one of these descriptions fits (e.g., a "nonhuman mage").

Once you've determined the character's chance to be a wild talent, roll percentile dice. Subtract 2 from the roll if the character is under the guidance of a psychic surgeon (see "psychic surgery" in Chapter 8). If the result is less than or equal to the modified chance, the character has at least one wild power. If the number is 97 or higher, the character suffers dire consequences. See "The Risks" below.

Example: Consider a 3rd level dwarf cleric with a Wisdom of 17, Intelligence of 9, and Constitution of 16. His chance to be a wild talent is 1 (base chance) + 2 (Wis 17) + 1 (Con 16) × 0.5 (because he's a dwarf). The final result equals 2%. The dwarf has a 2% chance of being a wild talent. The player rolls a 3 on percentile dice. The dwarf has no talent.

Determining Powers: If a character is a wild talent, the player should roll percentile dice again and consult Table 12, "Wild Devotions" to determine exactly what the character's psionic powers are. Most wild talents have only one power. A lucky few (those with high-rolling players) boast more than one. Furthermore, if a character gains any power with a prerequisite, he automatically gains the prerequisite, too. For example, if the wild talent knows a telepathic power which requires contact (an important telepathic power), he automatically knows contact, too.

Strength Points: Like an actual psionicist, a wild talent has psionic strength points. He receives the minimum number of PSPs necessary to use the power (or powers) once. If a power can be maintained, he receives enough additional points to pay the maintenance cost four times. Afterward, the character receives four additional PSPs every time he gains a new experience level (he receives no bonus for levels he already has).

The Risks: Characters who attempt to unlock their psionic potential are tampering with things they cannot begin to understand. If the dice roll is 97 or higher, the character suffers the following consequences:

Dice Roll	**Result**
97	Save vs. death or Wisdom reduced by 1d6 points—permanently
98	Save vs. death or Intelligence reduced by 1d6 points—permanently
99	Save vs. death or Constitution reduced by 1d6 points—permanently
00	Save vs. death with −5 penalty or Wisdom, Intelligence, and Constitution are all reduced to 3—permanently.

Table 12: WILD DEVOTIONS

Clairsentient Devotions

01	All-Round Vision
02	Combat Mind
03	Danger Sense
04	Feel Light
05	Feel Sound
06	Hear Light
07	Know Direction
08	Know Location
09	Poison Sense
10	Radial Navigation
11	See Sound
12	Spirit Sense
13	Choose any clairsentient devotion above
14	Choose any clairsentient devotion above

Psychokinetic Devotions

15	Animate Object
16	Animate Shadow
17	Ballistic Attack
18	Control Body
19	Control Flames
20	Control Light
21	Control Sound
22	Choose any psychokinetic devotion above

Psychometabolic Devotions

23	Absorb Disease
24	Adrenalin Control
25	Aging
26	Biofeedback
27	Body Control
28	Body Equilibrium
29	Body Weaponry
30	Catfall
31	Cause Decay
32	Cell Adjustment
33	Chameleon Power
34	Chemical Simulation
35	Displacement
36	Double Pain
37	Enhanced Strength
38	Ectoplasmic Form
39	Expansion
40	Flesh Armor
41	Graft Weapon
42	Heightened Senses
43	Immovability
44	Lend Health
45	Mind Over Body

46	Reduction
47	Share Strength
48	Suspend Animation
49	Choose any psychometabolic devotion above

Telepathic Devotions

50	Attraction
51	Aversion
52	Awe
53	Conceal Thoughts
54	Daydream
55	Empathy
56	ESP
57	False Sensory Input
58	Identity Penetration
59	Incarnation Awareness
60	Inflict Pain
61	Invincible Foes
62	Invisibility
63	Life Detection
64	Mind Bar
65	Phobia Amplification
66	Post-Hypnotic Suggestion
67	Psychic Impersonation
68	Psychic Messenger
69	Repugnance
70	Send Thoughts
71	Sight Link
72	Sound Link
73	Synaptic Static
74	Taste Link
75	Telempathic Projection
76	Truthear
77-78	Choose any telepathic devotion above

Psychoportive Devotions

79	Astral Projection
80	Dimensional Door
81	Dimension Walk
82	Dream Travel
83	Time Shift
84	Time/Space Anchor
85	Choose any psychoportive devotion above
86-87	Roll two times
88-89	Roll three times
90	Choose any two devotions
91-99	Roll on Table 13: Sciences
00	Choose any devotion. Then roll again and consult Table 13.

Table 13: WILD SCIENCES

Clairsentient Sciences

01-02	Aura Sight
03-04	Clairaudience
05-06	Clairvoyance
07-08	Object Reading
09-10	Precognition
11-12	Sensitivity to Psychic Impressions
13-16	Choose any clairsentient science or devotion

Psychokinetic Sciences

17-18	Detonate
19-20	Disintegrate
21-22	Molecular Rearrangement
23-24	Project Force
25-26	Telekinesis
27-30	Choose any psychokinetic science or devotion

Psychometabolic Sciences

31-32	Animal Affinity
33-34	Complete Healing
35-36	Death Field
37-38	Energy Containment
39-40	Life Draining
41-42	Metamorphosis
43-44	Shadow-form
45-48	Choose any psychometabolic science or devotion

Telepathic Sciences

49-50	Domination
51-52	Fate Link
53-54	Mass Domination
55-56	Mindwipe
57-58	Probe
59-60	Superior Invisibility
61-62	Switch Personality
63-64	Mindlink
65-68	Choose any telepathic science or devotion

Psychoportive Sciences

69-70	Banishment
71-72	Probability Travel
73-74	Summon Planar Creature
75-76	Teleport
77-78	Teleport Other
79-82	Choose any psychoportive science or devotion
83-85	Roll two times
86-88	Roll three times
89-92	Choose any science or devotion
93-96	Choose any science and two devotions
97-99	Choose any science and three devotions
00	Choose any two sciences and four devotions

Combat featuring psionicists is no more complicated than a fight between one or more wizards. In fact, it's similar. During a battle, psionicists and wizards tend to employ the same tactics: they avoid enemy hackers and slashers, and focus their efforts on the strongest opponent or shore up defenses where needed.

A lone psionicist caught by enemy fighters is in serious trouble. Unless he can summon, create, dominate, or otherwise garner some help, he probably will be overpowered. For this reason, psionicists—especially NPCs—rarely travel without an escort if they are expecting trouble.

Using Powers

In general, a character can initiate only one psionic power per round. There are two key exceptions:

- Once a power is initiated, a character can maintain that power for as long as he can continue paying the maintenance cost. (This assumes that the power has a maintenance cost; if no such cost is mentioned in the description, the power cannot be maintained beyond its initial duration.)
- Psionic defense modes (mind blank, thought shield, mental barrier, intellect fortress, and tower of iron will) do not count against the one-power-per-round limit. A character can always use a defense mode and initiate one other psionic power in the same round.

Power Checks

The power check is fundamental to psionic combat. *In general, no psionic power functions unless the character first makes a successful power check.* (Chapter 1 explains how the check is made.) Modifiers apply for some

powers. Furthermore, several powers require an additional power check before they'll yield a specific result. Check the individual power descriptions in Chapters 3-8 for details.

Psychic Contests

Psionic powers often clash "head-on." For example, one psionicist may make a psionic attack against a character with an active psionic defense. Which power prevails? Does the attack break through the defense, or bounce off? A psychic contest determines the answers.

Resolving a psychic contest is simple when both powers are initiated in the same round. The two contestants just compare the die rolls for their power checks. The character with the *higher successful roll* wins the contest. If neither character's power check succeeds, or if both rolls are equal, the defender "wins" by default. (In other words, a tie goes to the defender.)

Example: An attacker is using ego whip. The defender has erected a thought barrier. The attacker's ego whip power score is 15, and the defender's thought barrier score is 12. The table below shows several possible outcomes of the psychic contest between these powers.

Attack Roll	Defense Roll	Result
11	6	Attacker wins because his die roll is higher.
3	9	Defender wins because his die roll is higher.
4	18	Attacker wins because his attack roll succeeded and the defender's roll did not—in effect, there is no defense this round.
16	10	Defender wins because his defense roll succeeded and the attacker's failed.
19	15	Neither power check succeeded. The defender *(table continues...)*

After months of trying, Hosni finally catches Gustafa at home.

		"wins" by default simply because the attacker didn't.
8	8	Tied rolls. Again, the defender wins by default because the attacker didn't beat the defense roll.
15	—	The attacker wins this automatically. His power check succeeded and his roll is higher than the defender's power score, so NO roll will let the defender win.

Maintained Powers: In the example above, powers were initiated in the same round as the conflict. Some psychic contests involve a power that is being maintained—i.e., a power that was initiated in a previous round. In this case, the player whose character is maintaining the power must make a *new* power check strictly to resolve the contest. He gains a +1 bonus to his power score because the power is being maintained. If the contest roll "fails," it doesn't mean the power fails. It's still being maintained—just not very well. For the contest, the character ignores the "failed" check and instead receives a "successful" result of 1.

Multiple Conflicts: In the thick of battle, a psionicist may be involved in more than one psychic contest per round. If he's using more than one power, the player must make a separate die roll for each power used that round.

If he's using a single power against more than one opponent, the player can make a separate die roll for each opponent. As soon as he rolls a number he likes, the player may use that result for all remaining psychic contests involving *that power*, in that round. (In other words, once he gets a power really well "tuned in" during a given round, he can stop "fiddling with the dial".) This rule applies to telepathic defense modes, as well as other powers.

Psychic Lock

In some psychic contests, there is no clear-cut defender. For example, two characters may try to use psychokinesis on the same object simultaneously. (They do a little psionic arm-wrestling.) In such a case, the character with the higher successful die roll still wins the contest that round. In our example, the winner would control the object.

If the power checks indicate a tie, however, the characters are deadlocked—or *psychically locked*. Neither character wins that round. To resolve the conflict, both characters should maintain the same powers during the next round, and engage in a new psychic contest. If either character fails to maintain his power (effectively giving up), he suffers a backlash and loses 4d4 PSPs immediately.

In any case, victory may be fleeting. If conditions are right, the loser can challenge the winner to a "rematch" in the next round.

The Combat Round

Psionic conflicts follow the standard AD&D® game combat sequence. All psionic powers—excluding defense modes—are used in order of initiative. For example, if a psionicist wants to attack, or plans to teleport to safety, he can do so when his normal chance to attack comes around. Psionic defenses work throughout the entire round, starting at the very beginning. Unlike spells, psionic powers do not have initiative modifiers.

Psionic powers require a certain amount of concentration. A character who uses one during a combat round can move at only half his walking rate. Furthermore, he can be disrupted like a mage casting a spell. A power that is being maintained from a previous round cannot be disrupted this way, nor can telepathic tangents that were established in previous rounds (see below). If a power is disrupted during a preparatory round, the time

invested in preparation is lost. No PSPs are expended when a power is disrupted.

Telepathic Combat

Before a psionicist can use a telepathic power, he must establish contact with the recipient's mind. "Contact" is a telepathic devotion which paves the way for other telepathic powers. Usually, a single use of this devotion is all that's required; the psionicist uses contact first, then follows up with another telepathic power. Beings with little or no psionic talent, including wild talents, can be contacted in this way. So can psionicists and psionic creatures, *provided they cooperate.*

The contact devotion never works against a psionicist (or psionic creature) who does not allow it to work. This is true even when he's sleeping or unconscious. Psionicists normally have *closed minds.* Before the contact power can work against them, they must intentionally open their minds. They can be selective, allowing contact with a friendly power while closing their minds to hostile characters or strangers.

When a subject's mind is closed, he can only be contacted through telepathic combat. The text below describes five telepathic assaults, or *attack modes,* that are used to establish contact with a closed mind. It also describes five telepathic defenses, which can help prevent such attacks from succeeding. Lastly, it explains what happens when these opposing powers clash.

Telepathic Attack Modes

There are five attack modes: mind thrust, ego whip, id insinuation, psychic crush, and psionic blast. (See Chapter 7, "Telepathy," for a complete description of each.) Against a mind that is open to contact, each of these powers has specific effects. For example, ego whip can make a character feel so worthless that he suf-

fers a penalty to all of this die rolls. None of these effects occur unless the subject's mind is open to contact, however. If the subject's mind is closed, an attack mode only serves to erode his resistance. If he is repeatedly struck with an attack mode, his mind can be forced to open, and contact will be established. (See "Tangents" below for details.)

Learning Attack Modes: A psionicist learns attack modes in the same way he learns other powers. The character must first have access to the telepathy discipline. Then he must allot one of his devotion slots to the power (only psionic blast is a science). A character could devote himself completely to learning the attack modes, and know all five by 2nd level. Or he could learn dozens of telepathic powers without ever picking up a single attack mode. This is the player's option.

The One-Two Punch: Attack modes differ from most other psionic powers in one key regard: a character using an attack mode gets one bonus attack with that power each round. (An attack mode packs a one-two punch.) The player rolls two power checks. Each of these rolls constitutes a separate attack and, if opposed, is conducted as a separate psychic contest. *Both attacks must be directed against the same target.* The initial cost of an attack mode includes this double attack.

Telepathic Defense Modes

A character with psionic powers is not defenseless against telepathic attack modes. Five telepathic powers, known as *defense modes,* help protect characters from unwanted contact. These powers are mind blank, thought shield, mental barrier, intellect fortress, and tower of iron will. (See Chapter 7 for a description of each.) Although these powers belong to the telepathy discipline, they are common to all members of the psionicist class. Psionicists develop these powers naturally as they gain experience levels, regardless of whether they have access to the telepathy dis-

cipline. (See "Defense Modes" in Chapter 1 for an explanation.)

When a character activates a telepathic defense mode, it becomes effective at the beginning of the round. The character conducts a psychic contest against every attack mode coming his way. (The initial cost of the defense mode covers all attacks in the round.) At any point during the round, if he rolls a number he likes, he can keep it for the rest of the round. Defense modes have no effect against any psionic powers other than attack modes.

Attack Modifiers

Each attack mode is more effective against some defense modes than others, and vice versa. This is represented by modifiers which apply to the attacker's power score. Table 14 lists these modifiers.

When an attack mode clashes with a defense mode, cross-index the attack with the defense on Table 14. The resulting modifier is applied to the attacker's power score. Thus, positive modifiers are bonuses and negative modifiers are penalties.

Tangents

Each time an attack mode overcomes a defense mode (or an attack mode succeeds against someone who was not using a defense mode), the attacker has established a partial contact called a *tangent*. Three tangents equal full contact. Thus, establishing contact with someone's mind through combat requires three successful attacks. (In common parlance, a single tangent is often called "one-finger contact" and two tangents "two-finger contact.") Remember that an attack mode allows two attacks per round, so it is possible to establish two tangents per round.

A tangent has no direct effects in and of itself, no matter which attack mode helps to establish it. It is only a "foot in the door." When the door is open—i.e., when three tangents have succeeded—full contact is established. This contact is the same condition that is achieved when the contact power is used successfully against a nonpsionicist. (In other words, the three effective attacks simply take the place of one successful use of contact.) The tangents no longer apply when contact is established. (That's why there's no such thing as "three-finger contact.")

When full contact is established, the attacker can make no more attacks against the defender that round. In the next round, he can use any telepathic power against the defender that he chooses—provided he's within range and pays the power cost, of course. Having contact does not make the use of another telepathic power automatic; it only makes it possible. Still, the subject is incredibly vulnerable once contacted. His only means of protection is an overwhelming counterattack (probably a nontelepathic attack) or ejection, which is quite risky. A contacted mind can be dominated, mindwiped, affected by any number of other telepathic devotions, or crippled by another assault.

Maintaining Tangents: Maintaining tangents (one or two) costs 1 PSP per round. A psionicist can maintain tangents with only one mind at any time. He can maintain *full contact* with any

Table 14: ATTACK VS. DEFENSE MODES

	Mind Blank	Thought Shield	Mental Barrier	Intellect Fortress	Tower of Iron Will
Mind Thrust	+5	−2	−4	−4	−5
Ego Whip	+5	0	−3	−4	−3
Id Insinuation	−3	+2	+4	−1	−3
Psychic Crush	+1	−3	−1	−3	−4
Psionic Blast	+2	+3	0	−1	−2

number of minds, however. A tangent is broken only when 1) the attacker voluntarily breaks it by simply announcing he is doing so; 2) the attacker fails to pay the maintenance cost of 1 PSP per round; 3) the attacker uses an attack mode against a different target, or; 4) the attacker is incapacitated.

Other Considerations

Line of Sight: Unless the description states otherwise, psionicists require a line of sight to their target when using a psionic power. Clairsentient powers are an obvious exception, as are many of the telepathic powers which list power score modifiers for targets which are outside the psionicist's field of vision.

Touch Attacks: Psionic powers with a range of "touch" can be used in combat, but they require a physical attack roll in addition to a power check to succeed.

Combat Cards

The use of combat cards is optional, but strongly recommended.

A combat card is a 3″ × 5″ index card (or something similar) listing pertinent information for one psionic power. Each player makes one card for each power his character knows. Pertinent information includes the power score, initial cost and maintenance cost, range, preparation time, area of effect, and a brief description of the power's effect.

Combat cards serve three purposes. First, they're a handy reference collection—a sort of "psionic spellbook" for a character. Second, they help speed up the game when psionic powers are used during combat. And third, they make psychic contests more equitable.

If a character intends to use a psionic power during combat, the player thumbs through his combat cards until he finds the card for that power. Then he places the card in front of him, face down on the table. When the power takes effect, he flips the card face up. This way, if two psionicists do battle, neither psionicist can detect what his opponent is doing before he chooses his own action. If a character maintains a power from round to round, the card remains face up on the table as a reminder.

Combat cards can also be used to hide psionic activity from other players. When a psionic power is put into use, the player can select the combat card and show it to the DM only, instead of announcing aloud something that he may not want everyone to know.

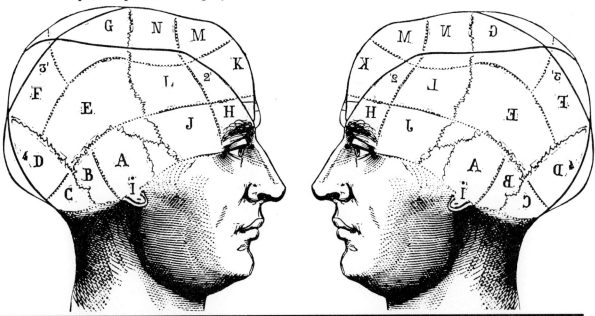

CHAPTER 3

Clairsentience

Clairsentient Sciences

Aura Sight

Power Score:	Wis −5
Initial Cost:	9
Maintenance Cost:	9/round
Range:	50 yds.
Preparation Time:	0
Area of Effect:	personal
Prerequisites:	none

An aura is a glowing halo or envelope of colored light which surrounds all living things. It is invisible to the naked eye. A creature's aura reflects both its alignment and its experience level.

When a psionicist uses this power, he can see auras. Interpreting an aura requires some concentration, however. With each use of this power, the psionicist can learn only one piece of information—either the subject's alignment or experience level, but not both simultaneously.

A psionicist can examine up to two auras per round. (He must be able to see both subjects.) Alternately, he can examine the same aura twice, to verify his first impression with a second reading or to pick up remaining information. In any case, the psionicist must make a new power check each time he attempts to interpret an aura.

The psionicist can be reasonably discreet when he uses this power. He doesn't have to poke at the subject or give him the hairy eyeball. However, he does need to gaze at the subject intently. Since the range of this power is the range of vision, the psionicist can go unnoticed by maintaining his distance. If he tries to sense auras on the people he is conversing with, they certainly will notice that he is staring and probably will be uncomfortable.

The level of the character being analyzed affects the psionicist's power check. The higher

---

Understanding Power Descriptions

■ **Statistics.** Each power in Chapters 3 through 8 begins with the following terms:

Power Score. This number or less must be rolled on a d20 whenever a character makes a power check. (See Chapter 1.) A character always makes a power check when attempting to activate a power.

Initial Cost. The number of PSPs expended when the power is first used. If a character fails his power check, he must expend half this many PSPs. Some telepathic powers list "contact" as their initial cost. That means the contact power must be established before these powers can be used. (See "Contact" in Chapter 7.)

Maintenance Cost. The number of PSPs expended per round (unless another time period is stated) to keep a power operating from the previous round. Maintaining a power does not require a new power check. If no maintenance cost is listed, then the power cannot be maintained. (A character could reactivate it round after round, however, making a new power check each time.)

Range. The maximum distance from the psionicist (psionics user) at which the power can have an effect. "Touch" means the psionicist must touch the target.

Preparation Time. How many rounds a character must spend preparing to use a power, before he can actually try to use it. For example, if a power has a prepa-

ration time of "1," the character must spend one full round preparing. (He can't initiate other powers during that round, but he can still maintain them.) After one round of preparation—i.e., in round number two—he can make a power check. If that check fails (or is delayed), the character can try to use the power again in round three. A power that has been prepared can be held ready for just one round; if it isn't used after that, preparation time is wasted (no PSP cost).

Area of Effect. The physical area or number of beings which the power affects. "Personal" means the power only affects the psionicist.

Prerequisites. Other sciences or devotions which a character must know before he can use this power.

■ **Optional Results:** Each power description ends with a section marked "Power Score" and another marked "20." The former describes what happens if a player rolls his character's power score exactly when making a power check. The latter describes what happens when the player rolls a natural 20 when making a power check. *Both results are optional.* DMs can use these results—or devise something similar—to add spice and a small element of risk to psionics.

■ **Psionicists.** The power descriptions in this book are written with psionicists in mind. Psionic creatures and wild talents often use these powers too—just as psionicists do.

Aura Sight: Mercenary hirelings reveal their true colors.

the subject's experience level, the tougher it is to interpret the subject's aura. This translates into a −1 penalty for every three levels of the subject, rounded down. For example, a psionicist reading the aura of an 8th level character would suffer a −2 penalty.

If the die roll for the power check is a 1, the psionicist's reading is incomplete or slightly incorrect. For example, the psionicist may learn only the chaotic portion of a chaotic neutral alignment. Or he may interpret the character's level with an error of one or two levels.

Power score: The psionicist can examine up to four auras per round instead of two.

20: The initiator can't use this power again for 24 hours.

Clairaudience

Power Score:	Wis −3
Initial Cost:	6
Maintenance Cost:	4/round
Range:	unlimited
Preparation Time:	0
Area of Effect:	special
Prerequisites:	none

Clairaudience allows the user to hear sounds from a distant area. The psionicist picks a spot anywhere within range. He then can hear everything that he would be able to hear normally if he were standing in that spot. If the psionicist has enhanced senses, the senses apply to clairaudience as well.

The farther the "listening spot" is from the psionicist, the more difficult it is to use this power. The table below gives specifics.

Range	Power Score Modifier
100 yards	0
1,000 yards	−2
10 miles	−4
100 miles	−6
1,000 miles	−8
10,000 miles	−10
Interplanetary*	−12

* Players with the SPELLJAMMER™ boxed set should note that clairaudience works only within a given crystal sphere or plane.

Using clairaudience does not screen out background noise around the psionicist. If something in his own neighborhood is raising a racket, he may have trouble hearing what is happening somewhere else. Clairaudience also does not give the psionicist the ability to understand a foreign or alien language, nor does it help him interpret sounds. For example, if the psionicist hears furniture scraping across the floor, he can only guess whether it's a chair or something else—just as if he heard it while blindfolded.

Power Score: The psionicist automatically gains clairvoyance of the area as well.

20: The psionicist is deaf for 1d12 hours.

Clairvoyance

Power Score:	Wis −4
Initial Cost:	7
Maintenance Cost:	4/round
Range:	unlimited
Preparation Time:	0
Area of Effect:	special
Prerequisites:	none

Clairvoyance allows the user to see images from a distant area. The psionicist picks a viewing spot anywhere within range. He can then see anything that he could normally see if he were standing in that spot. His field of vision is no wider than usual, but he can scan the area by turning his head.

Clairvoyance does not replace the character's normal eyesight. The psionicist can still "see" what is actually before him, but the distant scene is superimposed. For this reason, most clairvoyants close their eyes to avoid the confusion of images.

The more distant the viewed area is, the more difficult it is to use clairvoyance. The table below shows how the range to a viewed area can diminish the psionicist's power score.

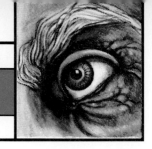

Range	Power Score Modifier
100 yards	0
1,000 yards	−2
10 miles	−4
100 miles	−6
1,000 miles	−8
10,000 miles	−10
interplanetary*	−12

* Players with the SPELLJAMMER™ boxed set should note that clairvoyance works only within a given crystal sphere or plane.

Clairvoyance does nothing to enhance the character's vision. Unless some other power or magic is at work, he still cannot see objects that are invisible, hidden in shadow, or behind other objects. This power also provides no sound, so the character actually sees a kind of silent movie (without subtitles, of course).

Once the viewing spot is chosen, it is fixed in space. To enjoy the view from another location, the psionicist must use this power another time, and make a new power check.

The psionicist's clairvoyant presence is undetectable by normal means. It cannot be dispelled, repelled, or kept away by any form of magic.

Power Score—The psionicist automatically gains clairaudience, too, for the duration of the clairvoyant vision.

20—The psionicist is blind for 1d4 hours.

Object Reading

Power Score:	Wis −5
Initial Cost:	16
Maintenance Cost:	na
Range:	0
Preparation Time:	1
Area of Effect:	touch
Prerequisites:	none

Object reading is the ability to detect psychic impressions left on an object by its previous owner, including his race, sex, age, and alignment. The power can also reveal how the owner came to possess the item, as well as how

he lost it. The amount of information gained depends on the result of the power check. If the psionicist's power check is successful, he learns the information listed beside that result in the table below, plus all the information listed above it.

Power Check Result	Information Gained
1-2	Last owner's race
3	Last owner's sex
4	Last owner's age
5	Last owner's alignment
6-7	How last owner gained and lost item
8+	All this information about all owners

An object can be read only once per experience level of the psionicist; additional readings at that level reveal no additional information. When the clairvoyant gains a new experience level, he can try reading the same object again, even if his object reading score has not changed.

Power Score—The psionicist automatically learns all information on the table above.

20—The psionicist becomes obsessed with the object; he strives to keep it until he can attempt to read it again.

Precognition

Power Score:	Wis −5
Initial Cost:	24
Maintenance Cost:	na
Range:	0
Preparation Time:	5
Area of Effect:	na
Prerequisites:	none

Precognition enables the psionicist to foresee the probable outcome of a course of action. This foresight is limited to the near future—no more than several hours from the time he uses the power. Furthermore, the character must describe the intended course of

action in some detail in order to establish the course of events.

The DM makes the power check secretly. If the check fails, the character gains no information. If the roll is 20 exactly, the character sees himself meeting his own death in a particularly nasty and grisly way and must make a saving throw vs. petrification. If the character fails the save, he is so completely shaken up by the vision that all his psionic power scores are reduced by three for 1d6 hours.

If the power check succeeds, the character sees the most likely outcome of the actions described. The DM has some liberty in describing the scene and should use the d20 roll as a guide to how much detail to include. High rolls get more detail.

Even when it's successful, precognition offers no guarantees. The psionicist sees only one possible (albeit likely) outcome to a specific course of action. If the characters involved deviate from the actions the psionicist describes, then they are changing the conditions and the lines of time, thereby making other outcomes more likely. Die rolls (particularly for surprise, initiative, and normal combat) also play a large part in a precognition's inaccuracy. The DM cannot be expected to engineer die rolls to the players' advantage, and even events with 95% certainty fail to occur 5% of the time. Anyone who relies on precognition to the exclusion of caution and common sense is asking for trouble.

Precognition is tiring. Regardless of the outcome, a psionicist who has used this power must rest for at least one turn before he can use any other clairsentient powers (the use of other disciplines is not affected).

Power Score—The psionicist's player may reroll three die rolls to maintain the precognition's validity.

20—See above. (Not an optional result.)

Sensitivity to Psychic Impressions

Power Score:	Wis −4
Initial Cost:	12
Maintenance Cost:	2/round
Range:	0
Preparation Time:	2
Area of Effect:	20-yard radius
Prerequisites:	none

With this power, a psionicist gains a sense of history. He perceives the residue of powerful emotions which were experienced in a given area. These impressions offer him a picture of the location's past.

Battles and betrayals, marriages and murders, childbirth and great pain—only events which elicited strong emotional or psychic energy leave their impression on an area. Everyday occurrences leave no residue for the psionicist to detect.

To determine how far into the past a psionicist can delve, divide the result of his power check by two and round up. This is the number of strong events which he can sense. Only one event can be noted per round, however, beginning with the most recent and proceeding backward through time.

The character's understanding of these events is vague and shadowy, as if he were viewing a dream. The dominant emotion involved—anger, hate, fear, love, etc.—comes through very clearly.

Power Score—The character gains an unusually clear understanding of each event.

20—An angry ghost comes forward and attempts to use *magic jar* against the psionicist.

Clairsentient Devotions

All-Round Vision

Power Score:	Wis −3
Initial Cost:	6
Maintenance Cost:	4/round
Range:	0
Preparation Time:	0
Area of Effect:	personal
Prerequisites:	none

This power gives the psionicist "eyes in the back of his head"—and in the sides and top, as well. (Of course, this is figurative; he does not literally sprout eyeballs.) In effect, the character can see in all directions simultaneously. Besides its obvious application when combined with the clairvoyance power, all-round vision prevents anyone from sneaking up on the character without some sort of concealment. On the down side, the psionicist suffers a −4 penalty against all gaze attacks while using this power.

Power Score—Infravision is also gained.

20—The psionicist is blind for 1d4 hours.

Combat Mind

Power Score:	Int −4
Initial Cost:	5
Maintenance Cost:	4/round
Range:	0
Preparation Time:	0
Area of Effect:	personal
Prerequisites:	none

A character using this power has an unusually keen understanding of his enemies and their fighting tactics. As a result, the psionicist's side in combat gains a −1 bonus when making initiative die rolls. This is cumulative with any other modifiers which may apply.

Power Score—The psionicist (but not his companions) also gains a +1 AC bonus.

20—The psionicist and his companions suffer a +1 initiative penalty.

Danger Sense

Power Score:	Wis −3
Initial Cost:	4
Maintenance Cost:	3/turn
Range:	special
Preparation Time:	0
Area of Effect:	10 yards
Prerequisite:	none

When using danger sense, a psionicist will experience a slight tingling sensation at the back of his neck when a hazard or threat is near. The DM must make a successful power check on the psionicist's behalf before the character detects the danger. This power does not give the psionicist any specific information about the type of danger. He does not learn how or when it will strike. However, he does learn the general direction of the threat (i.e., to the right, left, ahead, or behind).

The character's power check results determine how much warning he gets. If the roll is 12 or more, he knows whether danger is lurking anywhere in the immediate area. If the roll is 8 or more, he enjoys a full round of warning before that danger strikes. If the roll is 7 or less, however, the psionicist isn't alerted until moments before danger strikes. If the roll is 1 exactly, he still has several moments' warning but the direction is off; e.g., if the attack is coming from the left, he thinks it is coming from ahead, behind, or the right (DM's option).

If the psionicist and his companions have enough warning, they can do something to prepare—getting into defensive positions, preparing spells, or running away, for example. If they have less than one round of warning, the DM must decide how much preparation is possible. In any case, they always gain a +2 bonus on their own surprise rolls.

Power Score—The psionicist learns how far away the danger is.

20—The psionicist cannot sense danger successfully for 1d6 hours.

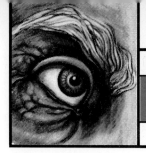

Feel Light

Power Score:	Wis −3
Initial Cost:	7
Maintenance Cost:	5/round
Range:	0
Preparation Time:	0
Area of Effect:	special
Prerequisites:	none

This extrasensory power allows the psionicist to experience light through tactile sensations (by touch). His entire body becomes a receiver for light waves. In effect, his body replaces his eyes; he can see what his eyes would normally reveal. (His field of vision does not change.) This power does not allow him to see in the dark, since there must be light for him to feel. Nor does it counter magical darkness, which actually destroys or blocks light waves. The character gains a +4 bonus when saving against gaze attacks.

Power Score—The character can feel light in all directions.

20—The psionicist becomes overly sensitive to light for 1d10 rounds. Exposure to light causes 1 point of damage per round, and the character cannot see.

Feel Sound

Power Score:	Wis −3
Initial Cost:	5
Maintenance Cost:	3/round
Range:	0
Preparation Time:	0
Area of Effect:	special
Prerequisites:	none

This power is almost identical to feeling light, but it makes the psionicist's body sensitive to sound. It allows him to continue hearing when his ears are disabled. This power does not detect sound where there is none, however, nor is it effective inside magical silence. The psionicist gains a +2 bonus against sonic attacks or effects, including a siren's song.

Power Score—The psionicist can detect noise like a thief of the same experience level.

20—For 1d4 rounds, any sound causes 1 point of damage per round and is garbled.

Hear Light

Power Score:	Wis −3
Initial Cost:	6
Maintenance Cost:	3/round
Range:	0
Preparation Time:	0
Area of Effect:	special
Prerequisites:	none

This extrasensory power resembles "feel light," but it relies on the character's hearing rather than his sense of touch. A character who has been blinded, either artificially, naturally, or by an injury, can "see" with his ears. Any light waves which reach him are converted to sound, and he "hears" the image. The image his mind perceives is just like an image offered by normal sight, and the character suffers no penalties for anything requiring vision.

Power Score—The psionicist can "hear" in the dark, as if he had infravision.

20—Bright light causes deafness, and all other light is just a buzz.

Know Direction

Power Score:	Int
Initial Cost:	1
Maintenance Cost:	na
Range:	0
Preparation Time:	0
Area of Effect:	personal
Prerequisites:	none

The psionicist becomes his own compass. By paying 1 PSP and making a successful power check, he knows which way is north.

Power Score—The power is automatically maintained for one day.

20—The psionicist is disoriented; he cannot use this power again for 1d6 hours.

Object Reading: A wheel spins a horrid tale of the past.

Know Location

Power Score:	Int
Initial Cost:	10
Maintenance Cost:	na
Range:	0
Preparation Time:	5
Area of Effect:	personal
Prerequisites:	none

This power is useful to characters who frequently travel by using teleportation, gates, or via other planes of existence. When it works, the power reveals general information about the character's location. The information is usually no more detailed than the response of a simple farmer when asked, "Where am I?" Typical answers include "a few miles southwest of Waterdeep...as the crow flies," "in the house of Kilgore the taxidermist," or "adrift on the Blood Sea."

The higher the result of the power check, the more precise the location will be. If the die roll is 8 or more, the location is specified within a mile or less. If the roll is 7 or less, the location is specified within 10 miles.

The character can get additional information that is *less* specific than the initial answer if his player asks for it. (The psionicist does not make another power check.) For example, if the DM's first response is "you're in the house of Kilgore the Taxidermist," the player might then ask where the house is. The DM might answer by saying Kilgore's house is in Chendl, in the Kingdom of Furyondy.

Power Score—The psionicist learns the exact location he's trying to determine.

20—Nothing within 100 miles can be located with this power for 24 hours.

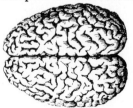

Poison Sense

Power Score:	Wis
Initial Cost:	1
Maintenance Cost:	na
Range:	0
Preparation Time:	0
Area of Effect:	1-yard radius
Prerequisites:	none

This power enables a psionicist to detect the presence of poison and identify its location within 1 yard of his body (or his presence, if he is using clairvoyance or traveling astrally). The type of poison is not revealed, only its presence. Any poison, including animal venom, can be detected.

Power Score—The psionicist determines the exact type of poison.

20—If poison exists, the sense of it mentally overwhelms the psionicist. The effects match those of actual exposure to the poison.

Radial Navigation

Power Score:	Int −3
Initial Cost:	4
Maintenance Cost:	7/hour
Range:	0
Preparation Time:	0
Area of Effect:	personal
Prerequisites:	none

As long as this power is in use, the psionicist knows where he is in relation to a fixed starting point. In other words, no matter how or where he moves, he still knows the exact direction and distance to his starting point.

He cannot necessarily tell someone how to get back to that starting point, however. If he is in a maze or dungeon, for example, he may know the starting point is 500 yards north, but he cannot retrace his steps through the maze automatically. Radial navigation *does* enhance his ability to do so, however. Every time the character comes to a decision point—e.g., "should I turn right or left?"—the DM makes a

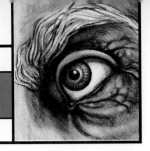

power check for him. If the check succeeds, the character knows which way he came. If the roll fails, he isn't sure. (He can still maintain the power normally, however.)

Radial navigation can be helpful in several ways that are not obvious. For example, teleportation and other extraordinary means of travel become simpler. Let's say a character cannot see a particular location because he's blindfolded. He leaves that location, but uses radial navigation to get a fix on it. That means he can still teleport back there. Furthermore, if the character has a fix on a place, he can reach it through the astral plane in just seven hours, the minimum possible (assuming of course that he can travel through the astral plane). And he can reach the same location by dimension walking (see the psychoportation discipline) with no chance of getting lost. Radial navigation can aid in telepathy, too. If the psionicist wants to make telepathic contact, and he has a fix on the target's location, he doesn't suffer the usual penalties for range.

If the character stops maintaining this power, he loses his fix on the location. He can get it back by resuming this power and making a successful power check within six hours. After six hours, the location is lost. Only one location can be fixed at a time unless the character pays the maintenance cost individually for each.

Power Score—The psionicist can automatically retrace his steps to the starting point.

20—The psionicist forgets where he is for 1d4 rounds.

See Sound

Power Score:	Wis −3
Initial Cost:	6
Maintenance Cost:	3/round
Range:	special
Preparation Time:	0
Area of Effect:	personal
Prerequisites:	none

This power enables a character to perceive sound waves visually—with his eyes—by converting the sound waves to light impulses. (It works in much the same way as feel light.) Only a character who can see normally can use this power. The psionicist can see sound even in darkness, because sound waves do not require light. The character can still be "blinded" by silence, however.

Power Score—The psionicist can maintain this power for 1 PSP per round.

20—Loud sounds cause "blindness," and all other sounds are as disturbing as bright lights.

Spirit Sense

Power Score:	Wis −3
Initial Cost:	10
Maintenance Cost:	na
Range:	0
Preparation Time:	0
Area of Effect:	15-yard radius
Prerequisites:	none

Using this power allows the psionicist to sense the presence of "spirits" within 15 yards—meaning ghosts, banshees, wraiths, haunts, heucuvas, and revenants. If a spirit frequently haunts the location at hand, the psionicist will know it. He will also know when a spirit is within 15 yards, but he won't be able to pinpoint its location.

Power Score—The psionicist knows the exact location of the spirits he senses.

20—The psionicist has aggravated the spirits (DM determines exact result).

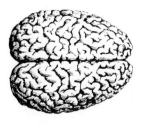

CHAPTER 4

Psychokinesis

Psychokinetic Sciences

Create Object

Power Score:	Int −4
Initial Cost:	16
Maintenance Cost:	3/round
Range:	20 yards
Preparation Time:	0
Area of Effect:	special
Prerequisites:	telekinesis

A psionicist with this power can assemble matter from air and the surrounding area to create a solid object. This object remains in existence as long as the psionicist pays the power's maintenance cost. When he stops maintaining it, the object breaks into its constituent parts.

An object created this way can have any shape, color, and texture the psionicist desires, provided it fulfills at least one of the following conditions:

- Fits entirely within a sphere no more than 4 feet in diameter.
- Fits entirely within a cylinder no more than 20 feet long and 1 foot in diameter.
- Fits entirely within a cylinder no more than 2 feet high and 6 feet in diameter.
- Weighs no more than 10 pounds.

Only available materials within 20 yards of the psionicist can be used in the construction. However, these materials can be rearranged or restructured if the psionicist also has the power of molecular rearrangement. By combining these two powers, he could manufacture diamonds from coal dust or a sword from rocks containing iron ore.

If the power check result is a 1, the item contains a flaw—e.g., a sword breaks when struck, a diamond contains impurities obvious to a jeweler, and so on.

Power Score—The object is permanent. No cost is expended to maintain it.

20—The power backfires, and a personal belonging (chosen randomly) disintegrates.

Detonate

Power Score:	Con −3
Initial Cost:	18
Maintenance Cost:	na
Range:	60 yards
Preparation Time:	0
Area of Effect:	one item, 8 cu. ft.
Prerequisites:	telekinesis, molecular agitation

Some psionicists can make a bush self-destruct, or cause a zombie to explode. With the detonate power, latent energy inside plants or inanimate objects can be harnessed, focused, and released explosively. The power even works against animated undead (skeletons and zombies). It does not affect noncorporeal undead, such as ghosts, because they aren't material. Furthermore, the science has no effect on animals of any sort, including intelligent creatures such as humans, or undead with free will.

The detonation inflicts 1d10 points of damage upon all vulnerable objects which the psionicist chooses to attack, within 10 feet. A saving throw vs. breath weapon reduces damage to half. To determine what percentage of the object was destroyed, multiply the result of the psionicist's power check by 10. If the product is 100 or more—i.e, 100% or more—the target has been completely destroyed. Anything less means a few significant chunks remain.

No more than 8 cubic feet of material can be destroyed with this power. A portion of a wall can be blown out, for example, but if the wall is 10 inches thick, an opening about 3 feet square will appear.

Power Score—Damage and range double, to 2d10 points and 20 feet, respectively.

Detonate: Bodo eliminates a bone of contention.

20—The air surrounding the initiator detonates; everyone within 10 feet of him is attacked.

Disintegrate

Power Score:	Wis −4
Initial Cost:	40
Maintenance Cost:	na
Range:	50 yards
Preparation Time:	0
Area of Effect:	one item, 8 cu. ft.
Prerequisites:	telekinesis, soften

The disintegrate science reduces an item or creature to microscopic pieces and scatters them. Anything is vulnerable unless it is protected by magical shielding such as a minor or regular *globe of invulnerability* or by an inertial barrier. The psionicist chooses his target, but he can disintegrate no more than 8 cubic feet of material with one use of this power.

If the target is an inanimate object, it must save vs. disintegration; success means it is unaffected. If the target is a living creature, character, or an undead creature with free will, it must make a saving throw vs. death magic. If it succeeds, the creature feels only a slight tingle, but is otherwise unaffected. If the save fails, the creature is disintegrated (or 8 cubic feet right out of its center, which should be enough to kill most anything).

Power Score—The power affects 16 cubic feet and saves are made with a −5 penalty.

20—The power backfires and it affects the initiator (save with +5 bonus).

Molecular Rearrangement

Power Score:	Int −5
Initial Cost:	20
Maintenance Cost:	10 per hour
Range:	2 yards
Preparation Time:	2 hours
Area of Effect:	one item
Prerequisite:	telekinesis, molecular manipulation

Molecular rearrangement is the psionic equivalent of alchemy. By toying with an object's molecular structure, the psionicist can change its fundamental nature or properties. This power cannot create matter or mass from nothing, however. Nor can it change a material's state from liquid to solid, gas to liquid, and so on. It is best suited to converting one sort of element into another, but it can also be used for more complex operations—neutralizing a poison, for example.

Converting one element to another is usually a simple operation, in which one ounce of material can be changed each hour. Typical conversions of this type include steel to lead, or any metal to gold. More complex rearrangement, like changing a metal to glass or changing a wooden goblet to a ruby goblet, takes four times longer.

The creation of gold coins from other metals is possible, but it's no way to get rich quick. At the rate of one ounce per hour, it would take 16 hours—about two work days—to change 10 copper pieces into 10 gold pieces, for a net profit of 9 gold pieces.

Molecular rearrangement is often used to create superior weapons. A psionically tempered weapon may receive a +1 on damage rolls (see "Weapon Quality" in Chapter 6 of the *DMG*). The process is time-consuming, however. For example, a typical short sword takes at least 40 hours to temper psionically. (The average short sword weighs 3 pounds, or 48 ounces, most of which is the blade.) A psionically tempered weapon does *not* automatically offer a +1 attack-roll bonus. In order to receive that bonus, the psionicist must 1) have the weaponsmithing proficiency and 2) make a successful proficiency check when he fashions the weapon.

The psionicist makes his power check when the process is complete. If it fails, he did not waste all his effort. The difference between the character's die roll and his power score, multiplied by 10, equals the percentage of work which must be redone.

If the roll is 1, the item seems perfect but contains a hidden flaw which will cause it to break, or fail, or simply look wrong when it is put to use (the ruby goblet might leak, for example, or the sword might contain a soft portion which causes it to bend).

This power has no effect against living creatures weighing more than one ounce. Creatures weighing one ounce or less are killed if their molecules are rearranged.

Power Score—The new material is extraordinary (DM's arbitration).

20—The item is seriously flawed and utterly useless.

Project Force

Power Score:	Con −2
Initial Cost:	10
Maintenance Cost:	na
Range:	200 yards
Preparation Time:	0
Area of Effect:	na
Prerequisites:	telekinesis

Some psionicists can push, shove, and otherwise bully an opponent from afar. Project force allows the psionicist to focus a psychokinetic "punch" against a target up to 200 yards away.

If used offensively, this punch causes damage equal to 1d6 points plus the target's armor class (negative armor classes reduce the damage). For example, a target with armor class 5 would suffer 6 to 11 points of damage (1 to 6 points, plus 5). A successful save vs. breath weapon reduces the damage by half.

This rather unsubtle blow can also be used to trigger traps, throw levers, open doors (if they aren't locked or latched), break windows, and the like.

Power Score—The blow also knocks down the target if it is roughly man-sized or smaller.

20—The blow strikes the initiator.

Telekinesis

Power Score:	Wis −3
Initial Cost:	3+
Maintenance Cost:	1+/round
Range:	30 yards
Preparation Time:	0
Area of Effect:	single item
Prerequisite:	none

Telekinesis, or "TK" for short, is the ability to move objects through space without touching them. All telekinetic efforts tend to be physically taxing, because they involve real work. Moving small, light objects is relatively easy. As the objects become more massive, the task becomes significantly more difficult.

The costs above (3 PSPs initially and 1 per round of maintenance) assume that the object being moved weighs 3 pounds or less. For heavier objects, these rules apply:

- The initial cost equals the object's weight in pounds.
- The maintenance cost is half the initial cost, rounded down.
- The character's power score is decreased by one-third of the object's weight in pounds, rounded down.

For example, to telekinetically snatch a 15-pound battle axe from a rack, a psionicist must pay 15 PSPs and make a power check with a −5 modifier to his score.

A psionicist using TK can move an object up to 60 feet per round. The object can serve as a weapon. In this case, the character attacks using his own THAC0 score, with a penalty equaling the object's weight modifier (one-third its weight, rounded down).

Power Score—The character can lift a second item of equal or lesser weight simultaneously for the same cost.

20—The psionicist "fumbles" the item, knocking it over, etc.

Psychokinetic Devotions

Animate Object

Power Score:	Int −3
Initial Cost:	8
Maintenance Cost:	3/round
Range:	50 yards
Preparation Time:	0
Area of Effect:	1 object, 100 lbs.
Prerequisites:	telekinesis

Inanimate objects can be "brought to life" with this devotion. The objects are not actually alive, but they move under the psionicist's control as if they were. For example, chairs may walk, trees may dance, and stones may waddle around.

The object being animated must weigh 100 pounds or less. The material being animated affects the difficulty of the task; stronger or more brittle materials are harder to animate than weak or floppy materials. Once animated, however, all materials become flexible to some extent.

Material	Ability Score Modifier
Cloth, paper	0
Live wood, dead animal	−1
Dead wood	−2
Water	−3
Thin metal	−4
Thick metal	−5
Stone	−6

Fluid motion is not common. The animated item moves more like a puppet. Its movements are jerky and clumsy, and if the item was rigid to begin with, it makes a loud creaking, groaning, or grating sound. It can move 60 feet per round (movement rate 6), in any direction chosen by the psionicist. It can attack as a club with a THAC0 of 20.

Power Score—Animation is smooth and lifelike.

20—No additional effect.

Animate Shadow

Power Score:	Wis −3
Initial Cost:	7
Maintenance Cost:	3/round
Range:	40 yards
Preparation Time:	0
Area of Effect:	100 sq. ft.
Prerequisites:	none

With this devotion the psionicist can animate the shadow cast by anyone or anything and make it seem to have life of its own. The shadow can even move away from the person or thing that cast it. It must, however, remain flatly cast along a surface. It can never be more than two-dimensional.

An animated shadow can't really do anything other than startle or amuse someone. It cannot attack or disrupt a mage's concentration. In this regard, it is similar to a *cantrip's* effect. It can serve as a diversion by entertaining someone or attracting a guard's attention.

Power Score—The range increases to 100 yards.

20—The shadow disappears completely for one round.

Ballistic Attack

Power Score:	Con −2
Initial Cost:	5
Maintenance Cost:	na
Range:	30 yards
Preparation Time:	0
Area of Effect:	1 item, 1 lb.
Prerequisites:	telekinesis

This power can make any psionicist a "David" when he's facing "Goliath." It's a special variation of the telekinesis science. Instead of moving any object relatively slowly, ballistic attack allows the character to hurl a small object at a target. The object, no more than 1 pound in weight, can achieve deadly speeds. It must be within sight of the psionicist and cannot be anchored or attached to anything else. A rock is the most common weapon.

The psionicist uses his regular THAC0 to determine whether he hits the target. If he succeeds, the missile inflicts 1d6 points of damage (assuming, of course, that the character made a successful power check in the first place).

Power Score—Damage increases to 1d12.

20—Ballistic boomerang. The psionicist becomes the object's target.

Control Body

Power Score:	Con −2
Initial Cost:	8
Maintenance Cost:	8/round
Range:	80 yards
Preparation Time:	0
Area of Effect:	individual
Prerequisites:	telekinesis

This science allows psychokinetic control of another person's body. In effect, the victim becomes a marionette. He knows that someone else is pulling his strings, though, and he's probably mad as all get-out.

Before this science actually works, the psionicist must engage in a psychic contest, pitting his power score directly against the victim's Strength. If the victim wins the contest, he breaks free (the psionicist still pays the power cost). In a tie, the contest continues into the next round, provided the psionicist maintains the power. The victim can't do anything else during this contest; all his effort is focused on retaining control of his own body.

If the power works, the psionicist has rudimentary control over the victim's limbs. He can make the victim stand up, sit down, walk, turn around, etc. The body can be forced to attack physically, but with a −6 penalty on attack rolls (using the victim's own THAC0). The victim can't be forced to speak. In fact, he keeps control over his own voice and can say whatever he likes.

The victim must stay within the 80-yard range or the psionicist's control is broken automatically. If the body is forced to do something obviously suicidal, like walking off a

cliff or poking at a red dragon, the victim can fight another contest with the psionicist to regain control (the adrenaline rush of imminent danger gives him renewed strength).

Power Score—The psionicist automatically wins the initial psychic contest.

20—The psionicist suffers partial paralysis (an arm or leg) for 1d10 turns.

Control Flames

Power Score:	Wis −1
Initial Cost:	6
Maintenance Cost:	3/round
Range:	40 yards
Preparation Time:	0
Area of Effect:	10 sq. ft
Prerequisites:	telekinesis

By controlling flames, a psionicist can make a normal fire bigger, smaller, hotter, or colder. He can even make it move around as if it were a living creature.

A fire's size can be increased by 100% or decreased by 50%. If the fire's heat is increased, it causes double damage. If its heat is reduced, the damage is halved. This applies to flaming torches, burning oil, and other normal fires, but not to magical fires such as *fireballs* or *burning hands*.

An animated fire can move up to 90 feet per round (MR 9). It can be shaped like a person or an animal, as long as it covers no more than 10 square feet of ground. If the fire moves away from its fuel, it can survive for only one more round, then dies out.

An animated fire can also attack by engulfing an opponent. The psionicist must make an attack roll using his regular THAC0. If successful, the attack causes 1d6 points of damage.

Power Score—Size can increase up to 200% or decrease to 0% (the fire is extinguished).

20—The psionicist burns himself, suffering 1d4 points of damage.

Control Light

Power Score:	Int
Initial Cost:	12
Maintenance Cost:	4/round
Range:	25 yards
Preparation Time:	0
Area of Effect:	400 sq. ft.
Prerequisites:	none

The psionicist can manipulate existing light with this devotion. He cannot create light from darkness, but he can create darkness from light. This power can accomplish the following, and anything else the DM allows:

- Deepen existing shadows, making them inky black. A thief hiding in this shadow gets a 20% bonus on his ability roll.
- Lighten existing shadows, reducing a thief's hiding ability by 20%.
- Brighten a light source until it hurts to look at it. This gives everyone exposed to the light a −2 penalty on attack rolls.
- Dim a light source so it resembles twilight. This does not affect anyone's attack rolls.
- Extend shadows into areas that are otherwise well lit. Only an existing shadow can be extended, but its size can be increased by 200% (i.e., its size can be tripled).
- Extend light into areas that are otherwise in shadow. Shadows can be reduced in size by 50%.

Power Score—The maintenance cost is reduced to 1 PSP per round.

20—The effect is the opposite of what is desired, and maintenance fails.

Control Sound

Power Score:	Int −5
Initial Cost:	5
Maintenance Cost:	2/round
Range:	100 yards
Preparation Time:	0
Area of Effect:	na
Prerequisites:	none

This power allows the psionicist to shape and alter existing sounds. As a woman speaks, for example, the psionicist could change her words into a lion's roar, or even into different words. Or he could disguise the sound of 20 men marching past a guard as falling rain. Sounds can also be layered—so that one singing person sounds like an entire choir, for example.

If the character's power check is a 1, something about the sound he's altered isn't quite right, so it arouses suspicion. If he is trying to exactly duplicate another voice, this fault occurs on a roll of 1 or 2.

This power can also dampen a sound. The player must specify which sound the character intends to eliminate; the power has no area of effect. For example, the psionicist might quiet the sound of a hammer, muffle the words from someone's mouth, or eliminate the creaking of a door. He could not do all three simultaneously, however.

Power Score—The maintenance cost is reduced to 1 PSP per round.

20—A loud boom erupts from the psionicist's location.

Control Wind

Power Score:	Con −4
Initial Cost:	16
Maintenance Cost:	10/round
Range:	500 yards
Preparation Time:	2
Area of Effect:	1,000 yards
Prerequisites:	telekinesis

The psionicist can gain limited control over wind speed and direction with this devotion. The speed of any existing wind can be increased or decreased by 10 miles per hour or 25%, whichever is greater. The direction of the wind can also be changed by up to 90 degrees.

These changes are temporary, lasting only as long as the psionicist pays the maintenance

cost. The changes occur within moments after he wills them, and die out in less than a minute when he stops maintaining them.

Winds above 19 miles per hour prevent anything smaller than a man or a condor from flying and impose a −4 modifier on missile fire. They also whip up waves on the sea and make sailing difficult. Winds gusting at over 32 miles per hour cause minor damage to ships and buildings. These gusts also kick up clouds of dust, and prevent all but the largest creatures from flying. Winds over 55 miles per hour prevent all flight, knock down trees and wooden buildings, and threaten to swamp ships. Winds over 73 miles per hour are hurricane gales.

Power Score—The psionicist gains total direction control and can change speeds by up to 25 mph or 50%, whichever is greater.

20—No additional effect.

Create Sound

Power Score:	Int −2
Initial Cost:	8
Maintenance Cost:	3/round
Range:	100 yards
Preparation Time:	0
Area of Effect:	na
Prerequisites:	telekinesis, control sound

Unlike the control sound devotion, this power allows a psionicist to create sound from silence. That means the psionicist can choose the source or location of the sound. For example, he can make rocks sing, weapons cast insults, and trees sound as if a battle is occurring inside. The sound can be as soft as a whisper or as loud as several people shouting in unison. Once the sound is created, the psionicist can control it without expending additional PSPs (other than normal maintenance).

If the die roll for the character's power check is a 1, the sound is not quite true and may arouse suspicion in listeners. If a specific hu-

man voice is being mimicked, this happens on a roll of 1 or 2.

Created sounds cannot have any magical effect. The psionicist might duplicate a banshee's wail, for example, but it cannot harm anyone.

Power Score—Sound volume can be up to that of a dragon's roar.

20—A loud boom erupts near the initiator.

Inertial Barrier

Power Score:	Con −3
Initial Cost:	7
Maintenance Cost:	5/round
Range:	0
Preparation Time:	0
Area of Effect:	3-yard diam.
Prerequisites:	telekinesis

The inertial barrier is a defense. The psionicist creates a barrier of "elastic" air around himself and anyone else within 3 yards. Like an unpoppable, semipermeable bubble, this barrier helps soften missile blows and can shield those inside from many forms of damage.

Specifically, the barrier helps protect against the following, by absorbing some (or with luck all) of the potential damage:

- Any nonmagical missile weapon.
- Any physical missile which was created with magic.
- Any missile with magical pluses.
- Flames.
- Some breath weapon attacks, depending on the nature of the breath.
- Acid. The barrier stops or slows the attack. This doesn't matter much if the acid comes from above, because it just drips on the characters.
- Gas. The barrier turns it aside, at least partially (depending on the defender's die roll), but after a turn it will eventually work its way inside and take full effect.

- Falling. A psionicist with an inertial barrier in place suffers only one-half damage from a fall; the barrier absorbs a lot of the impact, but the character still gets banged around inside.

The inertial barrier has no effect against the following:

- Missiles conjured from pure magic.
- Raw heat or cold.
- Pure energy or light.
- Gaze weapons.

Furthermore, the barrier cannot keep enemies out, but it does slows them a bit. Anyone trying to cross the barrier must stop moving when he hits it. He can then cross inside (or outside) in the next round.

Handling Missile Attacks: The inertial barrier saps energy from missile weapons by tightening around them as they pass through. If a missile strikes its target inside the barrier, the attacker rolls damage normally. The defender then rolls the same type of die (as the attacker just did) to see how much damage the barrier absorbed. The defender does *not* include any magical pluses the weapon may have.

The defender then subtracts the result of his die roll from the attacker's damage. If anything is left over, the defender loses that many hit points. If the defender's roll equals or exceeds the total damage, the weapon falls harmlessly to the ground. If the missile is explosive, the barrier does prevent damage, but not the explosion.

The barrier does not differentiate the direction of travel. If a weapon is fired from the inside, the penalties above still apply.

Power Score—The barrier blocks an additional point per die.

20—The psionicist creates a bizarre windpocket that knocks him to the ground.

Levitation

Power Score:	Wis −3
Initial Cost:	12
Maintenance Cost:	2/round
Range:	0
Preparation Time:	0
Area of Effect:	individual
Prerequisites:	telekinesis

Levitation allows the user to float. It is the use of telekinesis on oneself.

A character can lift himself at the rate of 1 foot per second, or 60 feet per round. The character can descend as quickly as he wants by simply letting himself fall, then slowing down as he nears the ground.

Levitation is not flying; it doesn't provide any horizontal movement. The character can hover motionless, and will drift with the wind, however. He can also push himself off a wall or other fixed object and drift up to 60 feet per round in a straight line, but he can't stop until he meets another solid object or lowers himself to the ground.

Two other powers—control wind and project force—can help the levitating psionicist propel himself forward. Control wind allows him to determine the direction in which he drifts. Project force allows him to create a "wall" wherever it's wanted; movement is up to 60 feet per round, in any direction. Each change of direction or speed is a distinct use of the power, however, and costs PSPs.

A psionicist can always levitate his own weight. Additional weight, however, such as equipment or passengers, is a hindrance. Every 25 pounds of added weight reduces the character's power score by one point.

Power Score—The rate of levitation is doubled (to 120 feet/round).

20—The psionicist doubles his weight for one round. If he falls, he suffers an extra d6 points of damage.

Molecular Agitation

Power Score:	Wis
Initial Cost:	7
Maintenance Cost:	6/round
Range:	40 yards
Preparation Time:	0
Area of Effect:	1 item, 20 lbs.
Prerequisites:	none

Molecular agitation enables the user to excite the molecules of a substance: paper ignites, wood smolders, skin blisters, water boils, etc. The list below shows what's possible, depending on how many rounds the substance is agitated.

1 round: readily flammable materials (e.g., paper, dry grass) ignite, skin becomes red and tender (1 point of damage), wood becomes dark.

2 rounds: wood smolders and smokes, metal becomes hot to the touch, skin blisters (1d4 points of damage), hair smolders, paint shrivels.

3 rounds: wood ignites, metal scorches (1d4 points of damage), skin burns away (1d6 points of damage), water boils, lead melts (damage does not increase after this round, but does continue).

4 rounds: steel grows soft.

5 rounds: steel melts.

Where magical items are concerned, allow saving throws against destruction, but add a +10 penalty to the saving throw number (this heat is quite destructive, coming from inside the material rather than outside).

Power Score—After round one, the rate of agitation doubles (3 rounds of damage occurs in just 2, 5 rounds of damage occurs in 3).

20—An item belonging to the psionicist (chosen at random) is affected for one round.

Molecular Manipulation

Power Score:	Int −3
Initial Cost:	6
Maintenance Cost:	5/round
Range:	15 yards
Preparation Time:	1
Area of Effect:	2 sq. inches
Prerequisites:	telekinesis

This power allows the user to weaken the molecular bonds within an object or structure. When someone stresses the object or strikes a blow it, it snaps.

The psionicist can create a "breaking point" of approximately two square inches per round. Deterioration occurs across a plane (in two dimensions, not three). One round's work is enough to fatally weaken most small objects—e.g., swords, ropes, saddle straps, belts, and bows. Larger objects require more time, and DM discretion.

DMs must decide how vulnerable this power makes larger, oddly shaped items like shields or doors. They should keep in mind that an object need not be in two pieces before it's virtually useless. For example, a little boat with a cracked hull is unsafe at sea. And a shield that is split halfway across offers little or no protection; if successive blows don't shatter it, they certainly will rattle the holder's arm unmercifully.

Power Score—Weakening occurs at twice the rate above.

20—The item is strengthened. Now it requires twice the normal effort to weaken.

Soften

Power Score:	Int
Initial Cost:	4
Maintenance Cost:	3/round
Range:	30 yards
Preparation Time:	0
Area of Effect:	1 object, 10 lbs.
Prerequisites:	none

This power resembles molecular manipulation, except that it weakens the entire object instead of small area across a single plane. The object softens overall, losing its rigidity and strength. Specific effects vary, depending on the material.

Metal: For each round of softening, weapons incur a −1 penalty to attack rolls and cause one less point of damage, cumulatively. The armor class of metal armor increases one point per round of softening. After 10 rounds, any metal becomes soft and rubbery, but retains its shape.

Wood: Like metal, weapons with wooden shafts or handles suffer a −1 penalty to attack rolls and damage per round of softening. After six rounds, wood becomes stringy and rubbery but retains its shape. After 10 rounds, the grain can be split easily and a punch can break through even the hardest and thickest doors or chests.

Stone: After two rounds, stone becomes noticeably soft to the touch. After five rounds, it can be worked like stiff clay, but this is as soft as it gets.

Magical Items: Save vs. crushing blow to escape the effect entirely.

Living Tissue: No effect.

DMs can use their own judgement and the examples above to handle other materials.

Power Score—All effects are doubled.

20—The item is strengthened, and can't be affected again until the psionicist gains one level.

A githyanki and an intellect devourer go head to head

Psychometabolic Sciences

Animal Affinity

Power Score: Con −4
Initial Cost: 15
Maintenance Cost: 4/round
Range: 0
Preparation Time: 0
Area of Effect: personal
Prerequisite: none

When the psionicist first learns this power, he develops an affinity for a particular type of animal. He cannot choose the animal; the affinity is dictated by his aura. To determine the nature of the affinity, the psionicist's player rolls 1d20 and consults the table below.

From that point on, when the character invokes this power, he can claim one of the animal's attributes as his own—temporarily. He can gain the animal's armor class, movement rate and mode, attacks and damage, THAC0, hit points, or any other special ability. Only one of these can be used at a time, however. The effect lasts as long as the psionicist maintains the power. Switching to a different ability means paying the initial cost of the power again, and making a new power check.

The character does undergo a physical change when this power is invoked. The extent of the change depends on the animal and the ability. For example, adopting a hawk's movement obviously requires wings, while attacking like a tiger calls for fangs and claws.

1	Ape
2	Barracuda
3	Boar
4	Bull
5	Crocodile
6	Eagle, giant
7	Elephant
8	Falcon
9	Griffon
10	Grizzly bear
11	Lion
12	Panther (black leopard)
13	Percheron (draft horse)
14	Peregrine falcon (hawk)
15	Rattlesnake
16	Scorpion, giant
17	Shark
18	Stag
19	Tiger
20	Wolf

Power Score—The character gains two abilities instead of one.

20—The character's skin takes on the appearance of the animal's skin until the power is used again successfully (no change in AC).

Complete Healing

Power Score: Con
Initial Cost: 30
Maintenance Cost: na
Range: 0
Preparation Time: 24 hours
Area of Effect: personal
Prerequisite: none

The psionicist who has mastered this power can heal himself completely of all ailments, wounds, and normal diseases. He places himself in a trance for 24 hours to accomplish the healing. The trance is deep, and cannot be broken unless the character loses 5 or more hit points. As he uses this power, the psionicist's body is repairing itself at an incredible rate. At the end of the 24-hour period, the character awakes, restored to complete health in every regard except for the 30 PSPs he expended to use complete healing.

If the character's power check fails, he breaks his trance after only one hour, having realized that the power was not working. Only 5 PSPs have been expended.

Power Score—The healing occurs in just one hour.

20—The psionicist awakes after the full 24 hours to discover that the attempt failed. He has expended 5 PSPs.

Chameleon Power: Leif makes like a tree and fells a goblin.

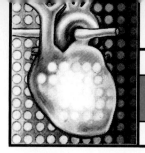

Death Field

Power Score:	Con −8
Initial Cost:	40
Maintenance Cost:	na
Range:	0
Preparation Time:	3
Area of Effect:	20 yd. rad.
Prerequisite:	none

A death field is a life-sapping region of negative energy. Only psionicists of evil alignment can learn this power without suffering side effects. If any other psionicist tries to learn the death field, his alignment will gradually be twisted toward evil as he explores this very dark portion of his psyche.

A successful death field takes it toll on everyone inside it, including the psionicist. Before he initiates this power, he must decide how many hit points he will sacrifice. If the power works, the loss is inevitable; he gets no saving throw. Every other living thing within the death field must make a saving throw vs. death. Those who succeed escape damage. Those who fail lose the same number of hit points as the psionicist. For the weak, that can mean death.

Power Score—The pionicist loses only half the number of hit points he specifies; victims who fail their saving throws lose the full amount.

20—The power fails, but the psionicist loses the hit points anyway.

Energy Containment

Power Score:	Con −2
Initial Cost:	10
Maintenance Cost:	na
Range:	0
Preparation Time:	0
Area of Effect:	personal
Prerequisite:	none

A psionicist with this power has trained himself to safely absorb and assimilate energy from electricity, fire, cold, heat, and sound—energy that would fry, freeze, or otherwise harm a normal character. Any physical assault based on these energy types can be drawn into the psionicist's body. The character transforms the energy, and safely releases it as visible radiance (light).

In effect, this protects the psionicist against energy attacks. If the psionicist makes a successful power check, he can double the result of his die roll when saving against an energy attack. If the character makes a successful saving throw, he suffers no damage from the attack. If he fails, he suffers only half damage, regardless of what the spell description (if applicable) states.

When the character absorbs energy, he radiates visible light for a number of rounds equal to the points of damage he absorbed. If he suffered half damage, he radiates for that many rounds. If he suffered no damage, roll for damage anyway to see how long he glows. This glow is definitely noticeable, but it is soft, and illuminates no more than an area with a 2-yard radius.

Power Score—All saves against energy attacks automatically succeed during the round in which the power is in effect.

20—The psionicist becomes an energy attractor for 1 turn. All saves vs. energy attacks fail, causing full standard damage.

Life Draining

Power Score:	Con −3
Initial Cost:	11
Maintenance Cost:	5/round
Range:	touch
Preparation Time:	0
Area of Effect:	individual
Prerequisites:	none

With this devotion, a psionicist can drain hit points from another character and use them to recover his own. This transfer occurs at the rate of 1d6 points per round.

The character can absorb up to 10 more hit points than his healthy total, but these bonus

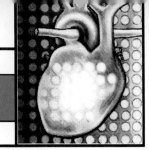

points last only one hour. After that, if the psionicist still has more hit points than he should, the excess points vanish.

Power Score—Rate of drain increases to 1d20 points per round.

20—Backfire! Half of the psionicist's remaining hit points are absorbed by the target, reversing the power's effects.

Metamorphosis

Power Score:	Con −6
Initial Cost:	21
Maintenance Cost:	1/turn
Range:	0
Preparation Time:	5
Area of Effect:	personal
Prerequisites:	none

This science resembles polymorphing, but it has a much wider application. The psionicist can change himself into *anything* with approximately the same mass as his body: a wolf, a condor, a chair, a rock, a tree. While in this form, he retains his own hit points and THAC0, if possible, but gains the armor class the new form. The psionicist also gains all physical attacks that form allows, but no magical or special abilities. (This all depends on the new form; a tree cannot attack, so THAC0s and attacks are meaningless.)

Like any massive change of shape, however, this causes great physical stress. The psionicist must make a system shock roll to survive the change. If the roll fails, he does not die, but the PSPs are expended and he passes out for 2d6 turns.

Power Score—The system shock roll automatically succeeds, and the new form's mass can be up to three times that of the psionicist's body.

20—The psionicist must save vs. paralyzation. Failure means he changes to the new form permanently.

Shadow-form

Power Score:	Con −6
Initial Cost:	12
Maintenance Cost:	3/round
Range:	0
Preparation Time:	0
Area of Effect:	personal
Prerequisites:	none

A psionicist using this power actually transforms himself into living shadow, along with his clothing, armor, and up to 20 pounds of equipment. He can blend perfectly into any other shadow and travel with a movement rate of 6. He can only travel through darkness and shadow, however. Areas of open light are impassable.

While in shadow-form, the psionicist can be detected only by life detection, other types of psychic detection, or by a *true seeing* spell. He cannot harm anyone physically, or manipulate any corporeal object, but he can still use psionic powers.

If the psionicist rolls a 1 on his power check, he becomes shadow but none of his clothing or equipment makes the switch.

Power Score—The psionicist gains all desirable powers of the "shadow" monster for 1d4 turns.

20—The player must roll a save vs. lightning for the psionicist's most valuable item. If it fails, the item becomes shadow and drifts away, lost forever.

Psychometabolic Devotions

Absorb Disease

Power Score:	Con −3
Initial Cost:	12
Maintenance Cost:	na
Range:	touch
Preparation Time:	0
Area of Effect:	individual
Prerequisite:	none

This power lets the psionicist take the disease from another character's body, and absorb it himself. Presumably, the psionicist will then heal himself (using complete healing). This power can absorb magical diseases, but not curses, such as lycanthropy.

Power Score—The disease is automatically destroyed by the psionicist's immune system.

20—The disease remains in the victim while spreading to the psionicist.

Adrenalin Control

Power Score:	Con −3
Initial Cost:	8
Maintenance Cost:	4/round
Range:	0
Preparation Time:	0
Area of Effect:	personal
Prerequisite:	none

By controlling the production and release of adrenalin in his system, the psionicist can give himself temporary physical boosts on demand. When he increases his adrenalin, the character gains 1d6 points, which he can add directly to his Strength, Dexterity, or Constitution scores however he chooses. He enjoys all the normal bonuses for high physical attributes while this power is in effect.

If the psionicist's power check result is a 1, he overtaxes his system with this adrenalin. He still gets the boost, but he loses twice that many hit points, too.

Power Score—Instead of dividing the d6 result, the character applies that many points to each of the three attributes.

20—The psionicist must make a successful system shock roll or suffer a 50% loss in current hps and pass out for 1d8 hours.

Animal Affinity: Two ogres have an eye-opening experience.

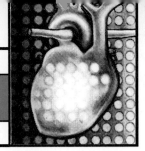

Aging

Power Score:	Con −5
Initial Cost:	10
Maintenance Cost:	na
Range:	touch
Preparation Time:	0
Area of Effect:	individual
Prerequisite:	none

With this power, an evil psionicist can cause unnatural aging by touch. (Other psionicists can use this power, too, but their alignment would begin to twist toward evil.) The victim ages 1d4 years instantly and must make a saving throw vs. polymorph. Failure means that the change was traumatic, and he ages another year automatically.

If the psionicist's power check result was a 1, there is a backlash and he, too, ages 1d4 years.

Power Score—The victim ages 1d20 years.

20—The psionicist ages 1d10 years.

Biofeedback

Power Score:	Con −2
Initial Cost:	6
Maintenance Cost:	3/round
Range:	0
Preparation Time:	0
Area of Effect:	personal
Prerequisite:	none

Biofeedback is the power to control the flow of blood through one's own body. This power has two key effects.

First, the psionicist can easily control bleeding. As a result, he suffers two fewer points of damage from every attack against him which causes physical injury.

Second, by flooding key portions of his body with blood, the psionicist effectively cushions blows against him and reduces their effect. The character's armor class is reduced by one.

Power Score—AC is reduced by three.

20—Excessive blood flow results in scattered bruises and a 10% hp loss.

Body Control

Power Score:	Con −4
Initial Cost:	7
Maintenance Cost:	5/turn
Range:	0
Preparation Time:	0
Area of Effect:	personal
Prerequisite:	none

This power allows a psionicist to adapt his body to a hostile enviroment. The change must be keyed to a specific surrounding: water, acid, extreme heat, extreme cold, an elemental plane, etc. If the power works, the psionicist not only survives, he fits in like a native organism. He can breathe and move normally, and he takes no damage simply from being in that environment.

An attack in any form does not constitute an environment. For example, a character who can survive subarctic temperatures is still vulnerable to a *cone of cold*.

Power Score—The psionicist can adapt himself to a new environment while maintaining the power.

20—The character becomes even more vulnerable, and the environment causes 1d4 points of damage per round. (A second use of body control halts damage.)

Body Equilibrium

Power Score:	Con −3
Initial Cost:	2
Maintenance Cost:	2/round
Range:	0
Preparation Time:	0
Area of Effect:	personal
Prerequisite:	none

Body equilibrium allows the user to adjust the weight of his or her body to correspond with the surface he's standing on. Thus he can walk on water, quicksand, or even a spider's web without sinking or breaking through. If the character is falling when he uses this

Expansion: Yuri will go to any length for a joke.

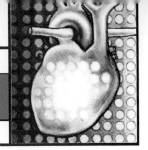

power, he will fall 120 feet per round—slow enough to escape injury.

Because of his lightness, the character must be wary of wind gusts, which can easily sweep him up and blow him away.

Power Score—The effect lasts up to a day without maintenance.

20—The psionicist's weight instantly rises by a factor of 10; he must use body equilibrium to fix the problem.

Body Weaponry

Power Score:	Con −3
Initial Cost:	9
Maintenance Cost:	4/round
Range:	0
Preparation Time:	0
Area of Effect:	personal
Prerequisite:	none

Body weaponry allows the psionicist to convert one of his arms into a weapon. Virtually any sort of weapon can be imitated—except a short bow, hand crossbow, light crossbow, or any weapon the psionicist cannot normally use. The arm actually becomes wood and/or metal, and assumes the weapon's form. It behaves in every respect like a normal weapon of the chosen type, with a bonus: it can never be dropped or stolen.

Power Score—The "armament" gives the psionicist a +1 attack bonus (but no damage bonus).

20—The psionicist must make a system shock roll or pass out for 1d10 rounds.

Catfall

Power Score:	Dex −2
Initial Cost:	4
Maintenance Cost:	na
Range:	0
Preparation Time:	0
Area of Effect:	personal
Prerequisite:	none

A character using this power can spring like a cat in the same round, and always land gracefully on his feet. He still suffers damage from falling, but the damage is halved. He can jump down 30 feet without risking any injury at all.

Power Score—The psionicist can jump 50 feet instead of 30 during this single use of the power.

20—No effect.

Cause Decay

Power Score:	Con −2
Initial Cost:	4
Maintenance Cost:	na
Range:	touch
Preparation Time:	0
Area of Effect:	60 lbs
Prerequisite:	none

This power works only against inanimate objects. The psionicist's touch causes instant decay: metal rusts, wood ages and splits, cloth falls to dust. The DM rolls a saving throw vs. acid for the item touched. If this fails, the item—or a maximum of 60 pounds of it—is consumed by decay within one round.

Power Score—The save automatically fails.

20—One of the psionicist's own items decays (no save)—either the first item touched, or an item chosen randomly by the DM.

Cell Adjustment

Power Score:	Con −3
Initial Cost:	5
Maintenance Cost:	up to 20/round
Range:	touch
Preparation Time:	0
Area of Effect:	individual
Prerequisite:	none

Cell adjustment allows the psionicist to heal wounds and cure diseases. Any sort of wound can be healed, but only nonmagical diseases are affected (e.g., this power cannot heal mummy rot, nor can it cure a lycanthropic curse).

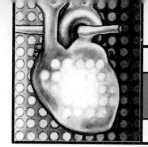

The psionicist can cure a disease in one round by spending 5 PSPs and making a succesful power check. If the die roll equals a 1, he succeeds but it's doubly taxing (10 PSPs). If it equals a 2, he fails because the disease is too widespread; he must spend another 5 PSPs and try again next round.

A "cure" doesn't automatically restore hit points lost due to illness; it merely arrests the disease. However, the psionicist can heal up to 4 points of damage in each subsequent round by spending 5 psionic strength points per hit point recovered. He cannot cure the disease and restore hit points during the same round.

Power Score—All disease—or up to 10 points of damage—is instantly healed at a cost of 5 PSPs.

20—The psionicist suffers 1d10 points of damage but the patient is unaffected.

Chameleon Power

Power Score:	Con −1
Initial Cost:	6
Maintenance Cost:	3/round
Range:	0
Preparation Time:	0
Area of Effect:	personal
Prerequisite:	none

The psionicist using this power actually changes the coloration of his skin, clothing, and equipment to match his background. The match is automatic; he does not choose the appearance. The change takes several seconds. As he moves, the coloration changes and shifts to reflect any changes in the surroundings.

In effect, chameleon power makes a psionicist very difficult to spot. If the character remains stationary, he can avoid detection simply by making a successful power check. If the character moves, his power score is reduced by three when he makes the check.

This power is most effective in natural surroundings, where one's coloration would logically conceal him. In an urban setting, or in an area without natural cover during broad day-light, the character's chameleon power score is halved (rounded down).

Power Score—The psionicist's power score gains a +3 bonus during "hiding" checks.

20—The psionicist's colorations strongly clash with the background; he sticks out like a sore thumb.

Chemical Simulation

Power Score:	Con −4
Initial Cost:	9
Maintenance Cost:	6/round
Range:	touch
Preparation Time:	1
Area of Effect:	varies
Prerequisite:	none

With this devotion, a psionicist can make his body simulate the action of acids. The character secretes an "acid" through his hand. Any item he touches and holds briefly must make a saving throw vs. acid or be dissolved. If used as a weapon, this acid cannot inflict more than two or three points of damage, though it can cause considerable pain.

Power Score—All saves for normal items fail; magical items still get a saving throw.

20—Acid oozes from the psionicist's sweat glands; all items touching his skin must save vs. acid.

Displacement

Power Score:	Con −3
Initial Cost:	6
Maintenance Cost:	3/round
Range:	0
Preparation Time:	0
Area of Effect:	personal
Prerequisite:	none

This power resembles the displacer beast's natural ability to make itself appear to be up to 3 feet from his actual location. The psionicist decides where this false image will appear. This is a very effective means of protecting oneself from attack, giving the psionicist a

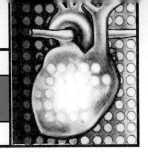

two-point bonus on his armor class (lowering it two points). *True seeing* will reveal the character's real location.

Power Score—The AC bonus is +4.

20—No effect.

Double Pain

Power Score:	Con −3
Initial Cost:	7
Maintenance Cost:	na
Range:	touch
Preparation Time:	0
Area of Effect:	individual
Prerequisite:	none

By touching another person, the psionicist greatly lowers that character's pain threshold. (Even a little scrape will feel like a serious injury.) The effect lasts one turn. During that time, all damage scored against that character is doubled. However, only half of this damage is real; the other half represents the amplified pain. When the character's total of real damage and pain reduces his hit points to zero or less, he passes out. He will regain consciousness 1d10 rounds later. At that time he also regains "fake" hit points—those lost only to pain.

If the victim does not pass out in one turn (the duration of this power's effects), damage scored against him is no longer doubled. However, the points of "pain damage" which he has an already incurred will remain in effect for another 1d6 rounds.

Power Score—The victim must make a system shock roll upon each hit, or pass out due to the excrutiating pain.

20—The power backfires and affects the psionicist for one hour.

Ectoplasmic Form

Power Score:	Con −4
Initial Cost:	9
Maintenance Cost:	9/round
Range:	0
Preparation Time:	1
Area of Effect:	personal
Prerequisite:	none

With this power a psionicist converts himself to ectoplasm, (a fine-spun, smoky substance). He becomes insubstantial, ghostlike, and able to walk through solid material as if it didn't exist. The psionicist is still visible as a whispy outline. He moves at his normal movement rate and in the normal fashion (e.g., if he couldn't fly before, he can't now).

The psionicist can also convert the following to ectoplasm: his clothing, armor, and up to 15 pounds of equipment that he's carrying.

Power Score—The maintenance cost is 3 PSPs per round.

20—The psionicist's items become ectoplasmic, but he doesn't. He must use this power again (successfully) to retrieve them.

Enhanced Strength

Power Score:	Wis −3
Initial Cost:	varies
Maintenance Cost:	varies
Range:	0
Preparation Time:	0
Area of Effect:	personal
Prerequisites:	none

A psionicist can increase his physical Strength score to a maximum of 18 through this devotion. The PSP cost is twice the number of points he adds to his Strength score. (If he fails, he loses half this amount; see Chapter 1.) The maintenance cost per round equals the number of Strength points he has added.

Physical Strength cannot be raised above 18 psionically. The psionicist does not qualify for exceptional Strength bonuses if he raises his Strength to 18.

Power Score—The psionicist can raise his strength to 18/00, with each 25% increase costing an additional PSP.

20—The power backfires and lowers Strength by 1d6 until arrested by this power.

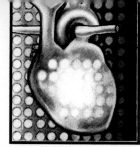

Expansion

Power Score:	Con −2
Initial Cost:	6
Maintenance Cost:	1/round
Range:	0
Preparation Time:	0
Area of Effect:	personal
Prerequisite:	none

The psionicist can expand his own body proportions in any dimension: height, length, width, or thickness. He can increase any or all of these proportions by 50% of their original size per round. Maximum expansion is four times original size.

This power has no effect on clothing or equipment. Ability scores don't increase either. In other words, the character does not grow stronger simply because he became taller. However, being very big often has other advantages.

Power Score—Maximum expansion becomes 10 times and the rate is 100% per round.

20—The psionicist shrinks by 50% until arrested by this power.

Flesh Armor

Power Score:	Con −3
Initial Cost:	8
Maintenance Cost:	4/round
Range:	0
Preparation Time:	0
Area of Effect:	personal
Prerequisite:	none

The psionicist transforms his own skin into armor. No one can see the change, but it's as if he had actually acquired some type of armor. The type of armor his body mimics depends on the result of his power check, as shown in the following table:

1	left hand functions as a shield, AC 9
2	leather, AC 8
3-4	ring mail, AC 7
5-6	scale mail, AC 6
7-8	chain mail, AC 5
9-10	banded mail, AC 4
11 +	plate mail, AC 3

Because this armor is part of his body, the psionicist can enjoy its benefits without suffering any penalty he might have if he were actually wearing that type of armor. The armor created by this power weighs nothing, has no magnetic properties, and in no way encumbers the psionicist.

Power Score—The psionicist gains a +1 bonus to the armor class listed above.

20—The power just grows ugly hair over his body, which must be shaved off or he loses 2 points of Charisma.

Graft Weapon

Power Score:	Con −5
Initial Cost:	10
Maintenance Cost:	1/round
Range:	touch
Preparation Time:	0
Area of Effect:	personal
Prerequisite:	none

With this power the psionicist can graft any one-handed melee weapon directly onto his body. He picks up the weapon, activates this power, and the weapon becomes an extension of the character's arm. Assuming the character is proficient with that type of weapon, he gains a +1 bonus to attack rolls and damage. If he is not proficient with the weapon, he suffers the usual nonproficiency penalties, but still gets the +1 bonus.

Power Score—The +1 bonus for attacks and damage increases to +4.

20—The weapon has been weakened; it will break on any attack roll of 1.

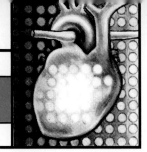

Heightened Senses

Power Score:	Con
Initial Cost:	5
Maintenance Cost:	1/round
Range:	0
Preparation Time:	0
Area of Effect:	personal
Prerequisite:	none

By means of this devotion the psionicist sharpens all five of his normal senses: sight, hearing, taste, touch, and smell. This has several effects, which are described below. The DM may allow additional applications as he sees fit.

First, the character has a good chance to notice thieves who are hiding in shadows or moving silently. The thief's skill chance is halved when someone with heightened senses is observing him. Even if the thief is already hidden, he must roll again when a character with heightened senses enters the picture.

Second, the psionicist can track someone like a bloodhound. He must make an Intelligence check every turn to stay on the trail or recover the trail if it is lost. His movement rate when tracking is 6. The trail can be no more than 24 hours old.

Third, the psionicist's ranges for hearing and seeing are tripled. He can, for example, identify a person (in daylight) at a range of 400 yards.

Fourth, the character can taste poisons or other impurities in quantities which are much too small to cause any harm.

Fifth, the character can identify almost anything by touch. He can, for example, tell two gold pieces from each other after having previously handled just one of them. He can also tell if something has been handled in the last five minutes simply by handling it himself.

Power Score—One of the heightened senses (chosen randomly) stays with the psionicist for a full day.

20—One of the psionicist's five senses is lost for 1d12 hours.

Immovability

Power Score:	Con −5
Initial Cost:	9
Maintenance Cost:	6/round
Range:	0
Preparation Time:	0
Area of Effect:	personal
Prerequisite:	none

When a psionicist makes himself immovable, he is exactly that. A tremendous amount of force is required to uproot him from his spot.

Moving the psionicist requires a combined Strength total that is at least 10 times greater than his immovability score (Con −5). If a character is pushing the psionicist, and makes a successful bend bars roll, that character can double the Strength he's contributing to the total. Even if a group manages to move the psionicist once, they may not be able to move him any easier the next time. The psionicist remains immovable until he stops maintaining the power.

This power has nothing to do with weight. A character will not crash through the floor because he made himself immovable. He has instead attached himself to the fabric of the universe, which is considerably more powerful than the strongest castle. He does, however, need a horizontal surface as an anchor.

If the psionicist's power check results in a 1, he attaches himself so well that even he can't break free simply by shutting off the power. He must pay the initial cost again (9 PSPs) to free himself.

Power Score—Moving the psionicist becomes impossible.

20—The psionicist can't stop the power; he maintains it until he runs out of PSPs.

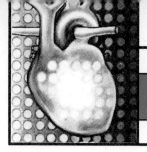

Lend Health

Power Score:	Con −1
Initial Cost:	4
Maintenance Cost:	na
Range:	touch
Preparation Time:	0
Area of Effect:	individual
Prerequisites:	none

Lend health is a power of healing. The psionicist who makes a succesful power check can transfer his own hit points to someone else he is touching. Each hit point transferred heals one point of damage. The character can transfer as many points as he wants to in a single round.

If the psionicist tries to transfer hit points when he has fewer than five remaining, he must make another power check. If this fails, he cannot transfer the points. In any case, he cannot transfer hit points if he has only one remaining.

The beneficiary of this power can never exceed his normal, healthy total of hit points.

Power Score—Every point drained from the psionicist heals two hit points in the beneficiary.

20—The psionicist suffers all the wounds which his target currently has. No one is healed.

Mind Over Body

Power Score:	Wis −3
Initial Cost:	na
Maintenance Cost:	10/day
Range:	touch
Preparation Time:	0
Area of Effect:	individual
Prerequisites:	none

Mind over body allows the user to suppress his body's need for food, water, and sleep. In exchange for one hour of meditation per day, all of the psionicist's physical needs are over-

come. He does not feel hunger, exhaustion, or thirst, nor does he suffer any ability reductions for privation.

The psionicist can also suppress the basic needs of others while suppressing his own. To do so, he must pay an additional 10 PSPs per person and spend an additional hour of meditation per person. Each person being aided must be in physical contact with the psionicist throughout the entire period of meditation. Usually, all the characters hold hands, forming a continuous line or circle.

The psionicist can survive in this fashion for a number of days equal to his experience level, or five days, whichever is more. At the end of that time, he collapses from exhaustion. He must then rest one day for every two days spent sublimating his body's needs. Or he can be restored through 24 hours of complete healing. These rules also apply to any characters the psionicist has aided.

Power Score—The psionicist need not rest after using this power.

20—The power fails, but the psionicist collapses with exhaustion and must rest for 24 hours.

Reduction

Power Score:	Con −2
Initial Cost:	varies
Maintenance Cost:	1/round
Range:	0
Preparation Time:	0
Area of Effect:	personal
Prerequisites:	none

This power is the reverse of expansion. The psionicist can reduce his body's dimensions along any or all axes: height, length, width, or thickness. The change amounts to 1 foot per PSP spent, until the dimension being affected is 1 foot or less. After that, the psionicist can halve his dimensions each time he spends a PSP.

For example, let's assume Magnilda (a dual-class psionicist and warrior maiden) stands 6 feet tall. Five strength points reduce her height to 1 foot. Three more strength points halve her size three times: to 6 inches, then 3 inches, and finally to 1.5 inches.

Now let's assume Magnilda only wants to make her arm thin enough to slide through a keyhole. At its thickest point, her arm measures 4 inches across. Three strength points will reduce the thickness of her arm to ½ inch (from 4 to 2, then to 1, then to ½) without altering its length at all. She can now slide her arm through the keyhole and unlock the door from the inside.

Power Score—Each PSP spent results in twice the described effect (if desired).

20—The psionicist doubles in size, and stays this big for an hour or until he uses this power again successfully.

Share Strength

Power Score:	Con −4
Initial Cost:	6
Maintenance Cost:	2/round
Range:	touch
Preparation Time:	0
Area of Effect:	individual
Prerequisites:	none

The psionicist can effectively lend his physical Strength to another character. The psionicist sacrifices *two* of his own Strength points (ability points, not PSPs) for every single point the recipient gains. This transfer remains in effect until the psionicist stops paying the devotion's maintenance cost; then all points return in one round. If the recipient is killed before the psionicist gets his Strength points back, the psionicist's Strength score is permanently reduced.

If the psionicist's die roll is a 1, he must expend three points for each point his pal gains, instead of two for one.

Power Score—The point transfer is 1:1.

20—The psionicist loses one Strength point for a day. If he fails a save vs. paralyzation, the loss is permanent.

Suspend Animation

Power Score:	Con −3
Initial Cost:	12
Maintenance Cost:	na
Range:	0/touch
Preparation Time:	5
Area of Effect:	individual
Prerequisites:	none

With this power a psionicist can "play dead"—bringing all life functions to a virtual halt. Only the most careful examination will show that the character is still alive. Even psionic powers such as life detection and ESP will not turn up any evidence of life unless those powers are maintained for at least three minutes. Use of the probe power will detect life immediately.

The psionicist can remain in suspended animation for a number of weeks equal to the results of his power check—or less. When he wishes to put himself to sleep, he first decides when he wants to wake. Then he makes his power check. If the number rolled is less than the time he hoped to be "suspended," he awakens prematurely.

Another willing character can also be suspended for the same PSP cost (not at the same time as the psionicist, however). This has a preparation time of one hour and a range of touch.

Power Score—The psionicist remains aware of his surroundings and can wake at any time he chooses.

20—The psionicist falls unconscious and only violent slapping can revive him.

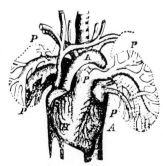

Heart and Lungs.

Psychoportive Sciences

Banishment

Power Score:	Int −1
Initial Cost:	30
Maintenance Cost:	10/round
Range:	5 yards
Preparation Time:	0
Area of Effect:	individual
Prerequisites:	teleport

With this power, the psionicist can teleport a creature against its will to a pocket dimension and hold it there. The creature being banished must be extremely close—within 5 yards. The pocket dimension is a featureless area with a benign environment—it may be hot or cold, dark or light, but not so much that it will cause injury.

Banishment has a boomerang feature. If the psionicist fails to pay the pay the maintenance cost, the banished creature automatically returns to its original location. The creature cannot reappear in a location that now contains other matter, however (e.g., to a doorway that has been closed, or to a spot that now has a sharp stakes upon it). If this happens, the creature returns to the nearest open space. In other words, psionicists cannot rely on the boomerang feature to kill or harm a creature.

As long as the psionicist pays the maintenance cost, the creature will not automatically return. If the creature has access to the astral or ethereal planes, or it can teleport between planes, it could try to return that way. If the banisher is still maintaining the power, however, a psychic contest takes place. If the banisher wins, the victim is prevented from returning.

Power Score—The banished figure cannot return of its own accord; it must wait until it is allowed to return.

20—Both the intended victim and the psionicist are banished to the same place. The other figure bounces back when the psionicist stops paying the maintenance cost, but the psionicist himself must return via some other method: teleportation, probability travel, etc.

Probability Travel

Power Score:	Int
Initial Cost:	20
Maintenance Cost:	8/hour
Range:	unlimited
Preparation Time:	2
Area of Effect:	individual +
Prerequisites:	none

With probability travel, a psionicist can traverse the astral plane physically as if he's in astral form. This power has a distinct advantage over magical astral travel. When a wizard uses the *astral* spell, he forms an astral body, which remains connected to his material body by a silvery cord. In contrast, a psionicist using probability travel never leaves his physical form; he brings it along. He has no cord, so, unlike the wizard, he can never die because his cord has been severed. (On the other hand, he can still be blown to bits.)

The astral plane boasts nothing that would attract tourists, but its two-dimensional color pools serve as highways to the outer planes. These pools, scattered randomly throughout the astral plane, provide connections to all surface layers of the outer planes.

Travel through the astral plane is speedy: 10 yards per minute per Intelligence point. However, distance on the astral plane does not equate to distance on other planes. After 1d6 + 6 hours of travel, the traveler reaches the color pool he sought. There is a flat 75% chance that this pool leads to the exact destination the character wants. Otherwise, it is at least 10 miles off target—maybe more.

The psionicist can take other persons (as defined by the *charm person* spell) along on his probability trip. Each passenger costs 12 extra PSPs initially, plus 4 extra PSPs per hour, and adds one-half hour to the time needed to find the correct color pool. Passengers must travel

Dimensional Door: Juan decides not to stay for dinner.

voluntarily; this power cannot drag a character into the astral plane against his will.

Combat on the astral plane is unusual. The traveler's physical body cannot affect astral bodies in any way. However, psionic powers do work against the minds of astral travelers. Most magical items do not work in the astral plane. Magical items which are keyed to a particular plane do function there, often with enhanced effect.

If the psionicist simply turns off this power while in the astral plane, he doesn't leave. Instead, he's stranded, unable to move except by physically pushing off of solid objects (which are extremely rare in the astral plane). He's also stranded if he runs out of PSPs or is knocked unconscious on the astral plane. The only exit from this plane is a color pool.

If you'd like to learn more about traveling on the astral plane, see the AD&D® handbook *Manual of the Planes*.

Power Score—The color pool is right where the character wants it to be.

20—The character attracts the attention of an astral creature, which may or may not be hostile, at the DM's discretion.

Summon Planar Creature

Power Score:	Int −4
Initial Cost:	45/90
Maintenance Cost:	na
Range:	200 yards
Preparation Time:	12
Area of Effect:	one creature
Prerequisites:	teleport

This science allows the psionicist to reach into another plane, grab whatever creature he happens to find there, and teleport it to his own plane. The victim will be disoriented for one round after arriving; as a result, he suffers a two-point penalty on die rolls for initiative, attacks, and saving throws.

A *magical* summons offers some control over a planar creature, and usually returns that creature to its home automatically. This psionic power does neither; it merely teleports something. To be rid of the creature, the psionicist must banish it, teleport it again, kill it, or control it somehow. If the creature is intelligent, the psionicist might reason with it. However, the creature is almost certain to fly into a murderous rage when it discovers its plight.

The psionicist can make the summoned creature materialize anywhere within 200 yards of his present position. This is a tremendous advantage, since the creature, at least initially, has no idea who summoned it. Its anger is likely to be vented against the first target it finds. However, if the psionicist's power check result was a 2, this range is reduced to 50 yards. If the result was a 1, the creature pops in within 10 yards. Obviously, some risk is involved.

The psionicist chooses the plane from which the creature will come. He does not choose the creature, however; that's determined at random. A creature from one of the elemental planes usually will be an elemental of the appropriate type. A creature from an outer plane probably will be a native of that particular plane, but it could also be a visitor, or even an adventurer who happened to be in the wrong place at the right time. In contrast, the astral or ethereal planes are a cornucopia of creatures, frequented by beings of every imaginable description. In any event, the DM decides which creature is summoned, drawing from the monsters for which he has game statistics. This book describes some extraplanar creatures. Many more are covered in the *Manual of the Planes* and various Monstrous Compendiums, especially the compendium featuring outer planar creatures.

It costs 45 PSPs to summon a creature from the astral or ethereal plane. If the psionicist is dipping into an inner or outer plane, the cost soars to 90 PSPs.

Power Score—The creature summoned enjoys this sort of thing and won't be angry with the psionicist.

20—The psionicist attracts the attention of a powerful, extraplanar creature without summoning it.

Teleport

Power Score:	Int
Initial Cost:	10+
Maintenance Cost:	na
Range:	infinite
Preparation Time:	0
Area of Effect:	personal
Prerequisites:	none

Teleport is the essential power within this discipline. It allows the psionicist to teleport to a familiar spot. The destination must be a place that the character knows and can picture mentally—even if he's never actually been there. For example, a psionicist may still know a location that he has seen through a crystal ball, via a sight link, or even by scanning someone else's mind for the information.

The psionicist can still teleport to a place even if it has somehow changed from the way he pictures it. For example, if a room has been rearranged, or is currently on fire, such changes won't affect the teleport.

Teleports always take characters to a fixed location. For example, if a character tries to teleport into a gypsy wagon which is on the move, he'll arrive at the wagon's location when he last knew it. The wagon itself may be miles away by then. Also, if the character was picturing the wagon's interior, he will teleport to the space corresponding to the wagon's interior—which is several feet off the ground! Because the wagon itself has moved, the teleporter will fall when he arrives. (Imagine teleporting to a room on the fifth floor of a tower, only to discover the tower has been razed by marauders since your last visit.)

Teleportation is instantaneous. The teleporting character simply ceases to exist in his previous location and springs into being at the destination. There is a slight, audible "pop" at both ends, as air rushes into the sudden vac-

uum or is instantly displaced.

Restraints do not affect teleportation. A character who is tied up, shackled to a wall, or buried up to his neck can still teleport. The restraints remain behind.

Clothing, on the other hand, does accompany a character who teleports. He may also carry small items in his grasp or wear equipment (e.g., armor) on his person, not exceeding one-fifth of his own body mass. If he doubles the amount of PSPs expended, he can carry up to three times his body mass, or take along one or two other characters on whom he has a firm grasp.

A character can teleport any distance, but as the distance increases, so does the chance of failure and the cost in PSPs. Ranges, point costs, and power score modifiers are shown below.

If the teleportation die roll is a 1 or 2, the character and anyone else with him are momentarily disoriented by the jump. They can do nothing during the round which immediately follows the teleport. After that, they suffer a 2-point penalty to the following for 1d6 rounds: initiative die rolls, psionic power checks, and attack rolls.

Distance	Initial Cost	Power Score Modifier
10 yards	10	+1
100 yards	20	0
1,000 yards	30	−1
10 miles	40	−2
100 miles	50	−3
1,000 miles	60	−4
10,000 miles	70	−5
planet to planet*	100	−6

* Players with the SPELLJAMMER™ boxed set should note that interplanetary teleports are possible only within the same crystal sphere. It is impossible to teleport between crystal spheres or different planes of existence.

Power Score—The PSP cost is reduced by 20 percent, rounded up.

20—No effect.

Teleport Other

Power Score:	Int −2
Initial Cost:	20+
Maintenance Cost:	na
Range:	10 yards
Preparation Time:	0
Area of Effect:	na
Prerequisites:	teleport

This power is identical to the one listed directly above, except it is used to teleport other characters. The psionicist stays where he is while someone else is teleported. The character must be willing to be teleported, or unconscious. PSP costs and power score modifications are the same as for teleportation. (In other words, cost and difficulty increase with distance.) If the psionicist pays twice the usual PSP cost, he can teleport up to three characters, provided they are firmly grasping one another.

Power Score—The PSP cost is reduced by 20 percent, rounded up.

20—All would-be teleporters are seriously disoriented. They cannot cast spells and suffer a −4 penalty on all die rolls for 1d4 turns.

Psychoportive Devotions

Astral Projection

Power Score:	Int
Initial Cost:	6
Maintenance Cost:	2/hour
Range:	na
Preparation Time:	1
Area of Effect:	personal
Prerequisites:	none

Astral projection is similar to probability travel, except the traveler is not accompanied by his physical body. Instead, an astral body is created. This astral body immediately leaps into the astral plane. Only creatures or characters who are also on the astral plane can see it.

A silvery cord connects the astral body to the physical body. Nearly all astral travelers have such a cord. It is visible as a translucent string which stretches 10 feet from the astral body, and then becomes invisible and intangible. If the cord is severed, both bodies die (so does the character). The silvery cord is nearly indestructible, however. Usually it can be severed only by the psychic wind at its most powerful, or by the *silver swords* of the githyanki.

Since the astral plane is a highway leading to other planes, a character who uses this power usually has another destination in mind—either a distant point on the prime material plane or an outerplanar locale. When the traveler reaches his destination, a temporary physical body is formed there. This body resembles the character's real body in every respect, and the two are still connected by the invisible, silvery cord.

If either the astral body or the temporary physical body is killed, the cord returns to the real body. This second physical body is not formed if the character travels to another location on the same plane where his real physical body is located. He can view that plane in astral form, but cannot affect it or even enter it physically, nor can he direct magical or psionic powers into it.

Magical items can be taken into the astral plane, but most lose their magical properties temporarily while in that plane.

If you'd like more detail on astral travel and the astral plane, see the *Manual of the Planes,* an AD&D® game handbook.

Power Score—The first color pool found is precisely where the psionicist wants it.

20—The psionicist attracts the attention of a powerful creature in the astral plane.

Dimensional Door

Power Score:	Con −1
Initial Cost:	4
Maintenance Cost:	2/round
Range:	50 yards +
Preparation Time:	0
Area of Effect:	na
Prerequisites:	none

Like teleportation, a dimensional door takes a character from one location to another. The similarity stops there, however. With dimensional door, the psionicist opens a man-sized portal which leads to the edge of another dimension. The edge acts as a lightning-quick transit system, carrying travelers to a destination chosen by the psionicist who uses this power.

When the psionicist uses this devotion, he creates a door leading into the alternate dimension. The door is a vaguely outlined portal, which appears in front of the psionicist. At the same time, an identical portal appears wherever he wants it, within range (see below). The door can have whatever orientation the psionicist chooses. If someone (including the psionicist) steps into either portal, he immediately steps out of the other. Both doors remain in place for as long as the psionicist maintains the power.

The dimension accessed by this power is not fully understood. Clearly, it has very different qualities of time and space, such that motion is greatly accelerated. For many years this transit was thought to be instantaneous, but arduous experiments by Larue d'jar Azif of Dhaztanar have proved that a very tiny bit of time does elapse. What this means is still unknown.

Travel via this power is disorienting. Presumably, exposure to the alternate dimension traumatizes the body in some way. As a result, a traveler is dazed and cannot attack or move for one round after stepping through a dimensional skip portal. Quick transit is advisable. People who shove only an arm through a portal suffer intense pain. Fools who poke their head through a portal must make a system shock roll; failure means they lose 50% of their current hit points and pass out.

Inanimate objects are not affected by exposure to the dimension's edge. In fact, a character can throw or fire objects through a portal, and they'll come out on the other side. Attackers suffer a −4 penalty on their to-hit rolls against targets on the other side of the dimension's edge.

Range: The normal range of this power— i.e., the maximum distance between the two portals—is 50 yards. The distance can be extended only with severe reductions to the character's power score, as shown below. Increasing the range does not increase the PSP cost, however.

Distance Between Doors	Power Score Modifier
50 yards	0
75 yards	−2
100 yards	−5
150 yards	−8
200 yards	−12

Power Score—Transit does not cause disorientation.

20—The psionicist is momentarily exposed to the transit dimension and is disoriented as if he had stepped through the portal.

Dimension Walk

Power Score:	Con −2
Initial Cost:	8
Maintenance Cost:	4/turn
Range:	na
Preparation Time:	2
Area of Effect:	personal
Prerequisites:	none

With dimension walk, a psionicist can travel from place to place in his own dimension by piercing other dimensions at right angles. This has two advantages over a

dimensional door: 1) a dimension walk is not physically traumatizing and 2) the range of travel is greater. On the other hand, dimension walk only allows the psionicist himself to travel, and he can easily get lost.

The dimension walker opens up a vaguely shimmering portal. Only the psionicist who opened the portal can enter it. As soon as he does, the portal closes behind him. He finds himself engulfed by an inky grayness that is virtually without features. The effect is one of extreme sensory deprivation.

The psionicist can travel through this gray realm at a speed of 7 leagues (21 miles) per turn. He cannot see where he is or where he's going while in the realm. He has only his instinct to guide him, and must make a Wisdom check every turn. If these checks succeed, he'll find himself at his chosen destination when he steps out of the realm. If any single Wisdom check fails, however, the character will stray off course by several miles. When the walker steps out of the gray realm, the DM can place him in any location, within the maximum distance from his starting point (e.g., if the psionicist walked for 10 rounds, he must be within 21 miles of his origin). It's up to the psionicist to figure out his location; this power doesn't help him gain his bearings.

Aside from getting lost, dimension walking is completely safe. Apparently anything that lives in the other dimensions crossed cannot interact with dimensional travelers. (Larue d'jar Azif of Dhaztanar postulated that these other dimensions teem with life just as much as our own, but because the traveler is crossing them "against the grain", as it were, they do not register on his senses.) The character can bring along as much as he can carry, but *bags of holding* and other dimensional storage devices spill their contents immediately if taken into this space.

Power Score—The psionicist receives a +2 bonus when making his Wisdom checks.

20—Overcome with vertigo, the character can do nothing but retch for three rounds.

Dream Travel

Power Score:	Wis −4
Initial Cost:	1/25 miles
Maintenance Cost:	na
Range:	500 miles
Preparation Time:	0
Area of Effect:	personal
Prerequisites:	none

Dream travel is a powerful but unreliable means of getting from here to there. The traveler journeys in his dreams, and awakes wherever his nocturnal wandering carried him. The psionicist can even take other characters with him, although it's more difficult than traveling alone. (See "Passengers" below.)

To use dream travel, the psionicist must be asleep. Once asleep, he begins fashioning a dream that involves traveling from his present location to his intended destination. At the beginning of the journey, the DM secretly makes a power check for the character. If the check succeeds, the psionicist will reach his destination. If the check fails, the character will fall short 10% for each point that the die roll exceeded the power score.

If the DM wants, this power check is all that's required to handle dream travel during a game. However, it's far more satisfying to actually role-play the dream. The player creates the setting and describes his intentions, with the DM interrupting to change things arbitrarily and throw obstacles in the character's path. If the player overcomes the obstacles and solves problems inventively, the DM is justified in giving a bonus to the character's power check. If the dream is dull and lifeless, the DM can also penalize the power check.

The DM should remember that this is a dream; terrain on the journey may not resemble actual terrain, the character may be completely different, and the world may be completely strange. The length of the dream journey should be approximately the same as the real distance, however, and the final destination should be at least similar to the real des-

Dream Travel: Five passengers set sail that day for a three-hour tour...

tination. Such dream adventures should minimize combat and maximize problems, puzzles, and surreal atmosphere. If combat does occur, it has no effect on the character physically, but if he is killed, he wakes up, right where he started. All dream journeys take approximately eight hours to complete, successful or not.

Passengers: The psionicist can bring other characters along with him in the dream. His power score is reduced by one for each passenger he carries. Passengers must also be sleeping. A single power check launches everyone on the dream journey. If the check fails, they still attempt the dream journey but fall short of their target. The psionicist must pay the PSP cost of the trip individually for each character accompanying him in the dream.

Intelligent animals can also be drawn into the dream, but normal animals (horses, dogs, falcons, whatever) are very difficult to bring along. The psionicist must make a separate power check to draw in each animal and his power score is halved, rounded down, when making this check.

When the dream travelers reach their destination, they awaken. In the place where they lay sleeping, their bodies and any equipment carried or worn fades away. At the same time, they fade into being at their new location, still in sleeping posture, but fully awake.

Power Score—No additional effect.

20—The dream is nightmarish. The psionicist must save vs. paralyzation or appear dead until violently struck.

Teleport Trigger

Power Score:	Int +1
Initial Cost:	0
Maintenance Cost:	2/hour
Range:	infinite
Preparation Time:	0
Area of Effect:	personal
Prerequisites:	teleport

A teleport trigger is a programmed event which causes the psionicist to instantly and re-

flexively teleport to a safe location. After making a successful power check, the psionicist must specify where he intends to go. He must also define very specifically what conditions will trigger the teleportation. These can be anything he wants, but the teleport will not be triggered unless he is aware that the conditions have been met. A volcanic eruption 500 miles away will not trigger teleportation unless the character has some way to know that the volcano is erupting.

For example, here are three typical triggers: being reduced to 10 or fewer hit points, seeing a mind flayer, and being attacked by a *magic missile* spell. When such predetermined conditions are fulfilled, the character instantly teleports to the programmed location.

When the teleport is triggered, the character must have enough PSPs remaining to teleport to that location, because he pays the cost just as if he were performing a normal teleport. (See "teleport.") He must also make a teleport power check, with penalties based on the distance traveled. If this power check fails, so does the programmed teleport.

No PSPs are spent when the trigger is defined, but the character spends two points per hour from that time just to maintain the trigger. The trigger remains in effect until the character stops paying the maintenance cost.

Power Score—The character can ignore power score penalties for distance.

20—No other effect.

Time Shift

Power Score:	Int
Initial Cost:	16
Maintenance Cost:	na
Range:	0
Preparation Time:	0
Area of Effect:	personal
Prerequisites:	teleport

Time shifting allows the psionicist to travel up to three rounds into the future and observe things until time catches up with him. He sees

everything frozen around him just as it will be when that moment in the future actually arrives.

The psionicist enters a different reality when he uses this power. No one in the "still life" that surrounds him can see or detect him in any way. He can move freely through the environment, putting himself wherever he wants to be when he returns to normal time. But he cannot affect anything around him, nor can anything affect him. Even two time-shifted characters are completely invisible to each other. To the people in real time, the character simply vanishes and then reappears sometime later.

The character does not exist for any normal game purpose during the period when he is time shifted. If, for example, a *fireball* spell detonates in the room while the character is time shifted, the character is completely protected against its effects. In fact, unless the blast leaves visible effects (charred walls or corpses or sulfurous fumes), the character won't even know it happened. He sees none of the intervening events.

This power cannot help a character escape contact, however. If someone has established contact or tangents (see Chapter 2) with the time shifter—and continues paying their maintenance cost—then the tangents or contact will still be in effect when the character returns to normal time.

Time shifting offers an obvious advantage in combat. A psionicist can leap one round into the future and maneuver into position for an attack. In that case, the shifter receives a +4 bonus to his attack roll. With enough time, he could even escape.

How long does a time shift last? If the psionicist travels one round forward, then he has one round in which to maneuver. If he travels two rounds forward, then it takes two rounds for reality to catch up. Three rounds is the limit. The farther (or longer) the trip, the more difficult it is to make, as shown in the table below.

Time Shifted	Psionic Strength Cost	Power Score Modifier
1 round	3	0
2 rounds	6	−2
3 rounds	12	−6

Power Score—No other effect.

20—The psionicist is disoriented, and suffers a −2 penalty on all die rolls for as many rounds as he intended to shift.

Time/Space Anchor

Power Score:	Int
Initial Cost:	5
Maintenance Cost:	1/round
Range:	0
Preparation Time:	0
Area of Effect:	3 yards
Prerequisites:	none

This power protects psionicists against unwanted teleportation. When a time/space anchor is in effect, the psionicist cannot be teleported against his will unless he loses a psychic contest.

Anyone and anything else inside the 3-yard radius is also protected using the psionicist's power score. Items are protected automatically, but living creatures or characters are protected only if the psionicist wants them to be. Each additional creature protected costs another PSP per round. This power cannot prevent someone from teleporting himself away; it only prevents teleporting from an outside source.

Power Score—The psionicist receives a +2 bonus in any resulting psychic contests.

20—The psionicist is rooted to the spot for 1d6 rounds. During that time his AC is penalized 5 points.

CHAPTER 7

Telepathy

Telepathic Sciences

Domination

Power Score:	Wis −4
Initial Cost:	contact
Maintenance Cost:	varies
Range:	30 yards
Preparation Time:	0
Area of Effect:	individual
Prerequisites:	mindlink, contact

With domination, a psionicist can project signals from his own mind into the mind of one other person or creature. As a result, the subject is forced to do nearly anything the psionicist wishes. The dominated subject knows what is happening, but he cannot resist the psionicist's will. Commands are given mentally and automatically.

The victim's abilities are neither diminished nor enhanced by this power. The subject can be forced to use any power or ability he normally can—assuming the psionicist knows about it. Domination does not reveal facts or secrets about a victim.

As soon as domination is attempted, the victim makes a saving throw vs. spells. If this saving throw succeeds, the victim is not dominated. If it fails, the victim has fallen under the psionicist's control. However, if the victim is later forced to do something completely ab-

horrent (against his alignment), he can make another saving throw to regain his free will.

Domination can exact a high price in PSPs. The cost to establish and maintain this power equals twice the cost to *contact* the victim.

Power Score—The maintenance cost is halved.

20—The victim knows that someone attempted to dominate him.

Ejection

Power Score:	Wis −4
Initial Cost:	varies
Maintenance Cost:	na
Range:	0
Preparation Time:	0
Area of Effect:	personal
Prerequisite:	none

Ejection is the final defense against unwanted contact. If one psionicist has forced contact with another's mind, or has been granted contact and is now doing things he should not be, he can be ejected.

The cost of ejection is twice the opponent's contact power score (even if contact was established through combat).

Ejection is risky for the user. If the power check result is 8 or less, consult the table below to see what "side effects" the psionicist suffers.

1   Lose access to all sciences for 1d10 hours
2   Lose access to one discipline, selected by the DM, for 1d10 hours
3   Lose 1d10 +10 additional PSPs
4   Lose 1d10 additional PSPs
5   Lose 1 point of Constitution permanently
6   Lose 1d10 hit points
7   Sever only one portion of contact (one successful attack reestablishes it)
8   Sever only two portions of contact (two successful attacks reestablish it)

Abbreviations

Telepathic attack and defense modes are often abbreviated as follows, especially in character or creature descriptions.

Attack Modes	Defense Modes
EW = ego whip	IF = intellect fortress
II = id insinuation	MB = mental barrier
MT = mind thrust	M- = mind blank
PB = psionic blast	TS = thought shield
PsC = psychic crush	TW = tower of iron will

Power Score—Roll 1d6 on the table above. The result applies to the ejected being.

20—Ejection fails, but the psionicist still makes a d6 roll on the table above.

Fate Link

Power Score:	Con −5
Initial Cost:	contact
Maintenance Cost:	5/turn
Range:	2 miles
Preparation Time:	1
Area of Effect:	individual
Prerequisite:	mindlink, contact

This power enables the telepath to intertwine his own fate with that of another creature. If either being experiences pain, both feel it. When one loses hit points, both lose the same amount. If either dies, the other must immediately make a saving throw vs. death to avoid the same fate.

Power Score—Range is unlimited.

20—Social regression. The psionicist loses 1d6 points of Charisma for a day.

Mass Domination

Power Score:	Wis −6
Initial Cost:	contact
Maintenance Cost:	varies
Range:	40 yards
Preparation Time:	2
Area of Effect:	up to 5 creatures
Prerequisite:	mindlink, contact, domination

This power is identical to domination except the psionicist can control up to five creatures simultaneously. Each one must be contacted and dominated individually. The maintenance cost—twice the victim's level or hit dice—must be paid for each dominated figure.

Power Score—The range is extended to 100 yards.

20—The intended targets are aware of the psionicist's efforts.

Mindlink

Power Score:	Wis −5
Initial Cost:	contact
Maintenance Cost:	8/round
Range:	unlimited
Preparation Time:	0
Area of Effect:	individual
Prerequisite:	contact

Mindlink allows the user to communicate wordlessly with any intelligent creature he can contact (Intelligence 5 or greater on a human scale). This is two-way communication. It is not the same as mind-reading because the psionicist only receives thoughts which the other party wants to send. Language is not a barrier. Distance affects the telepath's ability to make contact, but it has no other effect (see "contact").

Power Score—The mindlink allows one probing question (see probe).

20—The psionicist must save vs. petrification or be stunned for 1d4 rounds.

Mindwipe

Power Score:	Int −6
Initial Cost:	contact
Maintenance Cost:	8/round
Range:	touch
Preparation Time:	1
Area of Effect:	individual
Prerequisite:	mindlink, contact

Mindwiping is a crude form of psychic surgery which affects the subject's IQ. (It's like a temporary lobotomy.) The telepath systematically seals off portions of the subject's mind, making whatever knowledge was contained there inaccessible.

When a mindwipe is attempted, the victim saves vs. spells. If he succeeds, the mindwipe is thwarted for one round, but next round the psionicist can try again.

Each round of mindwiping has two important, immediate effects. First, it reduces the victim's Intelligence and Wisdom scores by 1

point. Second, it reduces his experience level or hit dice by 1 point.

These reductions have considerable impact. All characters may lose languages or proficiencies and their magical defense adjustment. Experience level and hit dice losses affect everything except hit points. The victim keeps all of his hit points regardless of what is wiped from his mind.

Intelligence and Wisdom losses affect wizards and clerics as if those losses were permanent. Clerics lose bonus spells, their chance of spell failure rises, and eventually they cannot cast spells. Wizards suffer reductions in their maximum spell level, their chance to learn spells, and their maximum spells per level.

When the number of available spells at a spell-level drops, a character must make an ability check before casting a spell of that level. Wizards roll an Intelligence check. Clerics roll a Wisdom check. Both use *current* scores. If the check succeeds, the character can cast the spell. If it fails, he has forgotten the spell and can't cast any spell that round.

Mindwipe only seals off information; it doesn't erase it. All of a character's lost Wisdom, Intelligence, and experience levels can be restored through psychic surgery (*q.v.*).

This power has no effect against creatures with neither stats nor hit dice.

Power Score—No saving throw allowed.

20—The power affects the psionicist instead of his intended victim.

Probe

Power Score: Wis −5
Initial Cost: contact
Maintenance Cost: 9/round
Range: 2 yards
Preparation Time: 0
Area of Effect: individual
Prerequisite: ESP, contact

A probe is similar to ESP (a telepathic devotion), but a probe allows psionicists to dig much deeper into a subject's subconscious. If the subject fails a saving throw vs. spells, then all his memories and knowledge are accessible to the prober—from memories deep below the surface to those still fresh in the subject's mind. The information gained is not necessarily true, but it is true as far as the subject knows.

The telepath can learn the answer to one question per round. DMs have some discretion in determining this rate. If the questions (or answers) become too complicated, each may take longer than one round to resolve.

Telepaths can probe a subject who is conscious, as well as one who resists. A probe can even be carried out in the midst of melee, provided the telepath can get close enough. If a probed wizard or cleric tries casting a spell, the telepath knows both that a spell is being cast and what the general effects of that spell are.

Power Score—Two questions may be asked per round.

20—The subject knows about the probe attempt and is not pleased.

Psychic Crush

Power Score: Wis −4
Initial Cost: 7
Maintenance Cost: na
Range: 50 yards
Preparation Time: 0
Area of Effect: individual
Prerequisites: mindlink

Psychic crush is one of the five telepathic attacks used to establish contact with another psionicist's mind. It is a massive assault upon all neurons in the brain, attempting to destroy all by a massive overload of signals.

If this attack is used against any mind that the psionicist has contacted, the victim must make a saving throw vs. paralyzation. Failure costs the target 1d8 hit points.

Power Score—The save automatically fails.

20—The victim is immune to further crushes by this psionicist for 24 hours.

Superior Invisibility

Power Score:	Int −5
Initial Cost:	contact
Maintenance Cost:	5/round/creature
Range:	100 yards
Preparation Time:	0
Area of Effect:	personal
Prerequisite:	mindlink, contact invisibility

Superior invisibility is like invisibility (see page 86), but it masks the character completely. The psionicist makes no sound and has no smell, though he can still be felt if touched. If he attacks someone physically, he automatically breaks contact with that character.

Power Score—Opponents affected by this power cannot detect the psionicist even if he touches or physically attacks them.

20—Everyone contacted becomes aware of the psionicist and his desire to be invisible.

Switch Personality

Power Score:	Con −4
Initial Cost:	contact +30
Maintenance Cost:	na
Range:	touch
Preparation Time:	3
Area of Effect:	individual
Prerequisite:	mindlink, contact

Some psionicists can literally put themselves in another man's (or woman's) shoes. This science allows the psionicist to switch his own mind with someone else's. In effect, they exchange bodies. The other person's mind inhabits the psionicist's body, while the psionicist's mind inhabits his subject's body. The switch is permanent, and lasts until the psionicist uses this power to reverse it.

Each character gains the other's physical attributes. However, both minds retain all their own knowledge and knowledge-based abili-

ties. For example, a telepath who switches minds with a 10th level fighter gains a body with that fighter's hit points and physical attributes (Strength, Constitution, and Dexterity). However, he retains his own THAC0, proficiencies, and so forth.

The switch takes a turn to complete, and the process is quite traumatic. At the end of the turn, both characters must make system shock saving throws using their new Constitution scores. A character who fails this roll lapses into a coma for 1-100 hours.

Bodies that have undergone a personality switch tend to degenerate. Both characters must make a Constitution ability check every day. If a check fails, the character loses one point of Constitution. If his Constitution drops to zero, he dies.

This Constitution loss is temporary, but it does not reverse itself until the personalities are restored to their proper bodies. At that point, both bodies recover one point of Constitution per day.

The psionicist does not lose his psionic powers if his Constitution drops below 11. However, if a power score is based on Constitution—like this power's score is—the score drops accordingly.

Power Score—System shock rolls automatically succeed, and the Constitution checks are made only once a week.

20—The psionicist lapses into a coma for 1d100 hours.

Tower of Iron Will

Power Score:	Wis −2
Initial Cost:	6
Maintenance Cost:	na
Range:	0
Preparation Time:	0
Area of Effect:	1 yard
Prerequisites:	none

Tower of iron will is one of the five telepathic defenses against unwanted contact. It relies only upon the superego to build an unassailable haven for the brain.

Like intellect fortress (a telepathic devotion), tower of iron will has an area of effect beyond the psionicist's mind. At 3 feet, it's very limited.

A psionicist can initiate one other psionic power during the round in which he uses the tower of iron will.

Power Score—The area of effect increases to 10 feet.

20—The psionicist is "lost inside himself" and cannot engage in psionic activity for 1d4 hours.

Telepathic Devotions

Attraction

Power Score:	Wis −4
Initial Cost:	contact
Maintenance Cost:	8/round
Range:	200 yards
Preparation Time:	0
Area of Effect:	individual
Prerequisite:	mindlink, contact

The opposite of aversion (see below), this power creates an overwhelming attraction to a particular person or thing—be it an item, creature, action, or event. A victim of this power will do whatever seems reasonable to get close to the object of his attraction.

The key word is "reasonable." The victim is completely fascinated, but he doesn't suffer from blind obsession. He won't leap into a fire or over a cliff, for example, or climb into the arms of a tarrasque (a bipedal killing machine). He can still recognize danger, but he will not flee unless the threat is strong and immediate. And if the danger is not apparent, (such as poison in a goblet of wine), the character could easily destroy himself in pursuit of the attraction.

Power Score—The effect borders on an obsession; the victim takes serious risks.

20—No additional effect.

Aversion

Power Score:	Wis −4
Initial Cost:	contact
Maintenance Cost:	8/turn
Range:	200 yards
Preparation Time:	0
Area of Effect:	individual
Prerequisite:	mindlink, contact

The victim of this power gains an aversion to a particular person, place, action, or event. He will do everything he can to avoid the object of his aversion. He will not approach within 20 yards, and if he is already within 20 yards, he will back away at the first opportunity.

The aversion is "planted" in the victim's brain for one turn. It cannot be maintained for another turn unless the psionicist maintains contact throughout that turn.

Power Score—The object of aversion affects the victim like a *fear* spell.

20—No additional effect.

Awe

Power Score:	Cha −2
Initial Cost:	contact
Maintenance Cost:	4/round
Range:	0
Preparation Time:	0
Area of Effect:	20 yards
Prerequisite:	mindlink, contact

A psionicist can use this power to make others hold him in awe. Each character contacted must make a saving throw vs. spells. Characters who fail are mentally cowed; they sense the telepath's "awesome might." They have no desire to serve or befriend him, but they won't attack him unless forced to do so. (For example, someone says, "You kill him or I'll kill you.") They'll do whatever they can to avoid angering or upsetting the psionicist. If possible, they'll avoid him altogether, and take the first opportunity to escape him.

Power Score—The save automatically fails.

20—All contacted characters view the psionicist as pathetic and ridiculous.

Conceal Thoughts

Power Score:	Wis
Initial Cost:	5
Maintenance Cost:	3/round
Range:	0
Preparation Time:	0
Area of Effect:	3 yards
Prerequisite:	none

This defensive devotion protects the psionicist against psionic or magical ESP, probes, mindlink, life detection, and other powers or spells which read or detect thoughts. To overcome thought concealment, an attacker must wage and win a psychic contest.

Power Score—All related psychic contests will automatically be won by the defender.

20—No additional effect.

Contact

Power Score:	Wis
Initial Cost:	varies
Maintenance Cost:	1/round
Range:	special
Preparation Time:	0
Area of Effect:	individual
Prerequisite:	none

Contact must be established before virtually any telepathic power can be used on another character or creature. It is just what its name implies—contact between the minds of the telepath and another character or creature. Contact does not allow communication by itself; it is merely the conduit for other telepathic exchanges.

Many telepathic powers list "contact" as their initial cost. That means contact must be established in a previous round before those powers can be used. As long as contact is maintained, the psionicist can use other powers which require it, and can even switch (using attraction and then mindlink on the same subject after contact was established, for example).

A psionicist can maintain contact with more than one subject at a time, but he must contact each one individually, and pay a maintenance cost for each use of the power. For example, if a psionicist wishes to inspire awe in two subjects, he must establish and maintain contact with each one separately.

Once contact is established, it costs 1 PSP per round to maintain. The psionicist can perform any other action while maintaining contact. *If he uses another telepathic power on the same subject while maintaining contact, the contact power is "free."* (The cost of maintaining contact is covered by the other power's cost.)

Establishing Contact: The initial cost of contact is based on the target's level or hit dice, as shown below.

1-5 levels or hit dice	3 PSPs/round
6-10 levels or hit dice	8 PSPs/round
11-15 levels or hit dice	13 PSPs/round
16-20 levels or hit dice	18 PSPs/round

A psionicist cannot contact a subject that he knows nothing about. In other words, he can't use this power to scan around and "see what's out there." He must either have his subject in sight or know specifically who or what he is looking for. He cannot, for example, try to contact any random orc which may or may not be standing behind a closed door. However, he can try to contact a *particular* orc which he has seen before.

If a psionicist fails to establish contact, he can try again the next round. Failure doesn't necessarily mean the target's mind cannot be contacted. Rather, it means the target has not been found yet. The psionicist can continue searching.

Several factors can make telepathic contact difficult to establish:

- how far the target is (distance)
- resistance by the target—especially if the target is a psionicist
- whether or not the target is an intelligent mammal

Each factor is described below.

Distance: The greater the distance between the two minds, the more difficult it usually becomes to make contact. If the psionicist can see the target—either with normal vision or by using psionic powers—distance is not a factor. If the psionicist cannot see his target, normal range modifiers apply. Simply knowing where to look does not constitute "seeing the target."

Separation Distance	Power Score Modifier
Line-of-sight	0
1 mile	−1
10 miles	−3
100 miles	−5
1,000 miles	−7
10,000 miles	−9

The maximum range for establishing contact is 10,000 miles when a psionicist cannot view his subject. Contact can be maintained across any distance, however; it is not broken if a contacted subject moves out of range. There is one exception: contact *cannot* be extended beyond a crystal sphere.

Resistance: An untrained character—i.e., a nonpsionicist—can actively resist intrusion, resulting in a −2 modifier to the psionicist's power score. To resist, the character fills his mind with a barrage of thoughts and emotions—much as a child avoids a lecture by plugging his ears and yelling. For example, a character might repeat a poem ad nauseam, or scream battle cries. However, even these efforts won't work unless 1) the character is specifically resisting psychic intrusion, and 2) resisting intrusion is his sole activity. If the character tries to fight or cast a spell, for example, his psychic defense has too many "holes" to be useful. Unless a wild talent knows a telepathic defense mode, he is as vulnerable to contact as any nonpsionicist.

Psionicists (and psionic creatures) are much better at resisting contact. In fact, this power won't work against them unless they intentionally drop their natural defenses. They must *allow* another psionicist to use contact on them, and can exclude some contacts while remaining open to others. If a psionicist resists, contact can only be established through mental attacks: psychic crush, ego whip, id insinuation, mind thrust, or psionic blast. See Chapter 2, "Psionic Combat," for more information.

Unusual Subjects: Contact can also be established with nonhuman minds, even plants. The further the subject is removed from mammals, the more difficult it becomes to establish contact. Modifiers that affect power scores are listed on the following page.

Probe: We have ways of making you think.

Life Order	Contact Score Modifier
Mammal (except marsupial)	−1
Marsupial	−2
Bird	−3
Reptile, amphibian	−4
Fish	−5
Arachnid, insect	−6
Monster	−7
Plant	−8

These modifiers are in addition to any distance modifiers that may apply. That means contacting a distant plant or monster is an uncertain proposition at best.

Breaking Contact: Contact is not severed until the psionicist breaks it off (fails to maintain it). If the person contacted is a psionicist, he may also do something to sever it. A psionicist often can eject an unwanted intruder (see "ejection").

Optional Rule: The minds of very intelligent beings are more difficult to latch onto. Increase the cost of contact by adding the creature's "# of Languages," minus two, as shown on Table 4 in Chapter 1 of the *Player's Handbook*. For example, a creature with Intelligence 17 knows six languages. The cost of contacting this creature's mind is increased by four.

Power Score—The contact is maintained for four rounds for free.

20—Further contact with this mind is impossible at this experience level.

Daydream

Power Score:	Wis
Initial Cost:	contact
Maintenance Cost:	3/round
Range:	unlimited
Preparation Time:	0
Area of Effect:	individual
Prerequisite:	mindlink, contact

By using this power, the telepath causes someone's mind to wander. This is only effective against characters with Intelligence 14 or less who are not concentrating hard on the task before them, but are just going about their business in a casual, relaxed manner.

Once affected, the daydreamer pays little attention to his surroundings, making it much easier for someone to pick his pocket, slip past him unobserved, or otherwise escape his notice. Thieves gain a 20% bonus on their pick pockets, move silently, and hide in shadows scores. Other characters can perform these tasks as an average 4th level thief (pick pockets, 45%; move silently, 33%; hide in shadows, 25%). The DM can assign chances for success to other types of skulking and skullduggery.

Power Score—Increase the bonuses to 30% for thieves and 5th level for others.

20—The victim realizes someone is toying with his mind.

Ego Whip

Power Score:	Wis −3
Initial Cost:	4
Maintenance Cost:	na
Range:	40/80/120 yards
Preparation Time:	0
Area of Effect:	individual
Prerequisites:	mindlink, contact

Ego whip is one of the five telepathic attacks used to establish contact with another psionicist's mind. (See Chapter 2.) The power assaults the victim's ego, leaving him with feelings of inferiority and worthlessness. If used against a contacted mind, the target is dazed for 1-4 rounds, during which all of his die rolls (psionic attacks, melee attacks, saving throws, etc.) are penalized five points (or 25%) and he cannot cast any spells above third level.

This power has three ranges: short, medium, and long. At medium range, the psionicist's power score is reduced by two. At long range, it is reduced by five.

Power Score—No additional effect.

20—No additional effect.

Empathy

Power Score:	Wis
Initial Cost:	contact (or 1*)
Maintenance Cost:	1/round
Range:	unlimited
Preparation Time:	0
Area of Effect:	20 ft. x 20 ft.
Prerequisites:	contact

By using empathy, a psionicist can sense the basic needs, drives, and/or emotions generated by any mind. Thirst, hunger, fear, fatigue, pain, rage, hatred, uncertainty, curiosity, hostility, friendliness, love—all these and more can be sensed.

*When used against nonpsionic targets, contact is not required.

Power Score—The subject of the emotion is revealed.

20—The target senses the attempt.

ESP

Power Score:	Wis −4
Initial Cost:	contact
Maintenance Cost:	6/round
Range:	unlimited
Preparation Time:	0
Area of Effect:	individual
Prerequisites:	contact

Extrasensory perception, or ESP, allows a psionicist to read someone else's mind (as the power is treated here). The telepath can only perceive surface or active thoughts. He cannot use ESP to explore someone's memories or delve into their subconscious.

Most intelligent creatures tend to think in words, so language *is* a barrier to understanding. Unintelligent creatures think in pictures. Magical thought, such as a wizard uses in casting spells, is also unintelligible. However, a telepath can easily recognize such thoughts as part of the spell-casting process.

Power Score—The first round of maintenance is free.

20—The psionicist develops a splitting headache and suffers a −1 penalty on all telepathic power scores for one hour.

False Sensory Input

Power Score:	Int −3
Initial Cost:	contact
Maintenance Cost:	4/round
Range:	unlimited
Preparation Time:	0
Area of Effect:	individual
Prerequisite:	mindlink, contact

This devotion allows the psionicist to falsify someone's sensory input—making the victim think that he sees, hears, smells, tastes, or feels something other than he really does. The falsehoods are somewhat limited. Nothing can be completely hidden or made to disappear, and everything must retain its general size and intensity.

For example, a human could be made to look like a dwarf, but not like a parrot. A slamming door could be made to sound like a thunderclap or a cough, but not like rustling paper. Oil could be made to taste like garlic, but not like water.

Power Score—Almost any false perception can be achieved.

20—The psionicist cannot see, hear, or otherwise sense the intended victim for 1d4 rounds, except psionically.

Id Insinuation

Power Score:	Wis −4
Initial Cost:	5
Maintenance Cost:	na
Range:	60/120/180 yards
Preparation Time:	0
Area of Effect:	individual
Prerequisites:	mindlink, contact

Id insinuation is one of the five telepathic attack modes. It seeks to unleash the uncontrolled subconscious of the defender, pitting it against his superego. The attack leaves the victim in a state of moral uproar.

Technically speaking, this power drives him nuts, at least temporarily. His id—the seat of primitive needs, animal drives, cruelty, and ferocity—seeks to launch him into a rage of violence and desire. His superego—the seat of moral conscience and the "civilized" part of his brain—struggles to maintain the upper hand. If this power is used against a contacted mind, the target can do nothing for 1d4 rounds.

Id insinuation has three ranges: short, medium, and long. At medium range, the telepath's power score is reduced by two. At long range, it is reduced by five.

Power Score—The victim's id overpowers his superego and he turns against his allies for 1d4 rounds.

20—The psionicist's id is unleashed; the resulting rage imposes a −1 penalty on all his attack rolls and power checks for one turn.

Identity Penetration

Power Score:	Wis −3
Initial Cost:	contact
Maintenance Cost:	6/round
Range:	unlimited
Preparation Time:	0
Area of Effect:	individual
Prerequisite:	contact

Identity penetration allows the user to determine the target's true identity in spite of polymorphs, illusions, disguises, etc.

Power Score—No additional effect.

20—Until he gains another level, the telepath cannot penetrate the identity of the current target.

Incarnation Awareness

Power Score:	Wis −4
Initial Cost:	contact
Maintenance Cost:	13/round
Range:	unlimited
Preparation Time:	0
Area of Effect:	individual
Prerequisite:	contact

By applying this power to another character, the psionicist can gain knowledge about past lives. One past life can be explored per round, starting with the most powerful personalities (usually these are also the most famous, but not always).

The psionicist also knows immediately how many times this particular personality has been killed and raised from the dead. It is up to the players to put this information to use.

Power Score—All past life information is gained in one quick mental blast.

20—Overwhelmed, the psionicist lapses into a trance until jolted or slapped—or for 1d4 hours, whichever comes first.

Inflict Pain

Power Score:	Con −4
Initial Cost:	contact
Maintenance Cost:	2/round
Range:	touch
Preparation Time:	1
Area of Effect:	individual
Prerequisite:	mindlink, contact

This is a particularly nasty form of torture. It causes no actual harm to the subject and leaves no marks or scars, but causes excruciating pain of any sort the telepath desires. Only evil characters can learn this power freely; others find their alignments twisting toward evil if they wish to inflict pain.

If the victim is an NPC who is being questioned, he must make a saving throw vs. paralyzation to withstand this agony.

If the psionicist finds a way to use this power in combat, the victim must also make a saving throw vs. paralyzation. Success means he grits his teeth and keeps on fighting. Failure means the pain imposes a four-point penalty on the character's attack rolls that round, or disrupts and ruins a spell.

Power Score—The pain is so excruciating that the victim passes out for 1d10 rounds.

20—This particular contact is broken.

Intellect Fortress

Power Score:	Wis −3
Initial Cost:	4
Maintenance Cost:	na
Range:	0
Preparation Time:	0
Area of Effect:	3-yd. radius
Prerequisites:	none

Intellect fortress is one of five telepathic defenses against unwanted contact. It calls forth the powers of the ego and superego to stop attacks.

Unlike most other defenses, intellect fortress has an area of effect beyond the psionicist's mind, offering protection to other minds within that radius. Every mind within that area defends against telepathic attack with the psionicist's intellect fortress power score.

A psionicist can initiate one other psionic power in the same round that he uses intellect fortress.

Power Score—No additional effect.

20—This defense falters and is not usable again for 1d4 rounds.

Invincible Foes

Power Score:	Wis −3
Initial Cost:	contact
Maintenance Cost:	5/round
Range:	unlimited
Preparation Time:	0
Area of Effect:	individual
Prerequisite:	mindlink, contact

The victim of this devotion believes that any blow struck against him will cripple or kill him. Even if the blow actually causes just one point of damage, the victim thinks he's dying, and that he can no longer fight. He falls to the ground in horrible pain.

A character who is struck while under the effect of this power won't recover until a turn later, even if the psionicist stops concentrating on him and turns his attention elsewhere. As long as the character was under this effect

when the blow was struck, he's out for 10 rounds.

Even if the victim of this power is never actually struck, his behavior is likely to change. Fully expecting the next blow to kill him, he may stop attacking and simply parry, or try to flee, or even surrender and beg for quarter. If the character has not been struck, however, the psionicist must keep renewing the power every round; otherwise future blows will affect him normally.

"Invincible foes" can also work in reverse. In other words, an attacker can be made to believe that every blow he strikes is fatal. The belief is strong enough to create an illusion: even if the attacker barely scratches his foe, he sees the "victim" lying down, mortally wounded. He will continue to imagine that opponent lying on the ground until the opponent attacks again (it doesn't matter whom he attacks; any attack breaks the illusion).

This reversal has several consequences. Characters who have been "killed"—i.e., struck—can simply walk away from the fight, leaving their "corpses" behind. Or they can move into position and attack again, gaining a +2 bonus to hit. After this happens three times, the affected character must make a saving throw vs. spells. If it fails, he becomes convinced that his foes are unkillable and reacts accordingly. (PCs, of course, are free to react as they see fit.)

Power Score—No other effect.

20—No other effect.

Invisibility

Power Score:	Int −5
Initial Cost:	contact
Maintenance Cost:	2/round/creature
Range:	100 yards
Preparation Time:	0
Area of Effect:	individual
Prerequisite:	mindlink, contact

Psionic invisibility differs significantly from magical invisibility. To make himself invisible,

the psionicist must individually contact each mind that he wants deceive. Once they are all contacted, he makes himself invisible to them only. He can still see himself, as can anyone who was not contacted. Only characters within 100 yards of the psionicist can be affected by this power.

Invisibility is a delusion affecting one or more select characters, not an illusion affecting everyone. The only real change occurs in the mind of the psionicist's targets. For this reason, the psionicist can make *anyone* invisible—not just himself. The "invisible" being must be approximately man-sized (or smaller), however.

The psionicist must make a separate power check for each delusion, and pay a separate maintenance cost for each. In this case, a delusion is one "invisible" creature or character, as perceived by one other character. For example, if the psionicist wants to make two things invisible to two people, he must make four separate power checks.

This power affects vision only. Observers may still be able to hear or smell "invisible" creatures.

Power Score—The power works like superior invisibility (a telepathic science).

20—All contacts are broken.

Life Detection

Power Score:	Int −2
Initial Cost:	3
Maintenance Cost:	3/round
Range:	100 yards
Preparation Time:	0
Area of Effect:	varies
Prerequisite:	none

A telepath can detect the presence of living, thinking creatures within a limited area. He must scan like radar. If he is scanning at short range, he can cover a large angle. At long range, the angle is significantly reduced. He can scan through 180 degrees to a range of 40 yards, 90 degrees to a range of 60 yards, or 30 degrees to a range of 100 yards.

One round of scanning will detect humans, demihumans, humanoids, mammals, and monsters with eight or more hit dice. A second round of scanning will detect birds, reptiles, amphibians, fish, and monsters with less than eight hit dice. In either case the character gets an accurate count of the creatures.

The DM should make this power check and keep the result secret from the player. If the psionicist doesn't detect anything, the player won't know whether that means there's nothing there, or the power didn't work. If the roll is 1, the psionicist gets faulty information. He detects what is there, but gets the numbers wrong by +/−50%.

Power Score—The psionicist can instantly detect everything within 100 yards, in every direction.

20—The telepath detects 1d6 creatures which aren't there.

Mental Barrier

Power Score:	Wis −2
Initial Cost:	3
Maintenance Cost:	na
Range:	0
Preparation Time:	0
Area of Effect:	personal
Prerequisites:	none

Mental barrier is one of five telepathic defenses against unwanted contact. It is a carefully built wall of thought repetition which exposes only one small area of the mind at a time.

A psionicist can initiate one other psionic power in the same round that he uses mental barrier.

Power Score—Contact during this round and the next is impossible.

20—The barrier fails, and the mental attempt disrupts any currently active powers.

Mind Bar

Power Score:	Int −2
Initial Cost:	6
Maintenance Cost:	4/round
Range:	0
Preparation Time:	0
Area of Effect:	personal
Prerequisite:	none

Mind bar is a magician's bane and the telepath's boon. It gives the psionicist 75% magic resistance against *charm, confusion, ESP, fear, feeblemind, magic jar, sleep,* and *suggestion* spells. It also offers complete protection against possession of any sort.

In addition, mind bar protects a psionicist against all telepathic powers, except the five contact-establishing attacks. No telepathic power can affect a barred mind unless the telepathic attack prevails in a psychic contest. (The defender uses mind bar.)

Power Score—The telepath gains a +5 bonus to his power score when defending in a psychic contest.

20—The telepath's saving throws vs. the spells listed above have a −4 penalty for one hour.

Mind Blank

Power Score:	Wis −7
Initial Cost:	0
Maintenance Cost:	0
Range:	0
Preparation Time:	0
Area of Effect:	personal
Prerequisites:	none

Mind blank is one of five telepathic defenses against unwanted contact. It attempts to hide the mind from attack, making its parts unidentifiable. This defense is particularly effective against a psionic blast and id insinuation. (See Chapter 2, "Psionic Combat," for details.)

Mind blank is unique. Unlike the other four defense modes, it costs nothing to maintain.

In fact, a character can still recover PSPs while using this power. That's because mind blank is almost instinctual; if a character knows it, it's nearly always active, even when he's sleeping or meditating. The power is inactive only if 1) the player announces it, or 2) the character uses another defense mode.

Even though mind blank has no PSP cost, it *still constitutes psionic activity*. If the power is active, a character is vulnerable to detection. He still may attract psionic feeders, or suffer some other unpleasant effect.

A psionicist can use one other psionic power (but not another defense mode) in the same round that he uses mind blank.

Power Score—No other effect.

20—The character cannot use mind blank for 1d4 hours.

Mind Thrust

Power Score:	Wis −2
Initial Cost:	2
Maintenance Cost:	na
Range:	30/60/90 yards
Preparation Time:	0
Area of Effect:	individual
Prerequisites:	mindlink, contact

Mind thrust is one of the five telepathic attacks used to establish contact with another psionicist's mind. It is a stabbing attack which seeks to "short" the synapses of the defender.

If the subject's mind has already been contacted, and he has psionic powers, then this power can do some damage. The subject loses the use of one power, chosen randomly, for 2d6 days. Beyond establishing contact, mind thrust has no effect on creatures or characters without psionic powers.

This power has three ranges: short, medium, and long. At medium range, the psionicist's power score is reduced by two. At long range, it's reduced by five.

Power Score—No other effect.

20—The telepath loses all tangents, but not contacts.

Phobia Amplification

Power Score:	Wis −2
Initial Cost:	contact
Maintenance Cost:	4/round
Range:	unlimited
Preparation Time:	0
Area of Effect:	individual
Prerequisite:	mindlink, contact

This power allows the psionicist to reach into someone's mind and discover his greatest fear, then amplify it to the point of irrationality. A victim who fails a saving throw vs. spells believes he is imminently threatened by the object of this fear, even if it is completely absurd. A character with a fear of falling, for example, is convinced he could pitch over a cliff at any moment—even while on an endless prairie—unless he stands absolutely still.

The reaction of the frightened character depends on the fear. He will defend himself if attacked (unless defending himself is somehow tied in to his phobia). A wizard may teleport away or use other spells to guarantee his safety. Other characters might freeze in place or flee for their lives. But all of their actions will be geared toward protecting against the fearsome object or situation.

This fear lasts as long as the psionicist maintains the effect. Once he stops, the fear fades back to its normal proportions, probably leaving the character slightly shaken and more than slightly chagrined.

Power Score—The target's save vs. spells automatically fails.

20—The subject has no detectable phobias.

Post-Hypnotic Suggestion

Power Score:	Int −3
Initial Cost:	contact
Maintenance Cost:	1/level or hit die
Range:	unlimited
Preparation Time:	0
Area of Effect:	1 creature
Prerequisites:	mindlink, contact

Any creature with an Intelligence between 7 and 17 can receive a post-hypnotic suggestion. (Very dim or very brilliant creatures are not susceptible.) The psionicist plants a suggestion of some reasonable course of action in the creature's subconscious, along with the situation that will trigger this action. When that situation arises, the DM makes a power check against the psionicist's post-hypnotic suggestion score, with a −1 penalty for each day that has passed since the suggestion was planted.

A "reasonable course of action" is one that does not violate the creature's alignment or class restrictions. It can be something that he would not normally do, but if it is too strange, he just won't do it.

The maintenance cost for this power is a one-time-only payment, made when the suggestion is implanted.

Power Score—The psionicist's power score is not reduced for the passage of time.

20—The intended victim is aware of the attempt.

Psionic Blast

Power Score:	Wis −5
Initial Cost:	10
Maintenance Cost:	na
Range:	20/40/60 yards
Preparation Time:	0
Area of Effect:	individual
Prerequisites:	mindlink

Psionic blast is a wave of brain force which can jolt a subject's mind like shocking news. This is one of the five telepathic attacks used to establish contact with another psionicist. (An illithid's mind blast is not the same.)

If this power is used against a mind that has already been contacted, the subject must save vs. death. Failure means he loses 80% of his remaining hit points, *but only in his mind*. The hit points are still there; he only thinks they're gone. He will pass out when the remaining 20% of his hit points are gone but won't die unless all of them are actually lost.

In any case, this effect wears off after six turns. At that time, an unconscious character awakens.

This power has three ranges: short, medium, and long. At medium range, the psionicist's power score is reduced by two. At long range, it is reduced by five.

Power Score—A victim who fails his save passes out for one turn.

20—No other effect.

Psychic Impersonation

Power Score:	Wis
Initial Cost:	10
Maintenance Cost:	3/hour
Range:	0
Preparation Time:	1 turn
Area of Effect:	personal
Prerequisite:	probe

This power enables a psionicist to mask his own aura and thought patterns, and make them match someone else's perfectly. To accomplish this, the psionicist must first probe the subject he wishes to impersonate.

Psychic impersonation does not alter any of the psionicist's other features. It only changes his identity to other creatures with psionic powers. Even then, a psychic contest with identity penetration or probe can penetrate the disguise.

While psychic impersonation is in effect, all of the user's psionic power scores are reduced by one.

Power Score—The disguise cannot be detected psionically and power scores are not decreased.

20—Until the psionicist reaches a new experience level, he cannot impersonate that subject.

Psychic Messenger

Power Score:	Con −4
Initial Cost:	4
Maintenance Cost:	3/round
Range:	200 miles
Preparation Time:	2
Area of Effect:	1 sq. yd.
Prerequisite:	none

This power allows a character to create an insubstantial, 3-D image of himself, which can appear anywhere within 200 miles and deliver a message. Everyone present can see and hear the messenger. Communication is one-way. The telepath has no idea what is happening around his messenger unless he's using some other power.

Power Score—The psionicist can make the messenger's appearance differ from his own.

20—No effect.

Repugnance

Power Score:	Wis −5
Initial Cost:	contact
Maintenance Cost:	8/round
Range:	200 yards
Preparation Time:	0
Area of Effect:	individual
Prerequisite:	mindlink, contact

With this power, a psionicist makes something—a particular person, place, or object—completely repugnant to another character. That character is overwhelmed with loathing for the "thing," and he will seek to destroy it as completely and quickly as possible.

If this destruction is strongly against the character's alignment (such as making a temple repugnant to its cleric), the character gets to make a saving throw vs. spells to shake off the effect.

Power Score—No save is allowed.

20—The victim is aware of the attempt.

Send Thoughts

Power Score:	Int −1
Initial Cost:	contact
Maintenance Cost:	2/round
Range:	unlimited
Preparation Time:	0
Area of Effect:	individual
Prerequisite:	contact

This is one-way communication, allowing the telepath to send his own thoughts to someone else's mind. The telepath can send information or simply distract the target.

If the target is a wizard casting a spell, he must make a saving throw vs. spells. The wizard applies a modifier to the save: the difference between his Intelligence and the telepath's power score. (If the wizard's Intelligence is higher, it's a bonus; if it's lower, it's a penalty.) If this save fails, the wizard's concentration is broken and the spell is spoiled.

If the target being distracted is someone involved in melee, he has a two-point penalty on all attack rolls (but not damage rolls).

Power Score—Wizards cannot make the saving throw.

20—If the receiver is a friend, he is distracted.

Sight Link

Power Score:	Con −3
Initial Cost:	contact
Maintenance Cost:	5/turn
Range:	unlimited
Preparation Time:	1
Area of Effect:	individual
Prerequisite:	mindlink, contact

Sight link allows the telepath to tap into another character's optical system. The telepath sees whatever his link sees. (His own vision is unaffected.) If the linked creature is subjected to a gaze attack, the telepath must make the appropriate saving throw or also be affected by the gaze.

Power Score—Sound link is also gained.
20—The psionicist is blinded for 1d4 hours.

Sound Link

Power Score:	Con −2
Initial Cost:	contact
Maintenance Cost:	4/turn
Range:	unlimited
Preparation Time:	1
Area of Effect:	individual
Prerequisite:	mindlink, contact

By means of a sound link, the telepath taps into the auditory system of another person or creature. He hears whatever his link hears. If the linked creature is subjected to an auditory attack (by sirens, shriekers, etc.), the telepath must make the appropriate saving throw or also be affected.

Power Score—Sight link is also gained.
20—The psionicist is deaf for 1d4 hours.

Synaptic Static

Power Score:	Int −4
Initial Cost:	15
Maintenance Cost:	10/round
Range:	0
Preparation Time:	0
Area of Effect:	20/50/90 yds
Prerequisite:	mindlink

Synaptic static interferes with all psionic activity within a given area. Even the psionicist is affected; when he creates static, he cannot use any other power simultaneously. However, he may also prevent others from using their powers. Anyone who tries to use a psionic power within the area of effect must fight the static's creator in a psychic contest. If an opponent succeeds, his power functions normally. If not, his power fails.

Exposure to synaptic static for more than five rounds will give anyone a splitting headache. This has no game effect, but it will make NPCs and animals irritable.

This power has three ranges: short, medium, and long. At medium range, the character's power score is reduced by two. At long range, it is reduced by five.

Power Score—The psionicist receives a +1 bonus in all psychic contests prompted by the current use of static.

20—The character has injured himself trying to create static. He immediately loses 1d20 PSPs and 1d6 hps.

Taste Link

Power Score:	Con −2
Initial Cost:	contact
Maintenance Cost:	4/turn
Range:	unlimited
Preparation Time:	1
Area of Effect:	individual
Prerequisite:	mindlink, contact

Could this be a dieter's dream? Taste link allows the telepath to tap into the flavor senses of another person or creature. The psionicist tastes whatever his link tastes.

If the linked creature takes poison orally, the telepath must make a saving throw vs. poison to avoid passing out and severing the link. The psionicist can't actually be poisoned this way, however.

Power Score—Scent link is also gained (not a defined power).

20—The psionicist has a bitter taste in his mouth, but no other effect occurs.

Telempathic Projection

Power Score:	Wis −2
Initial Cost:	contact
Maintenance Cost:	4/round
Range:	unlimited
Preparation Time:	1
Area of Effect:	10 yard diam
Prerequisite:	mindlink, contact

Telempathic projection allows the user to send emotions to everyone who has been contacted within a common 10-yard diameter. This power cannot radically change a character's emotional state, however. A character who is very angry could be made only slightly

angry, for example, but not happy. Empathic changes are a matter of degrees, no more.

Power Score—Emotions can be drastically altered (love to hatred, etc.) while this power is maintained.

20—All affected characters experience strong negative emotions toward the psionicist for 1d6 rounds.

Thought Shield

Power Score:	Wis −3
Initial Cost:	1
Maintenance Cost:	na
Range:	0
Preparation Time:	0
Area of Effect:	personal
Prerequisites:	none

Thought shield is one of five telepathic defenses against unwanted contact. It clouds the mind so as to hide first one part, then another.

A psionicist can initiate one other psionic power during the same round in which he uses thought shield.

Power Score—No other effect.

20—No other effect.

Truthear

Power Score:	Wis
Initial Cost:	4
Maintenance Cost:	2/round
Range:	0
Preparation Time:	0
Area of Effect:	hearing
Prerequisite:	mindlink

When a psionicist uses truthear, he can tell whether other people intentionally lie. He does not hear their words translated into truth; he merely knows whether or not speakers believe they are lying.

Power Score—The psionicist recognizes a falsehood even when the speaker does not.

20—The psionicist can't use this power effectively against this subject for 1d6 days.

Metapsionics

Metapsionic Sciences

Appraise

Power Score:	Int −4
Initial Cost:	14
Maintenance Cost:	na
Range:	0
Preparation Time:	0
Area of Effect:	personal
Prerequisites:	none

With this power, a psionicist can determine the likelihood that a specific course of action will succeed. He focuses on a course of action and examines the possibilities. He assigns probabilities. Then he mentally processes enormous calculations to arrive at an overall probability of success.

In game play, the character must first pass a power check. If he does, the DM must reveal the percentage chance for the plan or action's success. Exact odds may be difficult or impossible to determine, but the DM should provide his most accurate, honest appraisal.

No one, not even a psionicist, can foresee the future with assured accuracy. Like precognition, the success of this power depends on how closely the characters adhere to their plans. Do they act as they intended? React as they intended? What factors did they fail to foresee? Every deviation steers events away from the predicted path. If this power is used, the DM should give the best answer he can, based on information the characters have. Factors they don't know about, and therefore can't take into account while forming a plan, can change things dramatically.

Power Score—The player is allowed to re-roll any three die rolls to help make his character's forecast more accurate.

20—The psionicist can't use this power successfully again for 1d4 days.

Aura Alteration

Power Score:	Wis −4
Initial Cost:	10
Maintenance Cost:	na
Range:	touch
Preparation Time:	5
Area of Effect:	individual
Prerequisites:	psychic surgery, 5th level

With aura alteration, a psionicist can temporarily disguise a person's alignment, disguise his level, or remove aura afflictions like curses, geases, and quests.

Disguising a character's alignment or level is the easiest to do. The disguise is temporary, lasting only 1-6 hours. It has no effect on the character's real alignment or class, but a psionicist with aura sight will be fooled by the fake aura.

Because curses, geases, and quests are imprinted on the character's aura, they can be removed with this power. A psionicist who tries this suffers a −6 penalty to his power score and must expend 20 PSPs instead of 10. If the die roll is 1, the psionicist's patient must make a saving throw vs. spells to avoid losing one experience level. (A slip of the psychic scalpel can close off vital parts of the brain.)

Power Score—No other effect.

20—The full PSP cost of the power must be paid despite the lack of success, and this psionicist cannot alter this aura until he achieves a higher experience level.

Empower

Power Score:	Wis −12
Initial Cost:	varies
Maintenance Cost:	na
Range:	touch
Preparation Time:	0
Area of Effect:	1 item
Prerequisites:	10th level

This is not a tool for weak or inexperienced characters. Empower allows a psionicist to im-

bue an item with rudimentary intelligence and psionic ability. The process, which requires extraordinary time and effort, is described below.

Item Requirements. An item must meet two requirements before it can be empowered. First, it must be of exceptional quality—worth 250% to 500% of the normal cost for an item of its type. Second, it must be new. The process of empowering must begin within 48 hours after the item is manufactured. If it is delayed longer, the item cannot be empowered. (If the psionicist still tries, he automatically fails Step One below, expending 50 PSPs.) If the item meets these two requirements, the psionicist can begin the empowerment.

Step One. At the start of each day, the psionicist must first prepare the item to receive psionic power. This costs 50 PSPs and requires a power check. If this check fails, the day is wasted; no further progress can be made until the next day.

Step Two. If the item has been prepared, the psionicist can give it access to a discipline. It can have access to only one discipline, never more, and the psionicist himself must have access to it. This step costs 100 PSPs and requires a power check.

Step Three. The psionicist can attempt to empower the item with any single power he knows within the chosen discipline. (The item must have been properly prepared on the same day.) The psionicist must make two successful power checks: first, a check for the chosen power (using the appropriate power score), and second, another empower check. If both checks succeed, the item has that psionic power, with a score two points below the psionicist's. If Step Three is successful, the psionicist expends another 100 PSPs. (Failure means he expends half that amount, as usual.)

Step Four. The psionicist can imbue the item with other powers by repeating Step Three. The item can acquire *one* power per day, provided it has been properly prepared (see Step One).

Step Five. When the item has acquired all the powers which the psionicist intends to give

it, the psionicist can seal those powers within the item. To do this, he must prepare the item one more time (expending 50 PSPs), and make an endowment power check one last time. If the item is sealed successfully, it can never gain any additional powers—but it can't lose them, either. An item that has not been sealed will lose one power per month until it is just a normal object again.

An empowered object has 8 PSPs per devotion and 12 per science. It has Intelligence equal to its maker's Intelligence minus 1d6 points, with a minimum of 12. Its ego is 2 points per devotion and 3 points per science. Unless it was empowered with another telepathic power, it communicates as indicated on Table 113, "Weapon Intelligence and Capabilities" in the *Dungeon Master's Guide* (p. 186, A&D® 2nd Edition). Its alignment matches its creator's. The weapon has its own personality, however, and like all intelligent weapons, it will try to assert its independence at every opportunity.

The empowering process must be unbroken. *If a day passes in which the psionicist does not at least try to prepare the object, it is finished as is.* He cannot even try to seal the powers; they will wear off over the course of time.

Power Score—No other effect.

20—If three 20's are rolled during the empowering process, the item is a complete and utter failure.

Psychic Clone

Power Score:	Wis −8
Initial Cost:	50
Maintenance Cost:	5/round
Range:	60 feet
Preparation Time:	10 rounds
Area of Effect:	special
Prerequisites:	clairaudience, clairvoyance, psychic messenger, 5th level

When this power is initiated, a clone of the psionicist steps out of his body. It is in every

way identical to the original form, except that it has no substance. The psionicist can see and hear what the clone sees and hears. The clone will do anything the psionicist wants it to (as if it were actually him). Furthermore, the psionicist's psyche goes with the clone, thus enabling it to perform all of his psionic powers.

This power has a serious drawback. As long as the clone exists, the psionicist himself is practically a turnip. He retains only three senses: smell, taste, and touch. He cannot move, see, or hear. All his psionic powers are transferred to the clone. In effect, the immobile character is no longer a psionicist; not even psionic sense will reveal his true nature. He can be slain without any combat rolls if an opponent wishes to do so.

The clone can travel up to 60 feet from the psionicist. It can go anywhere the psionicist himself could go. For example, it can walk down a corridor, walk across acid (the clone has no substance and cannot be hurt), and swim (provided the psionicist can). Because the psionicist could walk through an unlocked door, so can the clone—although the clone passes through like a ghost. However, a clone cannot travel through walls or walk on water, because the psionicist could not either.

The clone is impervious to all forms of attack and damage except psionic or mental attack (which will affect the psionicist).

Power Score—The clone can travel through walls and other solid objects.

20—No other effect.

Psychic Surgery

Power Score:	Wis −5
Initial Cost:	contact
Maintenance Cost:	10/turn
Range:	touch
Preparation Time:	10
Area of Effect:	individual
Prerequisite:	telepathy, contact

Psychic surgery allows a telepath to repair psychic damage. He can even operate on himself if need be, though his power score is reduced by 5 in this case. Phobias, aversions, idiocy, comas, seizures—all these psychic ailments can be treated and cured, as well as several others. Curses or magical conditions—such as geases and charms—cannot be cured.

This power cannot cure possession, either. However, psychic surgery *can* confirm that the problem really is possession, and *can force the possessing entity into psionic combat* if the surgeon desires. This may be risky, since creatures capable of possession are often quite powerful and the psionicist cannot ascertain their power beforehand. On the other hand, psychic surgery could cure the possession indirectly by forcing a psionically weak entity to flee rather than face combat.

Most psychic ailments can be cured in one turn or less. However, if the psionicist's power check result equals 1 or 2, the problem is particularly tricky and requires another turn to repair. If the power check fails, the problem is too great for the psionicist to fix. He can try again after gaining another experience level.

Special Operations: Psychic surgery has two special uses. First, the surgeon can use this power to help nonpsionicists unleash their wild powers. If the psionicist performs this kind of operation successfully, the patient gains a −2 bonus to his wild talent roll. (See Chapter 1.)

The second operation can make the effect of any power in the telepathy discipline permanent with no maintenance cost. The patient is rarely grateful, because the *power* is not bestowed on the subject, only its effect. In this way, a person can be permanently dominated or fate-linked, for example. The following restrictions apply:

1) The power must be maintainable (i.e., it must have a maintenance cost).
2) The power must have a range of other than zero.
3) The surgeon must know the power and use it successfully on the patient.

4) A psionicist cannot use this type of surgery on himself or on another psionicist. If he tries, nothing happens.

5) At most, only one power can made permanent per turn. If the result of the power check is 1 or 2, the procedure takes two turns instead of one.

This procedure can also be reversed; i.e., psychic surgery can be used to remove a permanently implanted telepathic effect.

Power Score—The surgery takes only 5 rounds per "implanted" power.

20—The surgeon cannot use this power successfully again for 1d4 days.

Split Personality

Power Score:	Wis −5
Initial Cost:	40
Maintenance Cost:	6/round
Range:	0
Preparation Time:	1
Area of Effect:	personal
Prerequisites:	psychic surgery, 10th level

This is not a psychosis; it's the power to divide one's mind into two independent parts. Each part functions in complete autonomy, like two characters in one body. Both parts communicate fully. Both can use psionic powers, even at the same time. That means a split personality can use twice as many psionic powers per round. (The character's total number of PSPs remains the same, however, with both personalities drawing from it.) Alternately, one personality can use psionic powers while the other does something else—e.g., converse, ponder a puzzle, or control the body in melee. Thus, split personality allows a character to fight physically and psionically at the same time.

Mental attacks directed against the psionicist affect only half of the mind. Contact must be established separately with each half. If one half is destroyed, controlled, or subdued somehow, the other half can continue fighting

independently and retains control of the body.

Before he attempts to make his personality whole again, the psionicist must make a saving throw vs. paralyzation if any of the following is true: 1) he does not control both portions of his mind, 2) he has unrepaired psychic damage, or 3) is suffering unwanted contact. A successful save means that his mind returns to complete health and throws off all undesired influences. Failure means that the afflicted portion of his mind becomes dominant and he passes out for 1d6 turns, but regains consciousness free of undesired influences.

Power Score—The mind splits into three parts instead of two.

20—The character passes out for 1d6 turns.

Ultrablast

Power Score:	Wis −10
Initial Cost:	75
Maintenance Cost:	0
Range:	0
Preparation Time:	3
Area of Effect:	50' radius
Prerequisites:	10th level

A character using psionic ultrablast can overwhelm and damage nearby psyches. To do this, he casts thought waves in all directions. In laymen's terms, the psionicist "grumbles" psychically for three rounds. Then his consciousness bursts forth and a horrid, psychic scream penetrates all minds within 50 feet. Victims may never be the same again.

All characters within 50 feet of the psionic ultrablast must save vs. paralyzation. Failure means they pass out for 2d6 turns. Those who pass out must immediately save vs. paralyzation again. If they fail a second time, they lose all psionic power. Only psychic surgery can help them recover this loss.

Although the blast does not affect the initiator, the risks are great. If the power check fails, he becomes comatose for 1d10 days. Some characters may think he's dead.

Power Score—Creatures of 3 hit dice or less die if they fail their save.

20—The initiator must save vs. paralyzation or die. If he lives, he loses the use of all his psionic powers for 2d6 days.

Metapsionic Devotions

Cannibalize

Power Score:	Con
Initial Cost:	0
Maintenance Cost:	na
Range:	0
Preparation Time:	0
Area of Effect:	personal
Prerequisites:	5th level

This power allows the character to cannibalize his own body for extra PSPs. When it is used, the character can take any number of Constitution points and convert them directly to PSPs at a ratio of 1:8. (One Constitution point becomes eight psionic strength points.) The psionicist can use these points anytime, as if they were part of his total.

The Constitution reduction is not permanent, but it *is* debilitating and long-lasting. The character immediately loses bonus hit points. His system shock and resurrection survival chances are reduced. Most importantly, all of his psionic power scores which are based on Constitution are reduced by the appropriate amount.

A psionicist can recover one cannibalized point of Constitution per week of rest. Rest means staying quietly at home (safely indoors). Adventuring is not allowed.

Power Score—The psionicist gains 8 PSPs without reducing his Constitution.

20—The character loses 1d4 Constitution points, but can regain them by resting.

Convergence

Power Score:	Wis
Initial Cost:	8
Maintenance Cost:	0
Range:	10 yards
Preparation Time:	1
Area of Effect:	10 yards
Prerequisites:	contact, 4th level

When psionicists put their heads together, the results can be impressive. Convergence allows psionicists to link their minds into one synergetic being—an entity more powerful than the sum of the individual parts.

There is no limit to the number of psionicists who join minds. Each participating psionicist must know the convergence power, however, and each must make a successful power check in the same round. Then they are linked. All their PSPs flow into a single pool, from which each draws his strength. If one participant knows a power, now anyone in the group can use it.

Each participant can use psionic powers at the normal rate per turn: one defense and one other power per round. If the group is attacked psionically, the attack must overcome *every* working defense. If it does, the attack affects every character in the convergence, or as many as possible.

When the convergence is discontinued, PSPs that remain in the pool are evenly divided among all the participants. Fractions are rounded down, and no individual can exceed his usual maximum (extra points are lost).

Power Score—No other effect.

20—The participant loses 1d20 PSPs.

Enhancement

Power Score:	Wis −3
Initial Cost:	30
Maintenance Cost:	8/round
Range:	0
Preparation Time:	5
Area of Effect:	personal
Prerequisites:	6th level

This power yields the same results as the Meditative Focus proficiency, in less time. When a psionicist learns this power, he selects one discipline to enhance. As long as he maintains the enhancement power, all of his power scores within the chosen discipline are increased by two. At the same time, all other power scores are reduced by one.

Power Score—Other scores are not reduced.

20—All power scores in the chosen discipline are reduced by one for 24 hours.

Gird

Power Score:	Int −3
Initial Cost:	0
Maintenance Cost:	2 × maintenance
Range:	0
Preparation Time:	0
Area of Effect:	personal
Prerequisites:	3rd level

Each time a psionicist girds another power, he can maintain that power automatically—i.e., without mental concentration. Thus, a psionicist who is maintaining only girded powers can sleep without disrupting those powers.

To use gird, the psionicist must first initiate and maintain the power he intends to affect. Then he must make a girding power check. If he succeeds, he automatically pays twice the normal maintenance cost for the girded power—or a minimum of 1 PSP per hour. To remove the girding, he must consciously decide to do so (no power check is required). Otherwise, the girding remains in place until the psionicist runs out of PSPs. That means a psionicist who's unconscious or sleeping could awaken to find all his psionic strength girded away. If the psionicist wishes to reestablish a gird that he discontinued, he must make a new power check.

Power Score—No other effect.

20—The gird attempt disrupts the power.

Intensify

Power Score:	Affected −3
Initial Cost:	5/increase
Maintenance Cost:	1/round
Range:	0
Preparation Time:	1/increase
Area of Effect:	personal
Prerequisites:	3rd level

Intensify allows the psionicist to improve either his Constitution, his Intelligence, or his Wisdom for psionic applications. To improve one—for psionic purposes only—he must weaken the other two—for *all* purposes. Each point of increase in the targeted ability decreases the other two abilities by the same amount. In addition, each point of increase costs 5 PSPs.

For example, Zenita is a psionicist with Con 15, Int 16, and Wis 17. She wants to intensify her Intelligence by 4 points. To do so, she must spend 20 PSPs initially (5 PSPs for each bonus point of Intelligence). Her Intelligence is raised 4 points to 20. Meanwhile, her Constitution and Wisdom scores drop 4 points (to 11 and 13, respectively). The increase in Intelligence affects psionic powers only. The drop in Constitution and Wisdom affects everything applicable except psionic strength points: psionic power scores, hps, system shock rolls, saving throws, spell bonuses, spell failure, etc.

A psionicist can raise an ability score to a maximum of 25, provided he has enough PSPs and no other score is reduced below zero.

Empower: The sword can be mightier than the pen.

Power Score—The character's ability is raised to the level he intended, but the cost of this power is reduced to 3 PSPs per increased point.

20—The psionicist must make a system shock roll or the ability he intended to boost decreases by 1 point for 24 hours.

Magnify

Power Score:	Wis −5
Initial Cost:	25 × magnification
Maintenance Cost:	magnification/round
Range:	0
Preparation Time:	5
Area of Effect:	personal
Prerequisites:	6th level

Magnify allows the psionicist to magnify the effects of another power in all conceivable ways—e.g., double damage, double range, double modifiers, and so on. However, the affected power's initial cost is proportionately magnified, as is its maintenance cost.

The psionicist initiates the magnify power first. At the same time, he must designate which power he intends to improve. Unless he maintains the magnification, he must immediately use the power he wishes to improve (in the same round). Otherwise he can maintain the magnification until he uses the affected power (a costly endeavor). Once the power has been performed, magnify must be reinitiated to perform again.

The amount of magnification depends upon the psionicist's level, as follows:

Levels 6-10	× 2
Levels 11-15	× 3
Levels 16-20	× 4

Power Score—The magnification factor is one greater, with no additional cost.

20—The affected power becomes inoperative for a day.

Martial Trance

Power Score:	Wis −3
Initial Cost:	7
Maintenance Cost:	0 (free)
Range:	0
Preparation Time:	1
Area of Effect:	personal
Prerequisite:	3rd level

In some situations, the psionicist may find it useful to enter a trance before engaging in psionic combat. This trance focuses the character's complete attention on his psionic activity and tunes out all other distractions. While in the trance, he gains a +1 bonus on all of his Telepathy scores (all powers in the discipline).

The martial trance ends whenever the character chooses to end it. It is not deep; the character is brought out of it by any blow, shake, or slap. His attention is completely occupied, so any melee attack against him hits automatically and causes maximum damage.

Power Score—He manages to maintain enough awareness to dodge melee attacks.

20—No other effect.

Prolong

Power Score:	Con −4
Initial Cost:	5
Maintenance Cost:	2/round
Range:	0
Preparation Time:	0
Area of Effect:	personal
Prerequisite:	4th level

When this power is in effect, the range of all powers is increased by 50%, as is the radius of their areas of effect. This has no effect on powers with a range of zero or individual, nor does it alter personal, or single-item areas of effect. It does alter powers that affect a quantity of stuff; prolonged disintegration, for example, destroys up to 12 cubic feet of material instead of 8.

Power Score—The increase is 100%.

20—All ranges/areas of effect are halved for 1d4 hours.

Psionic Inflation

Power Score:	Wis −5
Initial Cost:	20
Maintenance Cost:	3/round
Range:	0
Preparation Time:	1
Area of Effect:	100-foot radius
Prerequisites:	3rd level

When a psionicist invokes this power, he sends out a powerful ring of psionic noise (extending to 100 feet). All psionic activity within this area requires twice the normal initial cost and maintenance. The initiating psionicist is not affected; the noise actually begins about an inch beyond his aura, creating a bubble of relative quiet around him.

Other psionicists in the area of effect will not realize anything is wrong until they have actually used a power. If they are maintaining a power, they discover the inflated rate after paying twice the normal maintenance cost.

If two psionicists initiate psionic inflation in the same area, the psionicists must conduct a psychic contest. The loser's psionic inflation ceases. If both characters fail, then both cease their power maintenance. Reroll ties.

Power Score—All psionic activity within the area requires three times the normal initial cost and maintenance.

20—The psionicist cannot recover PSPs for two hours.

Psionic Sense

Power Score:	Wis −3
Initial Cost:	4
Maintenance Cost:	1/round
Range:	0
Preparation Time:	0
Area of Effect:	200-yard radius
Prerequisites:	telepathy

With psionic sense, a character can detect psionic activity anywhere within 200 yards. Any expenditure of PSPs constitutes psionic activity, even if it is only to maintain a power. Use of the mind blank power is psionic activity, too, even though it expends no PSPs.

When the character makes his first successful power check, he learns whether or not someone—or something—is psionically active within range. If the psionicist makes a another successful power check in the following round, he also learns 1) how many PSPs are being spent, and 2) where the psionic activity is occuring (direction and distance). If psionic activity is occurring in more than one place, the psionicist gets a fix on all of it within 200 yards.

Power Score—Second-round information is gained in the first round.

20—This power cannot be used effectively for one turn.

Psychic Drain

Power Score:	Wis −6
Initial Cost:	10/person + contact
Maintenance Cost:	none
Range:	30 yards
Preparation Time:	0
Area of Effect:	up to 6 minds
Prerequisites:	telepathy, contact, 6th level

Psychic drain enables the psionicist to tap into the personal, psychic energy of other people to augment his own psionic strength. Up to six people can be tapped at one time.

Each subject, who is often called a *host*, must first be asleep. Next, the psionicist must make contact with the person's mind. Then he expends another 10 PSPs and makes a psychic drain power check. If he succeeds, the host falls into a trance which lasts 4-9 (1d6 + 3) hours. The character can be awakened with some difficulty before then, but he'll be groggy and disoriented for another hour.

While the host is in the trance, the psionicist can siphon psychic energy. Just as a vampire draws blood to grow strong, the psionicist

drains Wisdom, Intelligence, and Constitution points. He can drain as much as he desires. For every ability point the psionicist drains, he gains 10 PSPs.

Any PSPs gained cannot be banked (added to the psionicist's total). They cannot be siphoned any faster than they are used. In other words, when the psionicist expends PSPs, he automatically draws these points from his host(s)—unless he specifies otherwise. The psionicist must remain within range of the entranced characters in order to draw strength points from them.

If he exercises moderation, the psionicist does not harm his hosts. A host only begins to suffer ill effects when he loses more than 50% of his psionic potential. (Potential depends on Wisdom, Intelligence, and Constitution scores. See "Psionic Strength Points" in Chapter 1.) The table below shows the effects of excessive depletion. Psychic surgery can correct these problems.

Potential Lost	Effect on host
51-60%	Temporary amnesia (2-12 weeks)
61-70%	Permanent amnesia
71-80%	Intelligence reduced to 4
81-90%	Intelligence reduced to 4; put in coma for 1-12 days, must make system shock roll every day or die
91-100%	Save vs. death or die; if subject lives, Intelligence, Wisdom, and Constitution each reduced to 3, permanently

Power Score—The psionicist does not harm the subject(s) this time, regardless of how much he drains.

20—Contact broken.

Receptacle

Power Score:	Wis −5
Initial Cost:	0
Maintenance Cost:	0
Range:	touch
Preparation Time:	1 round/point
Area of Effect:	one item
Prerequisites:	empower or valuable gem

This power allows a psionicist to store psionic energy in a special receptacle. The psionicist can draw upon the energy later to fuel his other psionic powers. He cannot use these points when his total pool of psionic strength is at its maximum. However, he can keep the stored PSPs on hand until he's running low on psionic energy, and then use them immediately. (It's like storing a pint of your own blood at a hospital. With a little time, your body replaces the pint. Later, if you should lose blood in an accident or operation, you can use the stored blood to recover the loss quickly.)

Before powers can be stored, a receptacle must be prepared. Two types of containers are appropriate: a vessel prepared with empower (a metapsionic science), or a valuable gem that has been specially prepared using the receptacle power.

Empowered Vessel. Any vessel can serve as a receptacle for psionic energy if it is empowered first. The psionicist must perform the initial preparation and final sealing described earlier under "empower." He does not do anything further; the vessel needs no additional powers. It can hold PSPs equal to his psionic potential, multiplied by his experience level.

Valuable Gem. A gem can hold 1 PSP for every 100 gold pieces of its worth, rounded down. For example, a gem worth 650 gold pieces can hold 6 PSPs, and a gem worth 1,000 gold pieces can hold 10 PSPs. The gem still requires preparation, however. To do this, the psionicist must slowly fill the gem with PSPs—1 per turn—until the gem reaches maximum capacity ($1/100$ of its value). The psioni-

cist can do nothing else while filling the gem. When the task is complete, the psionicist must make a power check. If he fails, only one-half of the gem's capacity is useable.

Storing Points. Using his receptacle power, he can automatically place 1 PSP into a properly prepared container per round. When he is finished, the psionicist must make a receptacle power check. If it succeeds, all is well; if it fails, only half the points he expended are stored in the receptacle, while the rest are merely spent.

Using Stored Points. The psionicist can retrieve stored points automatically. The receptacle must be in contact with his flesh. He can never retrieve more points than the receptacle currently holds, *nor can he retrieve so many that it raises his current psionic point total above his maximum.* No matter how many receptacles he has, a psionicist can never store more PSPs than his maximum total. (For example, if his usual maximum is 100 PSPs, he can store no more than 100.) Only the psionicist who placed the points in the item can use them.

The danger of this power is receptacle loss. If the receptacle is damaged or destroyed, its contents (PSPs) are instantly subtracted from the psionicist's total possible points. This loss is temporary, but until the psionicist is once again back up to his full PSP score he recovers PSPs only half as fast as normal.

Power Score—No other effect.

20—No other effect.

Retrospection

Power Score:	Wis −4
Initial Cost:	120
Maintenance Cost:	na
Range:	0
Preparation Time:	10
Area of Effect:	personal
Prerequisites:	convergence, 7th level

Retrospection is a kind of psionic seance. It allows psionicists to delve into the past and lo-cate memories that have been loosed from other minds. A psionicist must join at least two other psionicists in a convergence before he can use this power. He—or one of the other participants in the convergence—then poses a question regarding a specific event in the past. To find the answer, the psionicist must make a successful power check.

When retrospection succeeds, the characters tap into a universal, pervasive memory. They have access to any information that ever existed in anyone's memory regarding the incident they are investigating. The amount of detail that comes to mind depends on power check results:

1	extremely vague and fragmentary
2	vague or incomplete
3-5	complete but not very specific
6+	reasonably complete and specific

Memories bear the mark of the personalities who created them. The DM should role-play the memories accordingly, not just recite information. If the psionicists' alignments differ significantly from the memories' alignments, reaction rolls are in order. Memories can be polite and helpful, or they can be cantankerous and downright rude. Memories which have lain undisturbed for centuries may be angered by the intrusion, or they may be delighted for the chance to air themselves out and bring the truth to light.

Power Score—No other effect.

20—No other effect.

Splice

Power Score:	Int −(2 × # spliced)
Initial Cost:	5 × # spliced
Maintenance Cost:	# spliced/round
Range:	0
Preparation Time:	# spliced
Area of Effect:	personal
Prerequisites:	2+ level (see below)

Splicing psionic powers is tremendously useful. In effect, the psionicist is splicing to-

gether two or more separate powers into one psionic release. This is very difficult, however, and it requires great precision. The more powers the psionicist attempts to splice, the more likely he is to fail.

First, the character must make a successful splice check. His power score is decreased 2 points for each power being spliced. For example, if he is splicing two powers, his score equals Intelligence −4. The initial cost of this endeavor is 5 PSPs for every power being spliced.

If the character passes this first power check, he must then initiate each spliced power in succession—without interruption. He does not have to make a separate splicing check for each of these powers, but he still pays their initial costs. Furthermore, each spliced power has absolutely no effect at this time.

Once all the powers have been initiated, the psionicist must make a second splice check. (His power score is still reduced two points for each power being spliced.) If he fails this check, all his efforts are lost; the PSPs he spent are gone, and none of the powers works. If the power check succeeds, the psionicist can maintain the splice by expending 1 PSP per spliced power per round.

At any later time (during which the splice has been maintained), the psionicist can unleash the spliced series of powers. In effect, he performs all of the spliced powers simultaneously—or with split second separations if desired. Success is not automatic. The psionicist must perform the individual power checks for these spliced powers when he releases them. He does not have to pay their initial costs again, however.

The maximum number of powers that a psionicist can splice equals his experience level. For example, a 2nd level psionicist can splice up to two powers, and a 3rd level psionicist can splice up to three. A complex splice is a long shot at best, however. As noted above, a psionicist's power score decreases two points

for every power he attempts to splice. That means a character who attempts a five-power splice has a score of Int −10.

Many psionicists use splice to combine just two powers: contact, and another power that requires contact. This is the most common combination.

Power Score—The character receives a +2 bonus on power checks when unleashing the spliced powers.

20—No other effect.

Stasis Field

Power Score:	Con −3
Initial Cost:	20
Maintenance Cost:	20/round or 1/round
Range:	0
Preparation Time:	3
Area of Effect:	max. 1 yard/level
Prerequisites:	8th level

A stasis field is a region in which time slows to a crawl and energy is reduced to a meaningless fizzle. When created, the stasis field surrounds the psionicist like a bubble. It can have any radius he desires, up to a maximum of 1 yard per each level of his experience. For example, a 10th level psionicist can create a field with up to a 10-yard radius.

From the outside, the stasis field looks like a slightly shimmering, completely smooth silver globe. When something presses against the edge, it gives slight resistance, but the object passes through.

Inside the field, all is murky and dim. Light filters through from the outside, but it turns gray. A light source inside is only about one-fourth as bright as usual.

Time is 60 times slower in a stasis field. That is, for every round (or minute) that passes inside, an hour elapses outside. (This dilation is not apparent to those inside the field, however.) Each round the psionicist spends inside, he must pay 20 points to maintain the stasis field.

Energy and motion also change inside a stasis field. Energy magicks—e.g., *fireball*, *magic missile*, *cone of cold*, and *flamestrike*—have no effect; the spells appear and then fizzle in midair. Movement is slowed down visibly, and swift objects are affected more than slow objects. Character and creature movement rates are halved. A dagger can easily be pushed through someone, but a lightninglike slash with a sword is slowed to a graceful arc, almost like slow motion. A missile weapon is useless; the missile drifts lazily through the air, only to bounce off an unwary target or be dodged by a target who's looking.

If the psionicist keeps the stasis field centered on himself, it moves with him. He can transfer the focal point of the field to anything he touches, however. Then he can move freely within the field, or even leave it. If he does leave the field, the cost to maintain it is reduced to 1 point per round. (From one perspective, this is actually an increase in cost, since it equals 60 points for every round which passes inside. Remember, one hour outside equals one round inside.) While outside the field, the psionicist can roam up to 100 yards from it and still maintain the field. However, he cannot move the field from the outside. To move it again, he must re-enter it.

Power Score—No other effect.

20—The psionicist pays the full initial PSP cost.

Wrench

Power Score:	Wis −4
Initial Cost:	15
Maintenance Cost:	8/round
Range:	30 yards
Preparation Time:	0
Area of Effect:	1 undead
Prerequisites:	none

This power affects only creatures which exist simultaneously on the Prime Material and another plane of existence. This includes most undead, and others as noted in the *Monstrous Compendium*. It specifically excludes gods, demigods, and avatars. When such a creature is wrenched, it is forced entirely into one plane or the other, at the psionicist's option.

If the creature is forced out of the Prime Material plane, it is trapped in the other plane for 2d6 turns. It can return to the Prime Material when that time has elapsed.

If the creature is wrenched entirely into the Prime Material plane, it is trapped only as long as the psionicist continues paying the maintenance cost. As soon as he stops, the creature's dual existence is immediately reestablished.

Except where contradicted by the *Monstrous Compendium*, a creature wrenched onto the Prime Material plane suffers any or all of the following effects, at the DM's option:

- Its armor class is penalized 1d6 points.
- Undead lose the ability to drain life energy.
- Magical pluses required to hit the creature are reduced by 1.
- The creature is killed permanently if it loses all of its hit points.

The DM should impose any other penalties which seem appropriate, considering the creature and the other plane involved.

Power Score—The creature is momentarily dazed. It has a −2 initiative penalty in the first subsequent round.

20—No other effect.

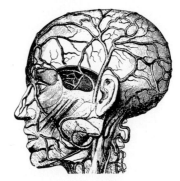

This chapter explains how to bring psionics into your AD&D® games. It examines the role of psionics in a campaign, the attitudes of NPCs toward psionicists, and the relationship between psionics and magic. It offers the DM advice for handling psionic villains and monsters. Finally, you'll find out what it's like to experience psionic power.

Look What I Got!

When something new and exciting comes along, the natural impulse is to rush back to the gaming group, toss it on the table, and let everyone rip into it with full vigor. But that's the wrong way to bring something as powerful as psionics into an existing AD&D campaign. Players are likely to react in one of two ways. First, everyone will want to play a psionicist. The whole atmosphere of the game will suddenly change—so much that players may eventually say, "This isn't like it used to be." The second reaction is that everyone will be skeptical about making a big change, so no one will want to play a psionicist. Either way, enthusiasm fizzles.

Like any new source of power, psionics should be approached with common sense and a bit of caution—especially by the DM. No matter how much experience the DM has, this material is completely new, and there's a lot of it. The DM who dives in with both feet may find himself drowning in details. If play bogs down every time a psionicist tries to do something because the DM must flip through this book, players will quickly lose interest in the class. It's best to start in the shallow end of psionics and advance slowly, rather than swamping players with the whole package at once.

An NPC psionicist is the perfect way to introduce psionics gradually. If the NPC is a hireling, a follower, or an ally, he might not even reveal his psionic powers right away—especially if he's a dual-class character. The DM can introduce as much or as little psionics as he wants, developing a feel for the powers

and how they mesh with other elements of the game. A particularly sly DM might not even mention that psionics is involved, but instead let the players try to puzzle out the unexplained events around them. (For example, some people currently believe that poltergeists are not troublesome spirits, but manifestations of untrained and often unconscious psychokinetic ability. An NPC with such powers could "haunt" players for along time.) Once the DM is satisfied and comfortable with his psionic NPC, the class can be opened to player characters.

Of course, in some games, secrecy may not be appropriate. Many DMs allow players to help develop the campaign background, and routinely discuss the game's direction with them. If you're that kind of DM, then your players should take part in the introduction of psionics. Slow and steady is still the best approach. Let one player have a psionic character. Debrief the player after each game session; get his reactions to both the rules and the way psionics is being used in the campaign. Ask other players for their opinions, too. When you and the players feel you have the bugs worked out, the class can be opened up in general.

Burn Him!

How do NPCs and society in general react to psionicists? The answer covers the gamut of emotions. A DM should choose whatever attitudes best suit his campaign. Some possibilities are as follows:

- Psionics is viewed no differently than magic. It is a tool, as good or as bad as the psionicist who wields it.
- Psionics is misunderstood by those who don't practice it, who generally believe it is magic and the psionicist is just another sort of wizard.
- Psionicists are feared and reviled, as witches were in medieval times.

Control Wind: Omar takes the enemy by storm.

- The practice of psionics is outlawed or restricted to officially sanctioned court practitioners.
- Psionicists are treated as a separate race entirely. They maintain their own small communities within the larger community.
- Psionicists have been driven underground. They maintain secret societies for their own preservation.

It is quite reasonable to mix these attitudes in a single campaign; viewpoints can vary from country to country or even town to town. When choosing a social attitude, however, keep several points in mind. Many fantasy novels involving psionics have a common thread: psionicists are segregated from the rest of society, often by choice, sometimes by force. There are several good reasons for this.

To most people, the heart of psionics is telepathy, and telepathy equals mind reading. Tapping directly into someone else's thoughts is the ultimate invasion of privacy, the ultimate violation of intimacy. Worst of all, the subject has no way to know when it is happening or how to prevent it from happening. He is not only invaded, but helpless.

Psionics lends itself to secrecy. Its use has no outward sign. Wizards must utter incantations, wave their hands through the air, and fling bits of dust and bone into sulfurous smoke to cast their spells. Clerics must pray and invoke their deities. All of these things clearly tip off the potential victim that something is about to happen, that a supernatural force is about to be released. The psionicist reveals nothing. His powers require no verbal, material, or somatic components. When psionic powers are used, anyone nearby could be the source, and sometimes even distance is not a restriction.

Nor does the psionicist's appearance reveal his nature. His pockets and purse do not bulge with strange concoctions. His fingers and sleeves are not stained with ink and chemicals.

He does not wear the robes or symbols of a holy order. Psionic characters who are careful can conceal their nature for a long time.

What this means to the common man is that anyone, even a friend or relative, could be reading your mind at any time—could, in fact, be influencing your actions, delving into your most intimate secrets, entering your home without leaving a trace. Who can be trusted with this sort of power, if power truly corrupts?

The answer, as far as the suspicious farmer or merchant is concerned, is no one. And if no one can be trusted with it, then anyone who has it should be controlled, or at least prevented from living among decent, normal folks.

This, of course, is the attitude among people with no real knowledge or experience of psionics. An enlightened populace or one that has benefitted from benevolent use of psionics would view psionicists in a positive light.

TSR's Campaign Worlds

The overall attitude toward and prevalence of psionics in each of TSR's published campaign worlds is described below. Bear in mind that these are general trends, and can vary significantly from region to region.

FORGOTTEN REALMS® game setting. Prior to the Time of Troubles, psionics were extremely rare in the Realms. The incidence of psionic abilities is now on the rise and the powers themselves seem to have become more stable. Most people have never heard of psionics or psionicists; those who have tend to confuse it with magic.

WORLD OF GREYHAWK® game setting. Psionics is an old and established facet of life on Oerth. Presumably it was brought there when an illithid spacecraft crashed on the planet ages ago. Psionicists are by no means common, but most people are at least aware of the existence of psionics and often consider it to be just another mystical pursuit, little dif-

ferent from magic. Psionic guilds and secret associations can be found in major cities.

Krynn, a DRAGONLANCE® game setting. No natives of Krynn exhibit any psionic potential whatsoever. What few psionicists live on that world undoubtedly came from somewhere else (via spelljamming vessels or other magical travel) or are the descendants of psionically-able ancestors who came from another world. Only the most widely-read sages and wizards will have any knowledge of psionics.

RAVENLOFT™ game setting. Psionics is known in Ravenloft. However, the nature of the Demiplane of Dread restricts the effectiveness of some psionic powers:

• No psionic power can breach the Mist. A character can teleport, travel through dimensions, travel through dreams, or travel any other way he chooses, but he will almost always emerge in the same domain. In those few cases where he emerges somewhere else, it will be in a bank of Mist which will lead him who knows where. The DM determines the exact location.

• No psionic power can bring another character into Ravenloft from outside. Some magical spells can do this; psionics cannot.

• All of the demiplane is so suffused with evil that it encroaches on everyone's aura. Examining a person's aura can reveal the character's alignment only so far as law and chaos are concerned, but not good or evil. Aura alteration cannot change a character's alignment with regard to good or evil.

• Any psionic power that gives the character access to remote or extrasensory information (primarily via clairsentient or telepathic powers) also creates a shadow presence of that character. This shadow presence can be detected by rolling the subject's level or hit dice or less on 1d20. Roll only once and use the level or hit dice of the most powerful creature or character begin affected.

SPELLJAMMER™ campaign setting. Psionic powers function normally in wildspace and the phlogiston. Psionics is not magic, however, and cannot power a spelljamming helm.

Psionics and Magic

Psionics and magic are completely separate forces. Some of their effects overlap, as might be expected, since some effects are so useful that everyone who can get them probably will try. For example, both psionicists and magic-users have a means of becoming invisible, traveling instantaneously, and controlling other people or creatures. But in their basic makeup, magic and psionics are like oil and water; they do not mix. The text below offers some general guidelines and specific rules for the interaction magic and psionics.

General Guidelines

• The essences of magic and psionics are wholly different. A wizard or cleric who can *detect magic* will never detect psionics. Nor will a psionicist who scans for psionic activity ever detect spell-casting. This holds true even if the effect of a particular magical and psionic skill is identical, or nearly identical. For example, a wizard can use *hold portal* to hold a door shut. In his own way, using psychokinesis, so can a psionicist. If a psionicist is holding a door shut, and a wizard casts *detect magic* on the door, the wizard will find nothing unusual about it. If the wizard casts *dispel magic*, the door will not open. No magical forces are at work on the door.

Exceptions do exist, but they're fairly easy to determine. For example, a wizard who casts a *detect invisibility* spell will see a character using psionic invisibility because the spell description states specifically that the spell does not discriminate between types of invisibility.

• Magic is capable of duplicating psionic effects like ESP, clairvoyance, clairaudience, teleportation, and levitation, among others.

Again, however, the energy involved is magical, not psionic. So normal psionic powers do not detect these magicks.

• Magical images and illusions manipulate light, sound, and scent. That means they can affect psionic powers which rely on or expand the normal senses: clairvoyance, clairaudience, all-round vision, feel light, etc. Using any psychometabolic, psychokinetic, telepathic, or psychoportive power against a magical illusion automatically gives the psionicist cause to make a saving throw vs. spells. Depending on the situation, the DM may rule that the use of such a power penetrates an illusion automatically.

• Magical phantasms, on the other hand, operate entirely in the mind of the viewer. A psionicist using any power against a phantasm automatically gets to make a saving throw vs. spells to penetrate the phantasm. (The psionicist is too tuned into his own mind to be easily fooled this way.)

Spells and Psionics

Anti-Magic Shell. This spell has no effect against psionics.

Detect Charm. This will detect telepathic control such as domination.

Detect Invisibility. This spell is effective against psionic invisibility, astral travelers, shadow form, and ethereal characters. It is not effective against characters in other dimensions.

Detect Magic. This never detects psionic activity.

Detect Scrying. When this spell is used against a clairvoyant psionicist, he must make a saving throw vs. spells. If successful, the clairvoyant avoids detection.

ESP. A psionicist always gets a saving throw against this spell with a +2 bonus. Success negates the spell.

False Vision. The psionicist is allowed a saving throw vs. spells to negate the effect of this spell.

Forbiddance. None of the teleportation or metabolic powers can breach this spell.

Free Action. This spell overcomes all psychokinetic effects against the subject's body, plus domination.

Globe of Invulnerability. Psionics are unaffected by globes.

Magic Jar. The psionicist uses his combined Wisdom and Constitution scores when determining the differential modifier.

Magic Missile. This spell has no effect inside a stasis field.

Mind Blank. The psionicist is allowed a saving throw vs. spells to overcome this spell.

Minor Globe of Invulnerability. Psionics are unaffected by globes.

Misdirection. This spell affects magical detection only.

Mislead. Any psionicist who tries to contact the wizard's mind will realize the deception immediately. That first contact attempt will fail automatically, however.

Nondetection. This spell is fully effective against psionic sensing.

Otiluke's Resilient Sphere. Psionic powers cannot penetrate this spell's protection.

Protection From Evil. All telepathic powers used against someone protected from evil have their power scores reduced by 2. Additionally, the spell prevents mental control such as domination.

Protection from Evil, 10' Radius. Same as *protection from evil.*

Reincarnation. Unless the new incarnation is allowable in the psionicist class, all psionic powers are lost.

Spell Immunity. This has no effect against psionic powers.

Telekinesis. If this spell is opposed by psychokinesis, conduct a psychic contest between the psionicist's power score and the wizard's experience level.

Trap the Soul. A psionicist trapped via this spell cannot use any of his psionic powers. (Although the character's body is trapped along with his soul, it is stored in a radically

altered, magical form. Thus the psionicist is denied access to the physical energy which is the basis for all his powers.)

Note: As stated in Chapter 1, all psionicists gain a +2 bonus when making a saving throw vs. any enchantment/charm spell.

Magical Items

The same guidelines which apply to spells also apply to magical items, their effects, and the interplay between them and psionics. One item in particular, however, deserves special mention—the *philosopher's stone*.

For reasons that are unknown, a *philosopher's stone* aids a psionicist in shaping energy. As long as the stone is in contact with the psionicist's flesh, all psionic power scores in his primary discipline are increased by one. If the stone is of the rare, crystalline salt variety, it increases his power scores in his primary discipline and one other discipline of the character's choice. If it is the extremely rare white powder stone, it boosts his power scores in his primary discipline and allows him to recover psionic strength points at twice the normal rate.

Monsters, Villains, and Other NPCs

Most of the common-sense rules that apply to regular monsters, villains, and NPCs apply equally to psionic figures. It never hurts to re-view, however, so some pointers follow.

Psionic NPCs make excellent major villains. But like any powerful, single entity—a vampire, a dragon, a lich, a beholder—they are much less effective in isolation than they are at the center of a web of minions. For this reason, most psionic villains will have numerous slaves, followers, mercenaries, and other vassals at their beck and call. Some of these may be minor psionicists in their own right. As well as acting as the master's eyes, ears, and go-

fers, they serve to wear down attackers before the final confrontation. (Or they buy time for the psionicist to escape if the opposition is overwhelming.)

Psionic monsters, on the other hand, tend to be solitary creatures. Many of them hunt by keying in on mental activity, or even on purely psionic activity. (They detect and track psionic activity the way a hound picks up the scent of a fox and mercilessly hunts it down.) A crowd of thinking beings tends to create interference (i.e., "jam the airwaves"), making it more difficult to notice an actual psionicist (or choice victim) who wanders into range.

Because they operate alone or in small groups, psionic creatures tend to strike quickly, inflict as much damage as possible, and then melt away before the victims can organize a counterattack. An excellent tactic, for example, is to teleport into a group, grab someone at random, and teleport away immediately. Suddenly, that one person can be dealt with alone, rather than in the midst of his comrades. Tactics like this can cause far more fear and destruction than a glance at the creature's statistics might inspire.

Even when they're friendly, NPCs with psionic powers tend to keep their those powers to themselves. Secrecy is always the best policy. Unless there is a good social or employment reason for it, never reveal that an NPC is a psionicist; let the players figure it out for themselves.

Living Psionics

Psionics—the harnessing and shaping of personal, internal energies—is a unique experience. Much like Zen, its essence cannot be described; it must be felt. At the heart of psionics is a tautology: only understanding brings understanding. Still, for the curious, what follows is an attempt to describe the psionic experience.

The first thing a psionicist learns is how to recognize internal energy. Everyone is filled

with it, but most people are completely unaware of it. It suffuses our being 24 hours a day, building up during times of rest and draining away during times of exertion or stress. The psionicist learns to turn his awareness inward and search for this energy. Gradually, he gathers it together, drawing it toward some spot. The notion of *drawing* is key, because this energy cannot be pushed or forced; it must be enticed to accumulate. An experienced psionicist can gather his energies continuously and unconsciously. For a beginner, however, this is the first and most important breakthrough.

Once an amount of energy has been gathered, the psionicist can begin shaping it. The closest description for this bundle of energy is a "warm spot" at the gathering point. Initially, warm spots are easiest to form at the front of the brain. As the budding psionicist practices, he learns to move it around. Eventually, he can gather energy anywhere: his head, his hand, his shoulder, his back. The precise location is important when using some powers, but not all.

The energy is not shaped in the normal sense of that word. Instead, *primed* may be a better label. The psionicist visualizes the effect he wants. The stronger the visualization, the more likely it is to succeed. When the gathering reaches its peak, the energy is usually realized in a single, explosive release.

Many psionicists describe this release as an instantaneous increase in the apparent temperature of the warm spot, accompanied by a "beat" sensation—as if the warm spot had fired spikes of energy in a radial pattern through the psionicist's body. This sensation is strongest when the psionicist is directing energy outward in an aggressive fashion—when moving an object, for example. If the power being used is directional, the spikes are strongest in that direction, and very minor in others. If power's effects continue for more than a few moments, the beat also continues, but at much lower intensity.

Contact, a common and vital power, has another physical manifestation. Rather than a warm spot, subjects describe the sensation of contact as a "thick spot" or a "heavy spot" somewhere in the mind. They usually have trouble locating it precisely (front, back, left, right), but feel nonetheless that it is a definite place. Forcible contact (as in telepathic combat) is similar, but much more extreme. Each tangent arrives "like a gallstone in the mind," according to Bezelar Mujarif, a prominent psionicist now residing in Calimshan. When contact finally comes, he adds, it feels "like a tiger has unsheathed its claws in your head."

Clairvoyant powers tend to operate one of two ways. Either the power simply layers over the psionicist's normal senses (clairaudience, clairvoyance) or brings information in snatches and bursts of insight (object reading, precognition).

Nonpsionicists often imagine that a telepath can "eavesdrop" on their thoughts. That not's quite true. If a psionicist uses telepathy, the target's thoughts do not flood into his mind, masquerading as his own thoughts, or interfering with them. Instead, the thoughts come forth as simple knowledge. The psionicist knows what the target is thinking, as if someone had told him hours before and he just now remembered.

Knights of the Floating Table

Most AD&D® game campaigns follow medieval themes and cultures, both historical and legendary. Players can easily find models for most character classes, from wizards to knights. But psionics is more often thought of as the property of science fiction and the future rather than the past. Historical examples are hard to find. Svengali is one possibility, in an evil vein. Modern figures like Kreskin and Uri Geller provide examples of extrasensory powers (allegedly), but these characters are thoroughly unmedieval.

To find models for the psionicist, one can delve into Indian and Asian folk tales. These contain many characters with abilities that mirror psionics, largely because Eastern mysticism emphasizes meditation and the harnessing of internal energy. Fantasy fiction also offers some good examples. The bibliography below includes several good sources which deal with psionics. Players with an interest in the subject are strongly urged to read some of these books for inspiration.

Related Reading

Fiction

Bester, Alfred; *The Demolished Man, The Stars My Destination*.

Bradley, Marion Zimmer; Darkover series: *The Bloody Sun, Children of Hastur, Darkover Landfall, The Forbidden Tower, Hawkmistress!, The Heritage of Hastur, The Keeper's Price, The Planet Savers, Sharra's Exile, The Shattered Chain, The Spell Sword, Star of Danger, Stormqueen!, The Sword of Aldones, Thendara House, Two to Conquer, The Winds of Darkover, The World Wreckers*.

Brunner, John; *The Whole Man*.

Del Rey, Lester; *Pstalemate*.

Henderson, Zenna; *The People, The People: No Different, Holding Wonder*.

Foster, Alan Dean; Flinx series.

King, Stephen; *The Dead Zone*.

Kurtz, Katherine; *Deryni Rising, Deryni Checkmate, High Deryni*.

May, Julian; Saga of the Pliocene Exile series: *The Many-Colored Land, The Golden Torc, The Non-Born King, The Adversary*.

Nourse, Alan E.; *Psi High and Others*.

Pohl, Frederik; *Drunkard's Walk*.

Russell, Eric Frank; *The Mindwarpers*.

Robinson, Frank M.; *The Power*.

Schmitz, James H.; *The Universe Against Her, The Lion Game*, stories.

Simmons, Dan; *Carrion Comfort*.

Sturgeon, Theodore; *The Synthetic Man*.

Tucker, Wilson; *Wild Talent*.

Van Vogt, A.E.; *Slan*.

Zelazny, Roger; *Creatures of Light and Darkness, The Dream Master, Lord of Light, Isle of the Dead, This Immortal, To Die in Italbar*.

Nonfiction

Brookesmith, Peter (ed.); *Strange Talents*, from the series "The Unexplained: Mysteries of Mind, Space, and Time;" Orbis Publishing, London, 1983.

Index of Possibilities: Energy and Power; Pantheon Books/Random House, New York, New York, 1974.

Mind Over Matter, Powers of Healing, Psychic Powers, Psychic Voyages, from the series "Mysteries of the Unknown;" Time-Life Books, Alexandria, Virginia, 1987.

Puharich, Andrija; *Beyond Telepathy*; Anchor Press/Doubleday, Garden City, New York, 1973.

Rhine, J.B.; *The Reach of the Mind*; William Sloane Associates, New York, New York, 1947.

Baku

CLIMATE/TERRAIN:	Semitropical/Forests
FREQUENCY:	Very rare
ORGANIZATION:	Solitary (or group)
ACTIVITY CYCLE:	Daytime
DIET:	Herbivore
INTELLIGENCE:	Exceptional to Genius (15-18)
TREASURE:	See below
ALIGNMENT:	Neutral (Any, See below)
NO. APPEARING:	1 (1d4 + 1)
ARMOR CLASS:	−2
MOVEMENT:	21
HIT DICE:	12 + 12
THAC0:	7
NO. OF ATTACKS:	3
DAMAGE/ATTACK:	3d6/2d6/2d6
SPECIAL ATTACKS:	Psionics, magical items, trumpet
SPECIAL DEFENSES:	Psionics, invisibility
MAGIC RESISTANCE:	20%
SIZE:	L (as 9' elephant)
MORALE:	Elite (13-14)
XP VALUE:	15,000

A baku looks like a strange elephant with a lizard's tail. It has an elephantine head, complete with trunk, but its trunk is rarely longer than 4 feet. Two upward thrusting tusks jut out from the creature's lower jaws, curving slightly. Its stout forelegs have a rhino-tough hide. The front feet are like an elephant's, but the rear feet have leonine pads equipped with claws. Dragonlike scales cover a baku's back and thick tail. On male baku, the scales continue over the back of the head.

Combat: Despite its size and bulk, a baku can move rapidly, attacking with a goring butt and two foreleg stomps. The stomp is used only against man-sized opponents, or those less than 6 feet tall. A baku can hold simple devices such as weapons or wands in its trunk, so a baku will often have some magical weapon or device when attacking.

Baku can use psionics to become invisible at will (see below). They expend no PSPs for this, and the power check always succeeds. Baku also boast a trumpeting roar, which affects creatures of certain alignments. Any vulnerable creature within 40 feet of a roaring baku suffers 1d8 points of damage; it must also make a successful save vs. paralyzation or flee in panic as if affected by *fear* (as cast by a 12th level wizard). Baku can trumpet once every four rounds. Neutral good baku affect only evil creatures, dark (evil) baku affect good creatures, and holy baku can affect either good and/or evil creatures at their discretion.

Neutral good baku are usually timid, peace-loving creatures, but they eagerly do battle with evil and malicious monsters.

Psionics Summary:

Level	Dis/Sci/Dev	Attack/Defense	Score	PSPs
12	4/6/17	MT,PsC/All	= Int	200

Common Disciplines/Sciences/Devotions:
- Clairvoyance - *Sciences:* Aura Sight*. *Devotions:* comprehend writing, danger sense.

- Psychometabolism - *Sciences:* animal affinity*, metamorphosis*. *Devotions:* absorb disease, cell adjustment*, ectoplasmic form*, lend health*, reduction*.
- Telepathy - *Sciences:* psychic crush*, superior invisibility*. *Devotions:* awe, conceal thoughts, contact*, invisibility (no cost)*, mindlink, mind thrust, telempathic projection, truthear.
- Psychoportation - *Sciences:* probability travel*. *Devotions:* dream travel, astral projection*.

* All baku have these psionic powers.

Habitat/Society: All baku come from the Concordant Opposition (an outer plane). They are seldom seen in desolate settings, and prefer to move invisibly among mankind.

Most baku (80%) are creatures of good will. They secretly dwell among humankind to serve its interests. Good baku favor societies in semitropical forests.

About 15% of all baku are of evil alignment. These baku, called "The Dark Ones" by their brethren, also move amongst humankind. However, they attempt to thwart the plans of their good brothers as well as cause general mayhem and suffering wherever they go.

The remaining 5% of baku are true neutral. Among other baku, they are known as "The Great Ones" or "The Holy Ones." Although they have no discernible abilities to set them apart from their brethren, they are reverently obeyed by other baku. These holy baku always have an Intelligence of at least 18.

Ecology: Baku tusks are worth 200 gp each. However, this treasure is greatly overshadowed by the magical item which a baku usually carries in its trunk.

Brain Mole

CLIMATE/TERRAIN:	Any/Below ground
FREQUENCY:	Very rare
ORGANIZATION:	Family
ACTIVITY CYCLE:	Night
DIET:	Psionic energy
INTELLIGENCE:	Animal (1)
TREASURE:	Nil
ALIGNMENT:	Neutral
NO. APPEARING:	1-3
ARMOR CLASS:	9
MOVEMENT:	1, Br 3
HIT DICE:	1 hp
THAC0:	Nil
NO. OF ATTACKS:	Nil
DAMAGE/ATTACK:	Nil
SPECIAL ATTACKS:	Psionic
SPECIAL DEFENSES:	Psionic
MAGIC RESISTANCE:	Nil
SIZE:	T (3″ long)
MORALE:	Unsteady (5-7)
XP VALUE:	35

These small, furry animals are nearly blind, and they look like normal moles. Brain moles are seldom seen, however. They live in underground tunnels, burrowing through rock as well as dirt. Usually, the only discernible evidence of a brain mole's presence is the network of blistered stone or mounded dirt above ground, which marks the tunnel complex. These creatures damage more than a landscape, however. Brain moles feed on psionic activity. From the protection of their tunnels, they can psionically burrow into a victim's brain, and drain his psionic energy.

Combat: A brain mole commonly attacks its victim in forests or underground; in either case, the creature is usually out of sight in a tunnel. The mole either waits for a psionically endowed being to appear above it, or burrows in search of prey.

A brain mole has an innate form of psionic sense; it can automatically detect psionic activity of any sort within 200 yards. However, it can only feed upon psionic energy when its victim nearby—within 30 yards if the victim is a psionicist or psionic creature, or within 30 feet if the victim is a wild talent. The mole can't get a fix upon its prey until the victim actually uses a psionic power.

Once it locates a victim, the brain mole attempts to establish contact. If contact is made, it will attempt to feed upon psionic energy. If the victim is a wild talent, feeding is accomplished using mindwipe. If the victim is a psionicist (or psionic creature), feeding is accomplished with amplification.

A brain mole does not attack maliciously. It must feed at least once a week or it will die.

Psionics Summary:

Level	Dis/Sci/Dev	Attack/Defense	Score	PSPs
6	2/1/4	MT/M-	12	100

Only has:
- Telepathy - *Sciences:* mindlink, mindwipe[1] *Devotions:* contact, mind thrust
- Metapsionics - *Devotions:* psychic drain[2] (no cost), psionic sense

[1] A brain mole can perform mindwipe up to a range of 30 feet.

[2] Strangely enough, a brain mole must establish contact before using psychic drain. Furthermore, it can only perform psychic drain upon psionicists or psionic creatures. However, it does not have to put them into a trance or sleep first. It just starts siphoning away psionic energy.

Habitat/Society: Brain moles live in family units that include one male, one female, and 1d6 young (one of which may be old enough to feed by itself). Large brain mole towns of up to 3d6 family units have been reported. Of course, these only occur in places frequently traveled by the psionically endowed.

Ecology: Though brain moles can be dangerous to some, while others keep them as pets. The moles are rather friendly, and easily tamed. They are favored by royalty, who enjoy the special protection which only brain moles can provide. Some sages claim that even a dead brain mole can offer protection from psionic attacks, provided the carcass is worn about one's neck as a medallion. Sometimes, nobles who have been harassed by a particular psionicist will send heroes out on quests for these little furry rodents.

On the open market, adult brain moles sell for 50 gp. Youngsters sell for 5 gp each.

Cerebral Parasite

CLIMATE/TERRAIN:	Any/Any
FREQUENCY:	Rare
ORGANIZATION:	Infestation
ACTIVITY CYCLE:	Any
DIET:	Psionic Energy
INTELLIGENCE:	Non- (0)
TREASURE:	Nil
ALIGNMENT:	Neutral
NO. APPEARING:	3d4
ARMOR CLASS:	Nil
MOVEMENT:	Nil
HIT DICE:	Nil
THAC0:	Nil
NO. OF ATTACKS:	0
DAMAGE/ATTACK:	0
SPECIAL ATTACKS:	Psionic
SPECIAL DEFENSES:	Only affected by *cure disease*
MAGIC RESISTANCE:	Nil
SIZE:	T (flea-sized)
MORALE:	Nil
XP VALUE:	35

These tiny psionic parasites float about in the air. Colorless and nearly transparent, they cannot be seen by the human eye. They drift in the wind until they come across a psionic being. Then they attach themselves to the host's aura, and slowly drain psionic strength.

Combat: A cerebral parasite's attack is so subtle that a victim may not notice it for some time. When a psionically endowed individual comes within 1 foot of a parasite, the creature is mysteriously drawn to the character's (or monster's) aura, and attaches itself. This initial "attack" usually will go completely unnoticed.

Only a few psionic powers can detect cerebral parasites: aura sight, life detection, and psionic sense. Magical spells which detect invisible or hidden objects are also effective. Of course, the infested host may realize that something is wrong when he uses his psionic powers.

Each time the victim uses a psionic power, the power costs 1 extra PSP for each parasite infesting an individual's aura. The power still works normally, but the parasite absorbs the extra PSP. After a particular parasite has absorbed 6 psionic points in this fashion, it can reproduce by splitting in two. Of course, both parasites will now feed, and the process continues. Eventually the victim may not have enough PSPs to feed the parasites when using a given power; in that case, the power fails.

Only two methods can rid a victim of cerebral parasites: 1) a *cure disease* spell or 2) refraining from spending PSPs until the threat of starvation forces the parasites to leave. Each day the victim refrains from spending PSPs, there is a 1% cumulative chance (95% maximum) that each parasite will detach itself. Since this check is made individually for each parasite, a heavily infested victim is not likely to shake all the pests unless he refrains from using his powers for three or four months.

Psionics Summary:

Level	Dis/Sci/Dev	Attack/Defense	Score	PSPs
1	2/1/2	Nil/Nil	18	unlimited

Only has:
- Psychometabolism - *Devotions:* ectoplasmic form, immovability.
- Psychoportation - *Sciences:* probability travel.

Habitat/Society: Psionic parasites, as these infestations are often called, have existed ever since psionicists have been around. Sages claim that an ancient sect of wizards created the parasites to rid the planes of "false mages"—i.e., psionicists. Of course, this tale is very popular even today among most wizards, but its validity is uncertain. The parasites' ability to enter the astral and ethereal planes does lend credence to this theory, however. (Entering the ethereal plane is an innate ability. They use probability travel to enter the astral plane.)

Every 15 years, a plague of cerebral parasites infests the prime material plane. Their frequency becomes common and 4d8 will be encountered at once. Psionicists dread this time, and call it "the year of weakness."

Ecology: Cerebral parasites, if captured, make a wonderful weapon to use against psionicists. The only problem is that they can eventually escape even the most tightly sealed jar. Each has a 1% cumulative chance of leaving the jar per day. Within several months, few if any will remain. Of course, this is because most of them will have left to search for food. Still, even a month of two of security is enough to prompt many to search the winds for these little clear specks.

Intellect Devourer, Adult

CLIMATE/TERRAIN:	Any/Subterranean or dark areas
FREQUENCY:	Very rare
ORGANIZATION:	Solitary
ACTIVITY CYCLE:	Any (if dark)
DIET:	Minds
INTELLIGENCE:	Very (11-12)
TREASURE:	D
ALIGNMENT:	Chaotic evil
NO. APPEARING:	1-2
ARMOR CLASS:	4
MOVEMENT:	15
HIT DICE:	6+6
THAC0:	13
NO. OF ATTACKS:	4
DAMAGE/ATTACK:	1d4/1d4/1d4/1d4
SPECIAL ATTACKS:	Psionics, stalk prey
SPECIAL DEFENSES:	Psionics, +3 weapon needed to hit
MAGIC RESISTANCE:	See below
SIZE:	S (brain sized)
MORALE:	Fanatic (17-18)
XP VALUE:	6,000

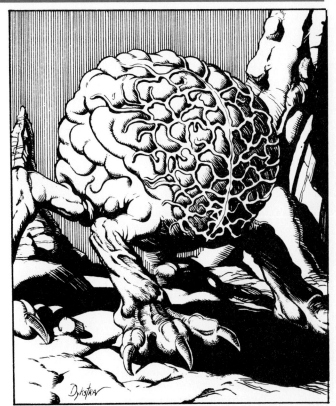

The term "intellect devourer" only applies to the adult form of this species. (The larval stage, or ustilagor, is covered on a separate page.) An intellect devourer looks like a large human brain standing on four legs. The "brain" has a crusty protective covering. The legs are bony and double-jointed. Each appendage ends in a foot with three great, stubby talons.

Combat: Intellect devourers are surprisingly capable in melee. Only magical weapons with a +3 bonus or greater can harm them. Even then, the weapons cause only a single point of damage per attack. Furthermore, these creatures can strike back with all four of their clawed legs simultaneously if they wish. To do this, they spring onto their opponent and rake.

However, the primary offensive of an intellect devourer is psionics. They hunt for psionic creatures and characters using a special version of psionic sense (60' range, no cost). If they locate a potential victim, they proceed to stalk him, waiting until they can attack with surprise. This attack is doubly potent if the creature uses split personality. With that power in action, the intellect devourer can rake a victim with its claws at the same time it attacks psionically.

The intellect devourer's most gruesome attack occurs just after it has killed a victim. Using reduction, an intellect devourer can enter a dead body. Then it will proceed to either devour the victim's brain, or control his body (using a special form of domination). In this fashion, the creature can seek opportunities to attack and devour other victim's brains.

Psionics Summary:

Level	Dis/Sci/Dev	Attack/Defense	Score	PSPs
6	4/4/13	EW,II/M-,TS,+1	= Int	200

Intellect devourers always have the following powers:

- Psychometabolism - *Sciences:* energy containment [1]. *Devotions:* body equilibrium, chameleon power, ectoplasmic form, expansion, chemical simulation, reduction.
- Metapsionics - *Sciences:* split personality. *Devotions:* psionic sense (only 60' range, no cost), psychic drain.
- Telepathy - *Sciences:* domination (even on dead, intact minds). *Devotions:* contact, ego whip, ESP, id insinuation, telempathic projection.
- Psychoportation - *Devotion:* astral projection.

[1] An intellect devourer's energy containment is superior to the one listed in this book. It is always "on"— without penalty or maintenance cost. Furthermore, even if the check fails against an attack, only one point of damage will be taken per die instead of half damage as is listed. The only exceptions are *death* spell, which has a 25% chance of success; *powerword kill*, which will slay the creature; and *protection from evil*, which keeps it at bay.

Habitat/Society: Intellect devourers dwell deep beneath the ground or in dark and dismal lairs in the wilderness. They rarely protect their young, and may even devour them. This race is so solitary that even the young ustilagor rarely stay together. However, occasionally up to two intellect devourers or three ustilagor will be found together.

Ecology: Adult intellect devourers are favored pets of mind flayers (illithids). They serve as watch dogs.

Intellect Devourer, Larva (Ustilagor)

CLIMATE/TERRAIN:	Dark, moist areas
FREQUENCY:	Rare
ORGANIZATION:	Solitary
ACTIVITY CYCLE:	During Darkness
DIET:	Emotions
INTELLIGENCE:	Not ratable
TREASURE:	Q (x1d20)
ALIGNMENT:	Neutral (evil)
NO. APPEARING:	1-3
ARMOR CLASS:	5
MOVEMENT:	9
HIT DICE:	3 + 3
THAC0:	17
NO. OF ATTACKS:	1
DAMAGE/ATTACK:	1d4 + 1 (save vs. poison or double)
SPECIAL ATTACKS:	Psionics
SPECIAL DEFENSES:	Psionics
MAGIC RESISTANCE:	Nil (See below)
SIZE:	T (Brain sized)
MORALE:	Unsteady (5-7)
XP VALUE:	650

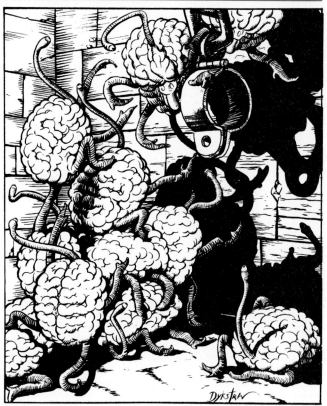

Ustilagor are the larval form of intellect devourers. Like their parents, they look like brains with four legs. However, they are much smaller, and their bodies are soft and moist. They lack the hard covering which they will eventually gain as adults. Ustilagor also have a 3-foot tendril which is very flexible and agile. Unlike their parents, they have coral-like legs with no feet, so they travel slowly (MV 9). Even so, they can jump and dart with amazing agility. (That's why their armor class is 5.)

Combat: Ustilagor can attack by striking an opponent with their tendril while performing their own version of chemical simulation. They never fail when using this power and expend only 1 PSP per attack. Moreover, the acid is so caustic that the victim must save vs. poison or suffer additional damage the next round (1d4 + 1).

Of course, this is not a highly effective form of attack, and the ustilagor prefers to use either id insinuation or its advanced telempathic projection power. Using the latter, it can force its victims into one of five states of mind during a round: hate for associates, distrust of associates, fear of fungi, loathing of area, or uncertainty. These projected emotions cause attack, bickering, desertion, or dithering, accordingly. Note that adult intellect devourers lose this enhanced power, and are only able to perform telempathic projection.

Though they are psionically endowed, ustilagor seem to have no intelligence as defined by humans. Thus, attacks that affect minds (psionically or magically) do not function upon them, with the exception of psionic blast. Due to an unusual fungal growth (see "Habitat/Society"), they are immune to fungal attacks and any attack that affects an aura.

Finally, ustilagor use their energy containment power to protect themselves from spells and other applicable forms of attack. A ustilagor does not have the advanced form of energy containment associated with their adult form.

All ustilagor are attracted to gems. No one knows why for sure, but it is suspected that ustilagor use the gems for energy containment. These creatures will attack a being who's carrying gems before they attack any others.

Psionics Summary:

Level	Dis/Sci/Dev	Attack/Defense	Score	PSPs
3	2/1/4	II/M-	10	150

Only have:
- Psychometabolism - *Sciences:* energy containment. *Devotion:* chemical simulation (see above).
- Telepathy - *Devotions:* contact, id insinuation, telempathic projection (see above).

Habitat/Society: Ustilagor are so moist that fungi usually grow upon them. It's a symbiotic relationship. The fungi prevent the ustilagor from drying out, and they also mask the creature's psionic aura. Thus, no power that affects an aura will work against a ustilagor covered with fungi. Cerebral parasites cannot penetrate this layer of protection, either.

No one knows when or how the ustilagor become intellect devourers, but it no doubt has something to do with minds and psionics. Sages theorize that fungi also plays a role.

Ecology: Mind flayers (illithids) view ustilagors as culinary delights. If they survive the encounter, adventurers view them as treasure troves. As noted above, ustilagors like to collect gems.

Shedu

	Lesser	Greater
CLIMATE/TERRAIN:	— Any (prefer hot)/	Any open region—
FREQUENCY:	Rare	Very rare
ORGANIZATION:	Herd	Herd Leader
ACTIVITY CYCLE:	— Hot part of the day—	
DIET:	Herbivore	Herbivore
INTELLIGENCE:	Exceptional (15-16)	Genius (17-18)
TREASURE:	G	Nil
ALIGNMENT:	Lawful good	Lawful good
NO. APPEARING:	2d4	1-2
ARMOR CLASS:	4	2
MOVEMENT:	12, Fl 24 (C)	15, Fl 30 (B)
HIT DICE:	9+9	14+14
THAC0:	11	5
NO. OF ATTACKS:	2	2
DAMAGE/ATTACK:	1d6/1d6	3d6/3d6
SPECIAL ATTACKS:	Psionics	Psionics
SPECIAL DEFENSES:	Psionics	Psionics, invisibility
MAGIC RESISTANCE:	25%	50%
SIZE:	L (as a mule)	L (as a draft horse)
MORALE:	Champion (15-16)	Fearless (19-20)
XP VALUE:	8,000	15,000

A shedu is a pegasus native to hot, arid climates. It has a powerful, stocky equine body with short but powerful feathered wings. Upon its short, thick neck is a large humanoid head. The face is rather dwarven in appearance, and it always has a beard and mustache. A shedu's hair is very bristly, and curls into tight waves or bands.

All shedu wear a simple headband made of braided cloth or rope, with a single button for adornment. The button is centered on the forehead, and its material represents the bearer's status. From the lowest rank to the highest, a button may be made of silver, gold, platinum, sapphire, ruby, or diamond. A lesser shedu almost never has a button above the platinum level. A greater shedu almost never wears one below sapphire status.

Shedu wander the prime material, astral, and ethereal planes. They further the cause of law and goodness, help allied creatures in need, and combat evil. Greater shedu typically lead herds of six or more lesser shedu.

Combat: All shedu attack with powerful front hooves. However, both forms of shedu prefer to use their psionic powers where applicable.

LESSER SHEDU

Languages: Lesser shedu speak shedu, lamia, lammasu, and most human tongues (although not common). Of course, they can always use their empathy power (a limited form of telepathy, see below).

Psionics Summary:

Level	Dis/Sci/Dev	Attack/Defense	Score	PSPs
9	4/4/13	All/All	= Int	100

Lesser shedu always have the five powers listed below (within three disciplines), and they can use them without expending PSPs. In addition to these powers, a lesser shedu knows any three sciences and five devotions desired (from these disciplines, or others). Each creature tends to specialize in a particular discipline to

complement the herd (each takes a different discipline).
- Psychometabolism - *Devotions:* ectoplasmic form.
- Telepathy - *Devotions:* contact, empathy, mindlink.
- Psychoportation - *Devotions:* astral projection.

GREATER SHEDU

Greater shedu radiate *protection from evil—10' radius.*

Languages: Greater shedu speak shedu, lamia, lammasu, common, and root languages (i.e., most human tongues). However, they can always rely upon their telepathy power, which they have mastered so well that rudimentary contact can be made even with plants.

Psionics Summary:

Level	Dis/Sci/Dev	Attack/Defense	Score	PSPs
14	5/12/15	All/All	= Int	200

Common powers (* denotes powers they always have, [1] denotes powers which require no point expenditure):
- Defense - mind bar*[1]
- Clairvoyance - *Sciences:* aura sight, clairaudience, clairvoyance, object reading, precognition *Devotions:* danger sense, sensitivity to psychic impressions
- Psychometabolism - *Sciences:* energy containment, metamorphosis *Devotions:* body control, ectoplasmic form*[1]
- Psychokinesis - *Sciences:* telekinesis *Devotions:* molecular agitation, molecular manipulation
- Telepathy - *Sciences:* domination, mass domination, mindlink*[1] *Devotions:* contact*, invisibility*[1], post-hypnotic suggestion
- Psychoportation - *Sciences:* probability travel*[1], teleport*[1] *Devotions:* dimensional door, dimension walk*[1]

Thought Eater

CLIMATE/TERRAIN:	Ethereal Plane
FREQUENCY:	Rare
ORGANIZATION:	Solitary
ACTIVITY CYCLE:	Any
DIET:	Mental Energy
INTELLIGENCE:	Not ratable
TREASURE:	Nil
ALIGNMENT:	Neutral
NO. APPEARING:	1-3
ARMOR CLASS:	9
MOVEMENT:	6 (ethereal plane only)
HIT DICE:	3
THAC0:	Nil
NO. OF ATTACKS:	0
DAMAGE/ATTACK:	Nil
SPECIAL ATTACKS:	Psionics, absorb: psionics, spells, and Intelligence
SPECIAL DEFENSES:	Ethereal existence
MAGIC RESISTANCE:	absorb (See below)
SIZE:	S (3' long)
MORALE:	Unsteady (5-7)
XP VALUE:	1,400

Thought eaters are natives of the Border Ethereal, and they only survive in ethereal form. They appear as a sickly gray skeletal body with an oversized platypus head (to those who can observe it). They have webbed skeletal paws, suited to swimming through the ether.

A thought eater has only one desire in its existence, and that is to avoid death. For some reason, they die almost instantly on the prime material plane. Fortunately for them, they have several psionic powers which help prevent this from occurring.

Combat: Thought eaters have no combat abilities except their psionic powers, even on the Border Ethereal. Thus, they can be quickly and easily slain if encountered ethereally.

They are not harmless, however. Thought eaters are unique. Although they cannot survive outside the Border Ethereal, their psionic powers can extend into the prime material plane. This is the only known case of such a cross-over.

Thought eaters always have psionic sense operating. Because of their unique nature, they can sense psionic activity in the prime material plane, as well as the Border Ethereal. When they detect psionic activity of any kind, they proceed to the area (ethereally, of course).

Their only "attack" is to absorb psionic energy. (This is an innate ability.) They can perform this function when within 60 feet of a true psionicist (or psionic creature), or within 10 feet of a wild talent. They drain 10 psionic points per round. They can also absorb any spell cast in the area as well as memorized spells (they get 5 points per spell level). Finally, they can feed upon Intelligence, with each point converted to 10 PSPs which they absorb. They will thus feed until all victims die or escape, or until sated. They are sated at a number of points equal to their PSP maximum.

Although they feed on brain power, thought eaters are essentially stupid. Because they lack intelligence, they are immune to all telepathic attacks and controls (psionic or otherwise). They always feed in this order of preference, even if it's illogical: 1) psionic points being expended (causes power to fail), 2) magical energy being expended (causes spell to fail), 3) PSPs, 4) memorized spells, 5) Intelligence. Note that if a thought eater eats all of someone's Intelligence, they will become a vegetable (effectively dead). Also, the Intelligence loss is permanent, unless it is relieved by *restore* or psychic surgery. Spells can be rememorized, and drained PSPs can be recovered naturally.

All this feeding has the sole purpose of keeping thought eaters in the ether. Their bodies process PSPs the way people process food, at a rate of 3 PSPs/hour. If they ever run out of points, they drop out of the ether into the prime material plane and instantly die.

Note that ethereal beings are invisible to creatures on the prime material plane, so it is likely that the thought eater will attack uncontested until sated, or until its victims out-distance it. Although it only has a movement rate of 6, this is ethereal movement, allowing it to move through walls, trees, etc. as if they didn't exist.

Any defense mode except those with a 0 maintenance cost will prevent the thought eaters from feeding. This includes spells such as *mind blank*, and magical devices which thwart psionic attacks.

Psionics Summary: Thought eaters have 1d100 + 100 (101-200) PSPs. Their score is 18. They boast a special form of psionic sense (in a metapsionic power), which operates continuously with no PSP cost. They also absorb PSPs, as described under "combat."

Habitat/Society: Little is known about thought eaters, except that they exist solely in the ethereal plane and are very solitary beings. Magical research has indicated that they aren't malevolent; they simply desire to keep existing. Some claim that this is the fate of all psionicists once they die.

Ecology: Thought eaters carry no treasure. When one dies, it automatically drops out of the ether and materializes on the prime material plane. Of course, they are usually dismissed as a platypus which died from starvation.

Su-Monster

CLIMATE/TERRAIN:	Dark areas/Wilderness and subterranean
FREQUENCY:	Uncommon
ORGANIZATION:	Family/Clan
ACTIVITY CYCLE:	Dawn and Sunset
DIET:	Omnivorous
INTELLIGENCE:	Average (8-10)
TREASURE:	C, Y
ALIGNMENT:	Chaotic (evil)
NO. APPEARING:	1d12
ARMOR CLASS:	6
MOVEMENT:	9
HIT DICE:	5+5
THAC0:	15
NO. OF ATTACKS:	5
DAMAGE/ATTACK:	1d4/1d4/1d4/1d4/2d4
SPECIAL ATTACKS:	Psionic, ambush
SPECIAL DEFENSES:	Psionic
MAGIC RESISTANCE:	Nil
SIZE:	M (large ape)
MORALE:	Average (8-10)
XP VALUE:	650

Su-monsters look like big gray monkeys, 4 to 5 feet tall. They have large bones and muscular limbs, but they always look a bit underfed, because their ribs and vertebrae show prominently. Their long, prehensile tails can easily support their weight. Their hands and feet are virtually alike, each having three long, thick fingers and an opposable thumb, all equipped with claws. Like the tail, their hands and feet are very strong, allowing them to hang by one limb for several hours.

Short, dirty gray fur covers most of their body. Their face and tail are black, while their paws are always bloody red (making them look like they just finished killing something, which is the case more often than not). They frequently grin, but this is usually a sharp-toothed threat rather than a gesture of friendliness.

Combat: Su-monsters attack with all four legs when possible, raking their extremely sharp nails across their victim. They can also deliver a powerful bite with their canine-like mouth.

These creatures like to hunt in small packs (1d12 members). Their favorite hunting ground is a well-traveled trail through the jungle/forest. They search for sturdy branches that overhang the trail, and then perch in the trees, waiting patiently. When a potential victim passes into the midst of them, they all swing down, using their tails as anchors. This way they can attack with all four claws plus the bite. Victims of this kind of ambush suffer a −4 penalty to their surprise rolls.

What really makes these beings ferocious is their tribal protectiveness. Half the time (50% chance), the entire family takes part in the hunt: male, female, and two young. If the young are attacked or threatened, the females fight as if under a *haste* spell (i.e., double movement and number of attacks). Likewise, if the females are attacked, the males appear to fight with *haste*. A surge of adrenaline accounts for this ferocity. Females can maintain the effect for up to 6 turns (an hour), and males can maintain it for up to 4 turns.

Psionically, these creatures can be deadly. They know three attack modes. They are also impervious to telepathic attacks (that's why they have no defense modes). When su-monsters are using their enhancement power, they can attack both psionically and physically if they choose (instead of enjoying a double attack rate).

Psionics Summary:

Level	Dis/Sci/Dev	Attack/Defense	Score	PSPs
2	3/1/3(2/5)	PsC,MT,PB/Nil	= Int	120

Su-monsters always know the following powers, and there is a 10% chance that they will have one more science and two more devotions in the psychometabolic discipline.

• Psychometabolism - *Devotions:* enhancement (no cost, see above).

• Metapsionics - *Devotions:* psionic sense (always on, no cost).

• Telepathy - *Sciences:* psychic crush. *Devotions:* mind thrust, psionic blast.

Habitat/Society: A su-monster family is composed of two parents (adult male and female) and two young. When two or more families live together, they form a clan. Su-monsters are very territorial and have a particular hatred for the psionically endowed.

According to legend, su-monsters were created by a powerful evil cleric or mage, who wished to guard his forest from intruders (especially psionic ones). The creatures do make a formidable attack force, which tends to support this theory. According to some sages (who point to the creatures' high Intelligence as proof), the creatures are magical hybrid made from humanoids and apes. In any event, many evil wizards and priests employ su-monsters as forest guards today.

Ecology: Su-monsters keep their valuables well hidden high in the trees of their territory. They have no food value, since their meat is mildly poisonous. Characters who eat su-monster meat must save vs. poison or become ill, and no natural healing is possible for 1 week.

Vagabond

CLIMATE/TERRAIN:	As host
FREQUENCY:	Very rare
ORGANIZATION:	Solitary
ACTIVITY CYCLE:	As host
DIET:	As host
INTELLIGENCE:	Genius to Supra-genius (17-20)
TREASURE:	As host + special
ALIGNMENT:	Neutral (any)
NO. APPEARING:	1
ARMOR CLASS:	As host
MOVEMENT:	As host
HIT DICE:	As host
THAC0:	As host
NO. OF ATTACKS:	As host
DAMAGE/ATTACK:	As host
SPECIAL ATTACKS:	As host, psionics
SPECIAL DEFENSES:	As host, psionics
MAGIC RESISTANCE:	As host, immune to mental spells
SIZE:	As host
MORALE:	Steady (11-12)
XP VALUE:	As host + 4 Hit Dice

It is difficult to say what a vagabond really looks like, because they can mimic countless other creatures in form. They are an alien life force of unknown origin. They are always encountered in the form of an intelligent, corporeal creature indigenous to the area (a creature with at least animal intelligence).

Vagabonds can assume such forms in one of three ways. First, they can simply form the body with their unusual powers. When this occurs, the vagabond looks like a small blob of ink which appears on the ground, then quickly enlarges into three dimensions, filling out, then forming the finer details. Such a change can be tremendously terrifying if the chosen form is something like a wolfwere. Secondly, vagabonds can take over a freshly dead body, curing it of all ailments. Lastly, they can inhabit a living body. In this last form, they are like back-seat drivers who make strong suggestions; they cannot do anything which the host life force does not want them to do. Thus, a possessed horse wouldn't jump off a cliff unless it felt safe or confident about the jump. As noted above, vagabonds take the form of any creature with at least animal intelligence. They rarely inhabit forms of higher intelligence, however, such as player character races.

Once they have assumed a form, vagabonds are locked into it and cannot leave, except with the typical psionic powers such as switch personality (which is one of their favorites).

If they are communicated with, it will soon become apparent that something is amiss, for they have none of their form's knowledge as to speech, behavior, customs, or expectations. However, they are able to use all of its attack and defense forms as well as movement and essential functions. Of course, many of these will be performed in strange and unique ways.

Combat: Vagabonds fight with the same skills as their form has. They are also completely immune to all forms of mental attacks and control which are not strictly psionic. Besides these adjustments, all vagabonds are psionically endowed. If their host body is slain, they will depart, never to return.

Psionics Summary:

Level	Dis/Sci/Dev	Attack/Defense	Score	PSPs
12	4/6/19	See below/All	= Int	1d100 + 200

Vagabonds never have psychokinetic powers. They have a particular affinity for these:

• Clairsentience - Any power which lets them learn things.

• Psychometabolism - Any power which allows them to change form or travel in difficult terrain.

• Metapsionics - They are masters of this discipline, having access to all its powers without regard to their total number of disciplines, science, and devotions.

• Telepathy - The creature can use any telepathic power to communicate or gain information, plus enough attack forms to psionically defend themselves.

• Psychoportation - Any which allows them to travel.

Habitat/Society: Habitat matches the form they assume. Society either matches the form, or the creature is a solitary wanderer. Vagabonds are never encountered together, and no one has ever heard of this occurring. All vagabonds can detect each other's presence up to a mile. At this point, they will separate if feasible.

Ecology: Vagabonds seem to have come to the prime material plane to gain information. They are extremely curious and inquisitive, often about mundane or personal details. If given the chance to adventure with the party, they are 90% likely to join. In exchange, they will use their considerable power to the party's benefit.

It can be great fun to have a vagabond secretly posses a PC's war dog or war horse (most of these will be true neutral). Evil and good vagabonds tend to side with forces of similar alignment, both aiding them and learning of their ways.

Many creatures in the AD&D® *Monstrous Compendium* series boast psionic powers. The text below brings those monsters up to date with the rules presented in this book. The creatures appear in alphabetical order. (Creatures from the Outer Planes are listed separately.) Each entry is organized as follows:

Level—How tough the monster is, in terms of a psionicist's experience level.

Dis/Sci/Dev—How many disciplines the creature can access, followed by the *total* number of sciences and devotions the creature knows (in all accessible disciplines).

Attack/Defense—Telepathic attack and defense modes the creature can use. (Defense modes are not included in the total number of powers the creature knows.) Abbreviations are as follows:

Attack Modes		*Defense Mode*	
PB	= Psionic Blast	M-	= Mind Blank
MT	= Mind Thrust	TS	= Thought Shield
EW	= Ego Whip	MB	= Mental Barrier
II	= Id Insinuation	IF	= Intellect Fortress
PsC	= Psychic Crush	TW	= Tower of Iron Will

Power Score: The creature's typical score when using a power that is not automatically successful.

PSPs: The creature's total pool of psionic strength points (the maximum available to it).

Type: The general type of powers the creature can use. Powers listed after this entry (if any) are *representative*; the list is not necessarily complete.

* *Creatures always knows a power that is distinguished by an asterisk.*

Level	Dis/Sci/ Dev	Attack/ Defense	Power Score	PSP s

Aboleth

		EW,II, PsC, +1/		
8	3/5/16	TS,IF,TW	= Int	250

Type: Powers which control others or manipulate minds.
 Telepathy: false sensory input*, mindlink*, mass domination*.

Couatl

9	4/5/18	Any/All	= Int	1d100+110

Type: Powers that allow them to gain information, travel, or disguise themselves.
 Clairsentience: aura sight*, all-round vision, see sound.
 Psychometabolism: metamorphosis*, chemical simulation, ectoplasmic form*.
 Psychoportation: teleport, time shift.
 Telepathy: mindlink*, ESP*, invisibility*.

Level	Dis/Sci/ Dev	Attack/ Defense	Power Score	PSP s

Dwarf, Duergar

		MT,EW,II/		
= HD	per level	M-,TS,MB	= Int	12×HD

Type: Powers of defense, escape, and underground movement.
 Clairsentience: feel sound, poison sense*.
 Psychokinesis: molecular agitation*, molecular manipulation.
 Psychometabolism: energy containment, expansion*, reduction*.
 Telepathy: identity penetration*, invisibility*.

Grey Ooze (only those creatures with over 20 hps)

1	2/1/1	PsC/M-	13	1d100+20

Type: Creatures have only those powers listed below.
 Telepathy: psychic crush*.
 Metapsionics: psionic sense* (only to 60', no cost).

Ki-rin

9	4/5/18	All/All	= Int	200

Type: Control of the nonliving, travel, mind reading.
 Psychokinesis: create object*, control flames, control wind.
 Psychometabolism: shadow-form*, body equilibrium, ectoplasmic form*.
 Psychoportation: banishment, probability travel*.
 Telepathy: mindlink*, ESP*, false sensory input*.

Mind Flayer (Illithid)

		MT/M-,		
7	3/5/14	TS,MB,+1	= Int	1d100+250

Type: Attack, mind control, travel.
 Psychokinesis: detonate, control body*, levitation*
 Psychometabolism: body equilibrium* (their only psychometabolic power).
 Psychoportation: probability travel*, teleport, astral projection*.
 Telepathy: domination*, awe, ESP*, post-hypnotic suggestion*.

Tarrasque

These creatures are totally immune to all psionics.

Level	Dis/Sci/Dev	Attack/Defense	Power Score	PSPs

Yellow Mold

Level	Dis/Sci/Dev	Attack/Defense	Power Score	PSPs
1	2/0/2	II/Nil (special)	15	1d10×5

Only sentient yellow molds (1 in 6 chance) have psionic powers. Such creatures are also immune to psionic attacks unless the attacker is being aided by one who can communicate with plants.
Type: Sentient yellow molds only have the powers listed below.
    Telepathy: mindwipe, id insinuation.
    Metapsionics: psionic sense (1d100+20' range, no cost).

Yuan ti

Level	Dis/Sci/Dev	Attack/Defense	Power Score	PSPs
HD−2	3/level	MT,II/M-,IF,TW	= Int	15×HD

Type: Related to snakes (see below).
    Clairsentience: danger sense, feel sound, poison sense*.
    Psychometabolism: animal affinity* (snake), metamorphosis (snake), chameleon power*, chemical simulation*, flesh armor.
    Telepathy: attraction (to snakes), aversion* (to snakes), false sensory input, inflict pain, invincible foes, life detection, phobia amplification*, post-hypnotic suggestion, repugnance (to snakes), taste link*.

Creatures from Outer Planes

All outer-planar creatures will be 1st level or greater when encountered. Telepathic attack and defense modes are listed in the order in which the creatures usually gain them. DMs should tailor an individual creature's repertoire of powers to its actual level, as desired.

Aasimon (only the 3 listed)

Level	Dis/Sci/Dev	Attack/Defense	Power Score	PSPs
= HD	per level	see below	= Int	see below

- Solar - All/All; 354 PSPs.
- Astral Deva - PB,MT,EW,PsC/M-,TS,MB; 210 PSPs.
- Planetar - All/All; 288 PSPs.

Type: Wide variety (nonhostile, except for control types).

Baatezu (all 4 greater)

Level	Dis/Sci/Dev	Attack/Defense	Power Score	PSPs
HD-1	per level	see below	= Int	see below

- Amnizu - MT,II/M-,TS,MB; 121 PSPs.
- Cornugon - MT,EW/M-,TS,MB; 113 PSPs.
- Gelugon - EW,II/M-,TS,MB; 166 PSPs.
- Pit Fiend - PB,EW,PsC/TS,MB,II; 213 PSPs.

Type: Powers of control and cruelty.

Gith

Level	Dis/Sci/Dev	Attack/Defense	Power Score	PSPs
= HD	per level	All/All	= Int	1d100+150

Type: Insubstantial (travel, energy), *not* mind-controlling powers.

Morti

Level	Dis/Sci/Dev	Attack/Defense	Power Score	PSPs
20	All/All/All	All/All		20,500

Tanar'ri

(Greater: babau; Lesser: succubus; True: all but vrock)

Level	Dis/Sci/Dev	Attack/Defense	Power Score	PSPs
HD-3	per level	see below	= Int	see below

- Babau - PB,PsC,EW/M-,MB,TW; 130 PSPs.
- Succubus - II/TS,IF;100 PSPs.
- Nalfeshnee - PB,EW,PsC/M-,TS,MB; 125 PSPs.
- Marilith - PB,PsC/M-,TS,MB; 175 PSPs.
- Balor - PB,MT,EW,PsC/M-,TS,MB; 250 PSPs.
- Glabrezu - II,EW,MT/M-,MB; 150 PSPs.
- Hezrou - II,MT/M-,IF; 100 PSPs.

Type: Powers of fire control, torture, shape change.

Titans

Level	Dis/Sci/Dev	Attack/Defense	Power Score	PSPs
HD+1	per level	MT,EW,II,PsC/Nil	= Int	1d100+100

Type: All types of powers.
Note: Titans are immune to psionic attacks.

Yugoloth (only Arcanaloth)

Level	Dis/Sci/Dev	Attack/Defense	Power Score	PSPs
13	5/7/24	All/All	= Int	1d100+200

Type: Powers of travel, combat.
Note: Lycanthropes never have psionic powers (except, possibly, in the Ravenloft™ campaign setting). Anyone contracting lycanthropy loses all psionic powers.

Score	IC	MC	Range	Prep.	A. of E.
Clairsentience					
Sciences					
Aura Sight, p. 28					
Wis −5	9	9/rnd.	50 yds.	0	personal
Clairaudience, p. 30					
Wis −3	6	4/rnd.	unlim.	0	special
Clairvoyance, p. 30					
Wis −4	7	4/rnd.	unlim.	0	special
Object Reading, p. 31					
Wis −5	16	na	0	1	touch
Precognition, p. 31					
Wis −5	24	na	0	5	na
Sensitivity to Psychic Impressions, p. 32					
Wis −4	12	2/rnd.	0	2	20-yd. rad.
Devotions					
All-Round Vision, p. 33					
Wis −3	6	4/rnd.	0	0	personal
Combat Mind, p. 33					
Int −4	5	4/rnd.	0	0	personal
Danger Sense, p. 33					
Wis −3	4	3/turn	special	0	10 yds.
Feel Light, p. 34					
Wis −3	7	5/rnd.	0	0	special
Feel Sound, p. 34					
Wis −3	5	3/rnd.	0	0	special
Hear Light, p. 34					
Wis −3	6	3/rnd.	0	0	special
Know Direction, p. 34					
Int	1	na	0	0	personal
Know Location, p. 36					
Int	10	na	0	5	personal
Poison Sense, p. 36					
Wis	1	na	0	0	1-yd. rad.
Radial Navigation, p. 36					
Int −3	4	7/hr.	0	0	personal
See Sound, p. 37					
Wis −3	6	3/rnd.	special	0	personal
Spirit Sense, p. 37					
Wis −3	10	na	0	0	15-yd. rad.
Psychokinesis					
Sciences					
Create Object, p. 38					
Int −4	16	3/rnd.	20 yds.	0	special
Detonate, p. 38					
Con −3	18	na	60 yds.	0	1 item, 8 cu. ft.
Disintegrate, p. 40					
Wis −4	40	na	50 yds.	0	1 item, 8 cu. ft.
Molecular Rearrangement, p. 40					
Int −5	20	10/hr.	2 yds.	2 hrs.	1 item
Project Force, p. 41					
Con −2	10	na	200 yds.	0	na
Telekinesis, p. 41					
Wis −3	3+	1+/rnd.	30 yds.	0	single item

Score	IC	MC	Range	Prep.	A. of E.
Devotions					
Animate Object, p. 42					
Int −3	8	3/rnd.	50 yds.	0	1 object, 100 lbs.
Animate Shadow, p. 42					
Wis −3	7	3/rnd.	40 yds.	0	100 sq. ft.
Ballistic Attack, p. 42					
Con −2	5	na	30 yds.	0	1 item, 1 lb.
Control Body, p. 43					
Con −2	8	8/rnd.	80 yds.	0	individ.
Control Flames, p. 43					
Wis −1	6	3/rnd.	40 yds.	0	10 sq. ft
Control Light, p. 44					
Int	12	4/rnd.	25 yds.	0	400 sq. ft.
Control Sound, p. 44					
Int −5	5	2/rnd.	100 yds.	0	na
Control Wind, p. 44					
Con −4	16	10/rnd.	500 yds.	2	1,000 yds.
Create Sound, p. 46					
Int −2	8	3/rnd.	100 yds.	0	na
Inertial Barrier, p. 46					
Con −3	7	5/rnd.	0	0	3-yd. diam.
Levitation, p. 47					
Wis −3	12	2/rnd.	0	0	individ.
Molecular Agitation, p. 48					
Wis	7	6/rnd.	40 yds.	0	1 item, 20 lbs.
Molecular Manipulation, p. 49					
Int −3	6	5/rnd.	15 yds.	1	2 sq. in.
Soften, p. 50					
Int	4	3/rnd.	30 yds.	0	1 object, 10 lbs.
Psychometabolism					
Sciences					
Animal Affinity, p. 50					
Con −4	15	4/rnd.	0	0	personal
Complete Healing, p. 50					
Con	30	na	0	24 hrs.	personal
Death Field, p. 52					
Con −8	40	na	0	3	20-yd. rad.
Energy Containment, p. 52					
Con −2	10	na	0	0	personal
Life Draining, p. 52					
Con −3	11	5/rnd.	touch	0	individ.
Metamorphosis, p. 53					
Con −6	21	1/turn	0	5	personal
Shadow-form, p. 53					
Con −6	12	3/rnd.	0	0	personal
Devotions					
Absorb Disease, p. 53					
Con −3	12	na	touch	0	individ.
Adrenalin Control, p. 54					
Con −3	8	4/rnd.	0	0	personal
Aging, p. 55					
Con −5	10	na	touch	0	individ.
Biofeedback, p. 55					
Con −2	6	3/rnd.	0	0	personal
Body Control, p. 55					
Con −4	7	5/turn	0	0	personal

Score	IC	MC	Range	Prep.	A. of E.
Body Equilibrium, p. 55					
Con −3	2	2/rnd.	0	0	personal
Body Weaponry, p. 57					
Con −3	9	4/rnd.	0	0	personal
Catfall, p. 57					
Dex −2	4	na	0	0	personal
Cause Decay, p. 57					
Con −2	4	na	touch	0	60 lbs.
Cell Adjustment, p. 57					
Con −3	5	up to 20/rnd.	touch	0	individ.
Chameleon Power, p. 58					
Con −1	6	3/rnd.	0	0	personal
Chemical Simulation, p. 58					
Con −4	9	6/rnd.	touch	1	varies
Displacement, p. 58					
Con −3	6	3/rnd.	0	0	personal
Double Pain, p. 59					
Con −3	7	na	touch	0	individ.
Ectoplasmic Form, p. 59					
Con −4	3	9/rnd.	0	1	personal
Enhanced Strength, p. 59					
Wis −3	varies	varies	0	0	personal
Expansion, p. 60					
Con −2	6	1/rnd.	0	0	personal
Flesh Armor, p. 60					
Con −3	8	4/rnd.	0	0	personal
Graft Weapon, p. 60					
Con −5	10	1/rnd.	touch	0	personal
Heightened Senses, p. 61					
Con	5	1/rnd.	0	0	personal
Immovability, p. 61					
Con −5	9	6/rnd.	0	0	personal
Lend Health, p. 62					
Con −1	4	na	touch	0	individ.
Mind Over Body, p. 62					
Wis −3	na	10/day	touch	0	individ.
Reduction, p. 62					
Con −2	varies	1/rnd.	0	0	personal
Share Strength, p. 63					
Con −4	6	2/rnd.	touch	0	individ.
Suspend Animation, p. 63					
Con −3	12	na	0/touch	5	individ.

Psychoportation

Sciences

Score	IC	MC	Range	Prep.	A. of E.
Banishment, p. 64					
Int −1	30	10/rnd.	5 yds.	0	individ.
Probability Travel, p. 64					
Int	20	8/hr.	unlim.	2	individ. +
Summon Planar Creature, p. 66					
Int −4	45/90	na	200 yds.	12	1 creature
Teleport, p. 67					
Int	10+	na	infinite	0	personal
Teleport Other, p. 68					
Int −2	20+	na	10 yds.	0	na

Devotions

Score	IC	MC	Range	Prep.	A. of E.
Astral Projection, p. 68					
Int	6	2/hr.	na	1	personal
Dimensional Door, p. 69					
Con −1	4	2/rnd.	50 yds. +	0	na
Dimension Walk, p. 69					
Con −2	8	4/turn	na	2	personal

Score	IC	MC	Range	Prep.	A. of E.
Dream Travel, p. 70					
Wis −4	1/25 mi.	na	500 mi.	0	personal
Teleport Trigger, p. 72					
Int +1	0	2/hr.	infinite	0	personal
Time Shift, p. 72					
Int	16	na	0	0	personal
Time/Space Anchor, p. 73					
Int	5	1/rnd.	0	0	3 yds.

Telepathy

Sciences

Score	IC	MC	Range	Prep.	A. of E.
Domination, p. 74					
Wis −4	contact	varies	30 yds.	0	individ.
Ejection, p. 74					
Wis −4	varies	na	0	0	personal
Fate Link, p. 75					
Con −5	contact	5/turn	2 mi.	1	individ.
Mass Domination, p. 75					
Wis −6	contact	varies	40 yds.	2	up to 5 creatures
Mindlink, p. 75					
Wis −5	contact	8/rnd.	unlim.	0	individ.
Mindwipe, p. 75					
Int −6	contact	8/rnd.	touch	1	individ.
Probe, p. 76					
Wis −5	contact	9/rnd.	2 yds.	0	individ.
Psionic Blast, p. 76					
Wis −5	10	na	20/40/60 yds.	0	individ.
Superior Invisibility, p. 78					
Int −5	contact	5/rnd./creature	100 yds.	0	personal
Switch Personality, p. 78					
Con −4	contact +30	na	touch	3	individ.
Tower of Iron Will, p. 79					
Wis −2	6	na	0	0	1 yd.

Devotions

Score	IC	MC	Range	Prep.	A. of E.
Attraction, p. 79					
Wis −4	contact	8/rnd.	200 yds.	0	individ.
Aversion, p. 79					
Wis −4	contact	8/turn	200 yds.	0	individ.
Awe, p. 80					
Cha −2	contact	4/rnd.	0	0	20 yds.
Conceal Thoughts, p. 80					
Wis	5	3/rnd.	0	0	3 yds.
Contact, p. 80					
Wis	varies	1/rnd.	special	0	individ.
Daydream, p. 83					
Wis	contact	3/rnd.	unlim.	0	individ.
Ego Whip, p. 83					
Wis −3	4	na	40/80/120 yds.	0	individ.
Empathy, p. 84					
Wis	contact	1/rnd. (or 1)	unlim.	0	20' × 20' × 20'
ESP, p. 84					
Wis −4	contact	6/rnd.	unlim.	0	individ.
False Sensory Input, p. 84					
Int −3	contact	4/rnd.	unlim.	0	individ.
Id Insinuation, p. 84					
Wis −4	5	na	60/120/180 yds.	0	individ.

Score	IC	MC	Range	Prep.	A. of E.
Identity Penetration, p. 85					
Wis −3	contact	6/rnd.	unlim.	0	individ.
Incarnation Awareness, p. 85					
Wis −4	contact	13/rnd.	unlim.	0	individ.
Inflict Pain, p. 85					
Con −4	contact	2/rnd.	touch	1	individ.
Intellect Fortress, p. 86					
Wis −3	4	na	0	0	3-yd. rad.
Invincible Foes, p. 86					
Wis −3	contact	5/rnd.	unlim.	0	individ.
Invisibility, p. 86					
Int −5	contact	2/rnd./ creature	100 yds.	0	individ.
Life Detection, p. 87					
Int −2	3	3/rnd.	100 yds.	0	varies
Mental Barrier, p. 87					
Wis −2	3	na	0	0	personal
Mind Bar, p. 88					
Int −2	6	4/rnd.	0	0	personal
Mind Blank, p. 88					
Wis −7	0	0	0	0	personal
Mind Thrust, p. 88					
Wis −2	2	na	30/60/90 yds.	0	individ.
Phobia Amplification, p. 89					
Wis −2	contact	4/rnd.	unlim.	0	individ.
Post-Hypnotic Suggestion, p. 89					
Int −3	contact	1/level or hit die	unlim.	0	1 creature
Psychic Crush, p. 89					
Wis −4	7	na	50 yds.	0	individ.
Psychic Impersonation, p. 90					
Wis	10	3/hr.	0	1 turn	personal
Psychic Messenger, p. 90					
Con −4	4	3/rnd.	200 mi.	2	1 sq. yd.
Repugnance, p. 90					
Wis −5	contact	8/rnd.	200 yds.	0	individ.
Send Thoughts, p. 91					
Int −1	contact	2/rnd.	unlim.	0	individ.
Sight Link, p. 91					
Con −3	contact	5/turn	unlim.	1	individ.
Sound Link, p. 91					
Con −2	contact	4/turn	unlim.	1	individ.
Synaptic Static, p. 91					
Int −4	15	10/rnd.	0	0	20/50/90 yds.
Taste Link, p. 92					
Con −2	contact	4/turn	unlim.	1	individ.
Telempathic Projection, p. 92					
Wis −2	contact	4/rnd.	unlim.	1	10-yd. diam
Thought Shield, p. 92					
Wis −3	1	na	0	0	personal
Truthear, p. 92					
Wis	4	2/rnd.	0	0	hearing

Metapsionics

Sciences

Score	IC	MC	Range	Prep.	A. of E.
Appraise, p. 93					
Int −4	14	na	0	0	personal
Aura Alteration, p. 93					
Wis −4	10	na	touch	5	individ.

Score	IC	MC	Range	Prep.	A. of E.
Empower, p. 93					
Wis −12	varies	na	touch	0	1 item
Psychic Clone, p. 94					
Wis −8	50	5/rnd.	60 feet	10 rnds.	special
Psychic Surgery, p. 95					
Wis −5	contact	10/turn	touch	10	individ.
Split Personality, p. 96					
Wis −5	40	6/rnd.	0	1	personal
Ultrablast, p. 96					
Wis −10	75	0	0	3	50 ft. rad.

Devotions

Score	IC	MC	Range	Prep.	A. of E.
Cannibalize, p. 97					
Con	0	na	0	0	personal
Convergence, p. 97					
Wis	8	0	10 yds.	1	10 yds.
Enhancement, p. 98					
Wis −3	30	8/rnd.	0	5	personal
Gird, p. 98					
Int −3	0	2× maint.	0	0	personal
Intensify, p. 98					
Affected −3	5/ increase	1/rnd.	0	1/increase	personal
Magnify, p. 100					
Wis −5	25 × mag.	mag./rnd.	0	5	personal
Martial Trance, p. 100					
Wis −3	7	0	0	1	personal
Prolong, p. 100					
Con −4	5	2/rnd.	0	0	personal
Psionic Inflation, p. 101					
Wis −5	20	3/rnd.	0	1	101 ft. rad.
Psionic Sense, p. 101					
Wis −3	4	1/rnd.	0	0	200-yd. rad.
Psychic Drain, p. 101					
Wis −6	10/person + contact	none	30 yds.	0	up to 6 minds
Receptacle, p. 102					
Wis −5	0	0	touch	1 rnd./ point	1 item
Retrospection, p. 103					
Wis −4	120	na	0	10	personal
Splice, p. 103					
Int −(2 × # spliced)	5 × # spliced	# spliced/ rnd.	0	# spliced	personal
Stasis Field, p. 104					
Con −3	20	20/rnd. or 1/rnd.	0	3	max. 1 yd./level
Wrench, p. 105					
Wis −4	15	8/rnd.	30 yds.	0	1 undead

Powers Index